The Caribbean in World Affairs

Foreign Relations of Latin America Series

The Caribbean in World Affairs

The Foreign Policies of the English-Speaking States

Jacqueline Anne Braveboy-Wagner

Westview Press • Boulder, San Francisco, & London

Foreign Relations of Latin America Series

Copyright © 1989 by Westview Press, Inc.

Published in 1989 in the United States of America by Westview Press, Inc., 5500 Central Avenue, Boulder, Colorado 80301, and in the United Kingdom by Westview Press, Inc., 13 Brunswick Centre, London WC1N 1AF, England

Library of Congress Cataloging-in-Publication Data
Braveboy-Wagner, Jacqueline Anne.
  The Caribbean in world affairs.
  (Foreign relations of Latin America series)
  Includes index.
  1. West Indies, British—Foreign relations—Research.
I. Title. II. Series.
JX1524.B73 1989   327'.09729   88-33783
ISBN 0-8133-7095-7

Printed and bound in the United States of America

The paper used in this publication meets the requirements of the American National Standard for Permanence of Paper for Printed Library Materials Z39.48-1984.

10   9   8   7   6   5   4   3

Contents

Tables and Figures

Figures

Preface and Acknowledgments

This book is intended not so much to supply new information concerning the external activities of the English-speaking Caribbean countries as to fill a large gap in the growing literature on the subject by integrating the known information into an analytical framework or model as a first step toward theory building. As such, the book complements the descriptive works on the Caribbean that are already available or in production. The book is also intended to reach the broader audience of those interested in small-state foreign policy in general, that is, those persons to whom the formulation of a model is useful in facilitating comparisons with other countries of similar size. Note that the aim is not to build a "grand theory" of small-state or Caribbean foreign policy, but rather to modify existing middle-range theories of international relations to suit the Caribbean region.

For readers unfamiliar with the region under study, a few explanatory notes are in order concerning the names of countries. *Antigua and Barbuda* is the full name of the country usually referred to in the book simply as Antigua. *Saint Lucia* is the preferred spelling for St. Lucia, but the second, more familiar spelling is frequently used in the text for reasons of brevity. Similarly, *Saint Vincent and the Grenadines* is generally abbreviated to St. Vincent. The country *St. Christopher/Nevis* is widely known in the Caribbean as St. Kitts/Nevis or simply St. Kitts, and these names are used interchangeably in the book. Finally, *Trinidad and Tobago* is often abbreviated in the text to Trinidad/Tobago or simply Trinidad. Related to the issue of country names is the designation used to refer to the administrative units in charge of foreign affairs in these territories. These units are formally called either Ministries of External Affairs or Ministries of Foreign Affairs. These terms are used interchangeably in the text, along with the broader designation "foreign ministry."

The research for this book was conducted primarily under a grant from the Research Foundation of the City University of New York. I am indebted to so many people for their assistance that I can name only a few here. Those not mentioned are, however, well remembered. I would like to thank first my good friends in the various diplomatic services for help cheerfully given: Marina Valere and Patrick Edwards (Trinidad and Tobago); Gloria Payne-Banfield (Grenada); Myron Dellimore (St. Vincent); Peter Laurie (Barbados); and Marilyn Zonicle (Bahamas), who came through with information solicited at the last minute. In addition, I must acknowledge the special help of Noel Sinclair (Guyana), who took time from his busy schedule while permanent representative to the U.N. to assist me generously. The Antiguan mission to the U.N. was also very cooperative, and I thank former Ambassador Lloydstone Jacobs and his wife. My stay in Saint Lucia was made most pleasant and intellectually rewarding through the cooperation of Earl Huntley from the Ministry of External Affairs. Other help that I would like to acknowledge came from Cecil John (St. Vincent); Lamuel Stanislaus, Ben Jones, and Denneth Modeste (Grenada); Harley Moseley, Sr. (Barbados); Colin Granderson (Trinidad); Patricia Durrant (Jamaica); Hillary Harker, the librarian at the Jamaican U.N. mission; Valerie McComie (Organization of American States); and Janet Bacon, who delved into the archives at the British Information Services. As noted in the relevant section, Humberto Garcia Muniz supplied considerable information on the military aspects of Caribbean external policy.

I must mention here that Caribbean foreign policy bureaucrats are extremely suspicious of researchers, especially fellow Caribbeaners bearing long, probing questionnaires. I hope that this book will help them to understand the need for more cooperation between academics and practitioners. Nevertheless, and in fact because of this, I would like to give special thanks to those persons who took time to complete and return my questionnaires, which were distributed to U.N. personnel. The only mission that was truly uncooperative was that of Belize. Fortunately, the Belize embassy in Washington, under Ambassador E. Laing, helped fill the gap.

I would like also to thank the students in my graduate class on Caribbean foreign policy in the Ph.D. program at the City University of New York. They helped clarify my ideas and sometimes supplemented my research. I must also indicate my appreciation for the efforts of my erstwhile assistant, Pius Bannis. Thanks too to Emily Hoffman and Allison Woods, who typed the tables and figures, and to the various editors at Westview, Barbara Ellington, Bruce Kellison, and especially Ida May Norton and Jane Raese. Finally, I wish to thank my husband, Jeffrey, and children, Justin and Jeremy, who put up with tremendous inconveniences and postponed family outings during the writing of this book. As has been the case with my other books, my husband, Jeffrey, has provided logistical and evaluative, as well as emotional, support. To the three Js, this book is dedicated, as well as to my Caribbean family who provided me with useful tips—Hilton and Josephine, as well as Kenneth S.

Jacqueline Anne Braveboy-Wagner

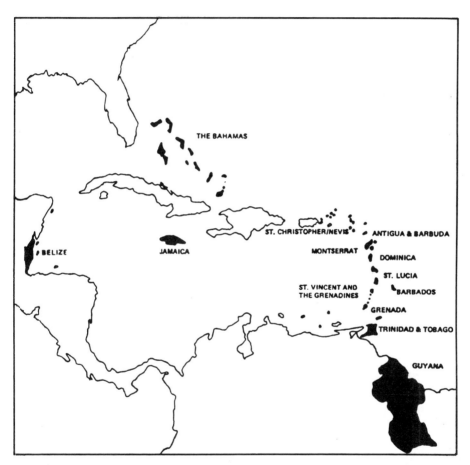

The English-speaking Caribbean
Source: Caribbean Community Secretariat

1. Introduction

Reviewing the literature on the foreign policy of Third World countries, Bahgat Korany noted in 1983 that studies of Third World foreign policies "can still be called 'the underdeveloped study of underdeveloped countries' . . . [even though] even general foreign policy theorists who do not concentrate on the Third World affirm its importance for theory building in foreign policy."[1] Of this "underdeveloped" field of research, it might be assumed that the study of Latin American foreign policies would be the most developed area, given Latin America's relatively long period of independence. Without actually applying methodological rigor to the question, it would seem that indeed studies of the foreign policies of Latin American nations are far more numerous than studies of African or Asian foreign policy. But there is still a problem here: Jennie Lincoln notes that the study of Latin American foreign policy is "not a theoretically well-developed field. Although scholars have studied 'the interAmerican [sic] system' for the past thirty-five years, a focus on *Latin American* foreign policies—as the product of *Latin American* foreign policy strategies—is a recent development."[2] For the most part, research has concentrated on case studies of the foreign policy behavior of individual nations.[3] The implication here is that not only are there relatively few studies from the Latin American perspective, but also the case study approach prohibits the development of more general theory.

The study of the foreign policy of the "newer" (primarily English-speaking) Caribbean[4] is of even more recent vintage, given the fact that independence for this region dates only from 1962. Until the 1970s, research in this area tended to concentrate on the theory and practice of economic integration, reflecting the creation of the Caribbean Free Trade Area in 1965. In 1966 the government of Trinidad and Tobago helped found the Institute of International Relations at the University of the West Indies. Affiliated then with the Geneva Institute of International Relations, the school began not only to train Caribbean diplomats but also to initiate research projects on Caribbean international relations. Much of the research in this field from a Caribbean perspective has thus been produced by those affiliated in some way with the institute. These scholars have included Roy Preiswerk, who produced the first

1

conceptual framework for Caribbean foreign policy in terms of goals and strategies used to obtain these goals,[5] and Basil Ince, who has to date been the only person to write on the foreign policy process in Trinidad and Tobago.[6] The institute has also produced various edited books and yearbooks on Caribbean international relations.[7] Other local research has not unexpectedly emerged from the regional University of the West Indies and the University of Guyana, while Caribbean scholars abroad have also turned their attention to issues in Caribbean international relations.[8]

A number of non-native scholars based outside the region have also produced useful works on Caribbean international relations. Interest in the Caribbean abroad was relatively muted until the mid- to late 1970s and 1980s, and the scholarly offerings on the region reflect this upward trend. One of the early foreign policy works was Robert Crassweller's 1972 book on U.S. policy toward the Caribbean community.[9] Atkins (1977) included the Caribbean, albeit marginally, in his *Latin America in the International Political System*; and Martin (1978) discussed U.S. policy in the Caribbean, including the English-speaking Caribbean.[10] Davis and Wilson, and Ferris and Lincoln included the Caribbean in their edited books on Latin American foreign policies.[11] In 1979, Millett and Will produced a text devoted to Caribbean international issues.[12] More recently, there has been a spate of books on the United States and the Caribbean, now popularly cenceptualized as the Caribbean Basin, especially in view of events in Nicaragua and Grenada.[13]

The study of the international relations of the Caribbean, including the English-speaking Caribbean, has therefore come a long way. As we scan the available works on the Caribbean, we find a reasonable amount of descriptive data on the conduct of diplomacy, the effects of small size on Caribbean activity, the role/perception of elites, the Caribbean's position in the East-West struggle, and issues of integration, immigration, and militarization, among others. What is missing are the same things that are missing in the study of Third World or Latin American foreign policy and international relations as a whole: Most of what is written is country-specific or issue-specific rather than general and comprehensive; most is descriptive rather than theoretical. The challenge is to put together what we know into a plausible whole, within a suitable theoretical *framework*, as a first step in developing theory and also to back up our analyses with reasonably rigorous and systematic analysis. Georges Fauriol's analysis of the foreign policy of Guyana, Haiti, and Jamaica[14] attempted to inject this type of rigor into Caribbean foreign policy analysis. However, Fauriol dealt with only two English-speaking nations, and his analysis is dated, ending in the mid-1970s. Also, in focusing on events data analysis, Fauriol sacrificed content for quantification. On the contrary, this work seeks to use quantification as a tool to buttress our contextual analysis.

But readers may well ask: Why is it important to engage in such a task, to study Third World policy with some rigor, an importance obviously assumed by Korany and others? Is it of any great significance to scholarly development for us to learn about the foreign policy processes and behavior of Third World states, especially small states such as the Caribbean states? Apart from the obvious value of supplying knowledge to those who want it, the study of Third World foreign policies should assist in the building and refining of international relations "middle-range" theory. The sub-field of international relations that is most clearly linked to such study is that of comparative foreign policy, which attempts to formulate general theories about foreign policy behavior. Also of relevance is the field of decision-making, a part of foreign policy studies but also a field unto itself.

Comparative foreign policy addresses several issues. It tries to identify and classify state behavior and "explain" this behavior (in the social science sense) in terms of various factors, including geography, economics, political and societal structures, the policymaking process (organizational factors), and systemic factors such as the influence of external events, the status of the country within the international hierarchy, and the strength of the various bonds/linkages among countries. Comparative foreign policy theorists are less concerned with foreign policy per se (that is, the guidelines or principles in accordance with which states act and react to the international environment) than with foreign policy *behavior*. Countries tend to develop written or unwritten guidelines for their international behavior. Often when a researcher asks a diplomat "What is your country's foreign policy?" the researcher is referred to various documents, election manifestos, speeches made by foreign ministers or prime ministers, and directives handed down by ministers or ambassadors. Over time even the smallest country develops a general pattern of response that forms the basis for evaluating reactions to specific events. Determination of goals and strategies is a part of this "pre-planned" aspect of the foreign policy process.

Foreign policy behavior (or international behavior) is different, referring, as Fauriol notes, to "purposive action directed at some external entity(ties) and initiated by individuals who are authoritative governmental decision makers or their representatives."[15] Here we are referring to actions, what states actually do, which may or may not conform to the established guidelines. The scientific literature on international relations even speaks of "behaviors," but we will try to refrain from this artificial construct in this book. Then there is the decision-making process, traditionally conceived as the "black box" between inputs and outputs. Clearly here we are in the realm of *process*, for we are studying how decision-makers arrive at their decisions, taking into account the many environmental and personal variables that affect them.

It seems obvious today that all states, whatever their size, are capable of formulating and producing responses to international stimuli. Of course small states, lacking financial and other resources, will generally have a lower level of international interaction and less input into major events and decisions made in the international system. Comparative foreign policy literature has, in fact, focused heavily on this question of the effect of size on foreign policy behavior. This is an issue that preoccupied scholars and decision-makers in the large countries during the 1960s, when decolonization produced a proliferation of independent entities with only minimal capabilities of conducting diplomacy, at least according to the accepted norms. A spate of studies addressed the issue, trying to define the limits of a "small" state, a "mini" state, and a "micro" state. For David Vital, smallness had an upper limit of 20 million to 30 million; for the authors of a United Nations study, a small state had 1 million or fewer inhabitants; for Taylor, the microstate range was from 100,000 to 1 million; for Blair, a ministate had 300,000 inhabitants or fewer; and Plischke provided various categories: small states, 300,000 to 1 million; microstates, fewer than 300,000; submicrostates, fewer than 100,000.[16] While this might all seem to be an exercise in numbers, there were two implications: first, that the population size of a state was relevant to its internal and international capabilities; and second, that special political and diplomatic arrangements had to be made for small states, arrangements that fell short of full self-determination either internally or internationally or both. Thus Plischke noted:

> Perhaps the time has come to consider adding to the current modes of government—dependence, self-government without full international statehood, and independence within sovereign equality—another category: independent self-management of internal and external policy and relations without full status and rights in the councils of the collective global community. This would mean that the family of nations would place some restraints on such states and exclude them from particular diplomatic forums and agencies.
>
> Alternatively, voluntary geographic and functional circumscription may be necessary. Small states may find it advantageous voluntarily to limit their active involvement to their immediate regions, maintaining relations with their neighbors but not participating in the broader international conferences, organizations, and affairs. In varying degrees, selective functional involvement has been practiced by all states, large and small, but the principle is not well served by the inclusion of microstates in hemispheric forums concerned with matters distant to their national interest. Thus the future participation of microstates as equals in such affairs might be restricted by the collective community.[17]

Written only ten years ago, these prescriptions no doubt sound quite condescending to the policymakers of small and developing states. They are also not necessarily diplomatically sound, for small states have often been able to overcome the limitations of size through vigorous and effective participation in international forums. Selectivity does not necessarily imply a foreign policy based simply on the local or regional environment. In today's interdependent world, a conference on nuclear issues or on terrorism or on the world economy carries implications for tiny states, even though the major actors are bound to be the largest countries. Finally, we should also consider the type of international system such an arrangement would produce: a system that would, as in the past, be completely managed by the large powers, an institutionalization of structural inequality.

The United Nations rejected this, and the argument that small states are not viable entities in international relations today sounds quaintly historical, although the large powers have predictably remained discontented. (A manifestation of this has been the U.S. contention in the 1980s that unless weighted voting on financial matters was introduced in the United Nations, U.S. aid would remain reduced.) By 1976, Lewis noted that the debate about size and sovereignty in the Caribbean "no longer takes precisely [the traditional] form." Instead the concern was with "autonomy":

> [That is,] the question whether in acting as a formally sovereign unit at the level of engaging in necessary relationships in the international environment, the state finds that it possesses sufficient instruments from its "sovereignty arsenal" to cope with the complexities of that environment. The further questions then arise of, in what locus or loci are such instruments to be sought; what institutional relationships are to be established between the sovereign state and the locus or loci in which such instruments are found; in other words, whether a new *system* is to be established and the extent to which system requirements will now determine *unit behaviour*.[18]

The question was whether the small politically independent state could pursue an autonomous foreign (or domestic, for that matter) policy, given the extent to which it is open to systemic influences. Rosenau reflected this concern in his "Pre-Theories and Theories of Foreign Policy"[19] when he included as important variables in foreign policy analysis the extent to which penetrative processes were at work in a country, and gave high rank to the systemic variable in small-state foreign policy. The *dependencia* school[20] contributed to this concern within the much broader perspective of underdevelopment. When, in the early 1970s, scholars asked "Does the Caribbean *have* a foreign policy?" the issue was not whether these states engaged in foreign behavior but the extent to which their policy and behavior were externally mandated. The question is still valid today, especially in terms of the smaller Eastern Caribbean territories. But the difference between the questioning then and now in the 1980s lies in the expansion of the range of choices.

In the rigid bipolar world of the 1950s and early 1960s, policy choices were limited for Third World states as a whole, small and large. In an ideologically competitive world, all countries were strategically important—Egypt as much as the Congo, Vietnam as much as Brazil—and their policy choices were significant for one superpower or another. Some states/regions were, of course, more strategically located than others, and hence their realm of action was more rigidly circumscribed. Again, much of the Third World was still colonized, hence the primary concern was with the achievement of political independence. Finally, even as concern about economic dependence emerged, the choices available were not clear: Given the structure of the economies inherited from the colonial powers, the economic survival of the new countries rested, at least in the short term, on the continuation of pre-independence international relationships.

In the late 1960s and early 1970s, the rigid bipolar system gave way to detente, facilitating the rise of Third World concerns (decolonization, disarmament, development) and providing Third World countries with more latitude on political and economic matters. The Non-Aligned Movement, initiated in 1961, was strengthened and broadened in terms of both membership and issues, and, under U.N. auspices, economic choices were discussed and broadened to include regional integration, diversification of economies and trade linkages, and tripartite trade among developing countries and Western and Eastern nations.[21]

Still, Third World countries were far from powerful. Although now initiating as well as reacting to international policy, their only real power lay in numerical strength (important in conference forums) and in their active neutralism.[22] In 1972, Marshall Singer noted that "unfortunately for the underdeveloped, weaker states of the world, the brutal truth is that they are simply too poor to be very good or very important customers of the industrial Powers."[23] This economic problem was about to take on new dimensions in 1973.

The oil crisis enlarged the economic power of the Third World, pointing the way to new economic strategies, in particular cartelization and collective self-reliance (South-South cooperation), and forcing the developed countries to open discussions with the Third World on various structural inequities in a variety of forums. By the end of the 1970s, international (and scholarly) concern turned to the issue of "interdependence," the fact that the developed countries had become quite dependent on the Third World not just in terms of strategic materials but also in terms of trade. For example, in 1977, the Overseas Development Council, a private Washington-based organization, reported that "27 percent of [U.S.] exports—more than we sell to the members of the European Community, Eastern Europe and the Soviet Union combined—now go to the non-OPEC [Organization of Petroleum Exporting Countries] developing countries."[24]

Thus the role of small states (in the sense of "weak" or "underdeveloped/developing" states) has been changing across time. With increasing power, they have become more active in the international system, and their economic and political activity has become more varied. Certain points should be stressed: First, these states are still not equal participants in the international system since major political and economic decision-making is dominated by the superpowers and others. Second, the activity of these states is still limited by economic and financial considerations, and the smaller the state the greater the limitations. Third, the power of these states is closely related to systemic considerations: Thus, for example, international market forces eventually eroded OPEC's economic power, and the rise of a less flexible administration in the United States was enough to produce in the Third World both economic changes (a mellowing of demands for international economic changes, a general return to the Western model of development) and political changes (a trend toward more conservative politics). Finally, and perhaps most importantly, the increase in Third World power of the 1970s was unevenly distributed. Although population size does not necessarily correlate with power, given the influence of wealth, it can generally be said that very small states moved up very little in the international hierarchy. Nevertheless, options were opened up to them, in particular greater possibilities of regional and international cooperation.

In sum, then, today the question of whether small states can conduct an autonomous foreign policy raises more complex issues than before. In the 1970s and 1980s, options have been developed to broaden the limited choices perceived earlier by decision-makers. Small states have greater opportunities for regional and global cooperation and diversification of external ties; they have greater knowledge about the international environment, and more precedents for small-state influence from which to choose. A very small state will still be highly vulnerable to systemic influence and will still have certain aspects of its policy determined by its "dependent" linkages, but it is still capable of adopting strategies to project an individual presence abroad and even to develop penetrative linkages of its own.

To look at the map of independent states today is to find that 40 percent of the independent nations have populations of 5 million or fewer (or are small states, according to the wholly reasonable cutoff point established by some writers already cited). The list of these countries in Table 1.1 includes all of the "newer" Caribbean countries. Can anything be said briefly about the importance of these states in the international system? The list of those with populations under 1 million, primarily island nations, contains few countries that spring to mind as having made a great impact internationally. But a closer look will show that the list includes Brunei, one of the richest nations in the world, whose leader has, under U.S. prodding, supplied considerable funding to Nicaraguan counterrevolutionaries. It includes Grenada, whose foreign policy openly antagonized the United States in the early 1980s. It includes Guyana, which has been very active in international forums. And it includes Vanuatu, which is becoming very visible in its attempt to pursue an independent policy in the Pacific area. Among the countries with larger populations are: Costa Rica, which is regionally well respected; Singapore, which is internationally respected and well represented in diplomatic forums; Nicaragua, which is pursuing a nationalistic internal

TABLE 1.1. Independent Countries with Populations of 5 Million or Fewer (1984)

	Population (in thousands)		Population (in thousands)
1 Million and Under		**1 Million+ to 3 Million**	
Antigua and Barbuda	78	Albania	2,900
Bahamas	226	Bhutan	1,213
Bahrain	407	Botswana	1,031
Barbados	255	Central African Republic	2,534
Belize	156	Congo, People's Republic	1,838
Brunei	216	Costa Rica	2,435
Cape Verde	321	Jamaica	2,289
Comoros	381	Kuwait	1,790
Cyprus	665	Lesotho	1,490
Djibouti	358	Liberia	2,122
Dominica	72	Mauritania	1,664
Equatorial Guinea	366	Mauritius	1,003
Fiji	677	Mongolia	1,852
Gabon	812	Oman	1,186
The Gambia	712	Panama	2,009
Grenada	92	Singapore	2,533
Guinea-Bissau	877	Togo	2,928
Guyana	806	Trinidad and Tobago	1,170
Iceland	240	United Arab Emirates	1,277
Kiribati	61	Uruguay	2,990
Luxembourg	365	Yemen, People's Democratic Rep.	2,021
Maldives	173		
Malta	360	**3 Million+ to 5 Million**	
Qatar	292	Benin	3,921
Saint Christopher/Nevis	46	Burundi	4,587
Saint Lucia	134	Chad	4,900
St. Vincent and the Grenadines	109	Finland	4,902
Sao Tome and Principe	106	Honduras	4,234
Seychelles	64	Ireland	3,533
Solomon Islands	263	Israel	4,172
Suriname	384	Jordan	3,372
Swaziland	730	Lao People's Democratic Rep.	3,738
Vanuatu	131	Libya	3,620
Western Samoa	163	New Zealand	3,249
		Nicaragua	3,116
		Norway	4,151
		Papua New Guinea	3,253
		Paraguay	3,291
		Sierra Leone	3,668

Total: 71 countries

Source: World Bank, World Bank Atlas 1986 (Washington, D.C.: World Bank, 1986).

and external policy; Jamaica, which is quite well known internationally; and Israel, Jordan, and Libya, all of which have pursued strong external policies with far-reaching consequences.

The point of this exercise is this: Despite the limitations under which small states labor, there are obviously conditions under which they can come to play relatively strong roles in international affairs. These may be geopolitical, that is, the country's importance in world affairs is inflated relative to its size because of its location and perceived centrality to the national interest of a superpower. But there are also other conditions at work. Thus Singapore is able to play a significant role partly because of domestic considerations (good management of its economy and polity) and partly because of the finely honed skills of its diplomatic community. Libya, on the other hand, has achieved importance (albeit, to many, notoriety) because it has set for itself wide-reaching regional and international goals—support for Islamic movements around the world, federation or unity with North African states, support for liberation groups around the world, and so on.

To sum up, states that are small in size not only engage in international behavior but specifically pursue foreign policies (goals, strategies, and purposive action in pursuit of goals). Their ability to pursue these effectively is surely circumscribed, for some states more than others, by both financial and resource limitations and by geopolitical and systemic considerations. Nevertheless, the area of choice for small states has widened over the years. Historically, small states made up for military and political limitations either by allying with a larger power or powers or by foregoing military involvement and adopting neutrality. Now, small states have added economic concerns to military ones and can choose among at least the following strategies, with the choice depending on their specific internal and external circumstances:

They can, as in the past, ally with a larger power—in today's world, this usually translates into alliance with one of the superpowers.

They can pursue moderate policies aimed at developing new ties while preserving the old.

They can pursue militant policies aimed at asserting their independence in world affairs.

They can pursue opportunistic policies aimed at playing off the superpowers against one another and shifting allies as they see fit.

As we look at the Caribbean countries, some of which have adopted militant policies but most of which have opted for moderation, we will address these questions of the effects of small size, the types of roles and strategies adopted, and the effectiveness of these in achieving goals. The book will not only analyze the international behavior, processes, and foreign policy influences on the English-speaking Caribbean subset of small states, but in the process attempt to determine the conditions under which they can achieve their goals and achieve international visibility.

Geographical Scope

Earlier, we referred to the "newer" Caribbean in making some points about Caribbean international relations. The focus of our research is actually narrower, for the "newer" Caribbean includes Suriname, which gained independence in 1975. Because of the differences in its historical and cultural development, Suriname is not included in this analysis. The Hispanic Caribbean and Haiti, usually included in Latin American analyses, are also excluded here. However, all these countries are discussed to the extent that they are targets of our core countries' foreign policies.

The core region with which we are concerned (and which, in this book, is frequently referred to simply as the "Caribbean") is therefore the English-speaking or Commonwealth Caribbean, a region whose relative homogeneity and political and economic closeness allow us to make certain generalizations about the members' policies. This is important in developing a level of theorizing about their international behavior. The countries studied are Antigua and Barbuda, Bahamas, Barbados, Belize, Dominica, Grenada, Guyana, Jamaica, Saint Christopher/Nevis, Saint Lucia, Saint Vincent and the Grenadines, and Trinidad and Tobago. Relevant introductory data—dates of independence, size, per capita gross national product (GNP), and other information—are given in Table 1.2. These countries share a common history of British colonialism, membership (except for Bahamas, Belize, and Guyana) in the British-imposed West Indies Federation (1958–1962),[25] and current membership in the Caribbean Community (Caricom), the region's integration movement.

In analyzing the foreign policies of these countries, the first concern is to draw on other theoretical frameworks to build our own within which to study Caribbean international relations. The next task is to analyze the general patterns of foreign policy behavior exhibited by these states to date. Later chapters look at the sources of and influences on foreign policy, the decision-making process, and the foreign policy machinery. As far as possible, quantitative data are used to bolster the descriptive analysis that has normally proliferated in the study of the Caribbean. The entire exercise is intended to give the reader a comprehensive picture of the role of the Caribbean in the world, from the Caribbean perspective.

The English-Speaking Caribbean:
A Foreign Policy Sketch

The more developed territories of the Commonwealth Caribbean—Jamaica, Trinidad and Tobago, Guyana, and Barbados—emerged to independence in the 1960s, at a time when the debate on the viability (external as well as internal) of small states was still vigorous. In addition, the options open to states were, or at the very least appeared to be, very limited. Colonialism had bequeathed to them a parliamentary system of government, an orientation toward moderate rather than radical change, and economic structures that fostered dependence on a few products and a few trading partners. As independence was not achieved with any long anti-colonial struggles, there was no strong antagonism toward the British (Western) model of politics and development. Caribbean leaders were also enchanted with the Puerto Rican "open" economy (industrialization by invitation) model, which achieved early growth in that island, although at enormous social cost.

Leaders were also faced with the important reality that they were in the U.S. sphere of influence at a time when the anti-Communist concerns of the United States were heightened by events in Cuba. In one of the Caribbean states, Guyana, the ideological competition had already reared its head. In 1950, the Marxist Cheddi Jagan and the moderate socialist L. Forbes Burnham had formed the People's Progressive Party (PPP). The party was victorious in the first general election held under adult suffrage in 1953. However, the government it formed lasted only 133 days as British troops were sent in to prevent the establishment of a "Communist-dominated state."[26] The U.S. Central Intelligence Agency was also, on its own admission, involved in fostering racial and economic disturbances in the country in the early 1960s. (Burnham formed his own party, the People's National Congress [PNC], in the mid-1950s and, under the system of proportional representation instituted with Jagan's approval, was able to achieve power in 1964.)

With an eye on geopolitics and on history, the Commonwealth Caribbean territories that gained independence in the 1960s adopted the conservative strategy of continuing the traditional patterns of external economic and political ties. The United Kingdom (U.K.) remained their most important trading partner, although, except for Barbados, the United States soon outstripped the U.K. in importance. Foreign aid was received primarily from the United States and the United Kingdom. Security and defense arrangements centered on the same two countries, and diplomatic ties were primarily with Western developed and pro-West developing countries.

In the 1970s, most of the Caribbean experienced major changes.[27] Systemically, the rapprochement between the superpowers and the rise of the Third World increased the choices open to the Caribbean countries. Third World and non-aligned ideas and concerns permeated the Caribbean, first at the popular level (except for Guyana, where the leadership undertook changes on its own) and then among the leadership. Guyana's leadership moved the country toward "cooperative" socialism in 1970 and proceeded to transform the economy into a state-run economy and the polity into one in which the party was "paramount."[28] In Trinidad

TABLE 1.2. Caribbean Countries: Basic Data

Country	Population (in thousands)	Area (sq. Miles)	Per Cap. GNP (current $US)	Major exports[a] Concentration	Life Expectancy (at birth)	Infant Mortality (per 1,000 at age one)	Literacy (percent)
Antigua/Barbuda	78	171	1,830	Manuf. goods/machinery/chem. (n.a.)	72	32	88
Bahamas	226	5,000	4,260	Petro. prod./pharm./crawfish (n.a.)[b]	69	33	93
Barbados	255	166	4,340	Sugar/elec. components/clothing (11.9)	72	23	99
Belize	156	8,866	1,150	Sugar/clothing/citrus (34.2)	66	30	91
Dominica	72	290	1,080	Bananas/laundry soap/toilet soap (41.3)	74	20	94
Grenada	92	133	880	Cocoa/bananas/nutmeg (46.3)	69	39	98
Guyana	806	83,000	580	Sugar/bauxite/rice (79.3)	68	36	92
Jamaica	2,289	4,411	1,080	Alumina/bauxite/sugar (83.4)	71	28	90

Saint Kitts/Nevis	46	101	1,390	Sugar (n.a.)c	63	56	98
Saint Lucia	134	238	1,130	Bananas/coconut oil/cocoa (46.2)	69	30	82
St. Vincent/Grenadines	109	150	900	Bananas/arrowroot/coconut (56.4)	70	45	96
Trinidad/Tobago	1,170	1,980	7,140	Petro. prod./crude petro. (46.4)	69	28	95

a Three major exports. "Concentration" refers to the index of commodity concentration, representing the percentage distribution of the three major commodities in total merchandise exports.

b Although the index is not available, according to Inter-American Development Bank (IDB) figures petroleum products account for more than 90 percent of exports. See IDB, Annual Report (1980s: various years).

c St. Kitts (Christopher)/Nevis has been almost entirely dependent on sugar until recently. It is currently diversifying into some light industry.

Sources: World Bank, World Bank Atlas 1986 for population and GNP (data are provisional for 1984), and for infant mortality and life expectancy (data are for 1983); Jack Hopkins, ed., Latin American and Caribbean Contemporary Record Vol. 2, 1982-3 (New York: Holmes and Meier, 1984): Appendix Table 2, p. 956 for area (except Trinidad and Tobago); Tom Barry, Beth Wood, and Deb Preusch, The Other Side of Paradise: Foreign Control in the Caribbean (New York: Grove, 1984): x-xi, for exports of all countries except Belize; World Bank, World Bank Tables (Baltimore: Johns Hopkins University Press for the World Bank, 1983): Table 8, p. 544 for index of commodity concentration; John W. Sewell, Richard E. Feinberg, and Valeriana Kallab, eds., U.S. Foreign Policy and the Third World: Agenda 1985-6 (New Brunswick: Transaction Books for the Overseas Development Council, 1985): 220 for literacy rate.

and Tobago, popular agitation in 1970 led to the government's adoption of a policy of localization of the economy. In Jamaica, the tide of change brought to power the Michael Manley government that introduced socialistic reforms. Barbados was the only country that did not undergo significant change.

The result of these changes, as far as the external dimension is concerned, was the emergence of new foreign policies. There was a general diversification of diplomatic ties toward the socialist bloc (especially by Guyana and Jamaica) and Afro-Asia. Ties with Latin America were already cemented through Caribbean participation in the Organization of American States (OAS), although Guyana and Belize were excluded from the OAS because of their border disputes with other Latin American members. Ties were established with Cuba; and Guyana, Jamaica, and Trinidad and Tobago joined the Non-Aligned Movement, with Guyana particularly active.

A new group of countries came to independence in the 1970s—the smaller countries of the Eastern Caribbean. The first to gain independence was Grenada, which achieved independence only after a considerable amount of popular agitation targeted against the Gairy leadership. Between 1973 and 1979, Grenada, led by Eric Gairy, maintained a pro-West stance, but the resurgence of the anti-Gairy opposition led in 1979 to his overthrow and replacement by the socialist People's Revolutionary Government (PRG). This produced a change in external emphasis toward the socialist countries, including Cuba and Nicaragua.

The Bahamas also achieved independence in 1973, but it maintained a pro-West stance despite periods of disagreement with U.S. policy. Conservative external and internal stances have also characterized the Eastern Caribbean countries that emerged to independence after 1973. However, the Bahamas, Barbados, and Saint Lucia, along with Belize, which gained independence in 1981, joined the Non-Aligned Movement in the early 1980s.

All the Caribbean states moved closer to the Third World in terms of their participation in international economic forums, including their support for the economic reforms embodied in the United Nations Declaration and Action Programme on the Establishment of a New International Economic Order.[29] Other Third World–oriented actions included Jamaica's leadership in the creation in 1974 of the International Bauxite Association, a cartel modeled along the lines of OPEC; the South-South cooperation embodied by Caribbean participation in 1975 with African and Pacific countries in negotiations to establish preferences for their agricultural products on the markets of the European Community; and, regionally, Caribbean support for the formation of the Latin American Economic System (SELA) in 1975, a grouping that was unusual in including Cuba but excluding the United States. Meanwhile, Trinidad and Tobago, its wealth having increased as a result of OPEC actions, assumed a new role as aid donor to the rest of the Caribbean.

The 1970s also saw another facet of Caribbean policy emerge, that is, a closer relationship with nearby Venezuela. Until then, Trinidad and Tobago was the only country with relatively close relations with Venezuela, relations engendered by geographical proximity. In the early 1970s, Venezuela began to perceive the Caribbean as important to its security interests and embarked on a political and economic thrust into the area just as the decolonization process was accelerating in the Eastern Caribbean. Initial Caribbean suspicions about Venezuelan intentions, primarily asserted by Trinidad's Dr. Eric Williams, were replaced by diplomatic, economic, and cultural ties.[30]

As the Caribbean moved into the late 1970s and 1980s, further changes occurred. In the international system, East-West tensions increased once more, and the new U.S. administration took a harder line toward militant socialist-oriented nationalism. By the time the Reagan administration assumed power, the Manley regime in Jamaica had already been voted out of power by a people tired of the economic hardship and violence engendered by misguided (if well-meaning) domestic policies and external economic pressures. Jamaica then turned to the right, an orientation reflected in its return to pro-West policies. Guyana, also suffering from economic malaise caused by mismanagement, a repressive political and social climate, and the effects of the world-wide recession, turned back (beginning in the late 1970s) to the West for economic and military assistance. Economic liberalization was affirmed after the death of Prime Minister Burnham in 1985. Mismanagement also led Trinidad and Tobago to seek a somewhat more open economy in the 1980s. In Grenada, internal elite instability led to U.S. intervention and the installation of a new pro-U.S. regime. At the same time, the Eastern Caribbean–U.S. relationship was cemented by the fact that it was these states that requested U.S. intervention in Grenada. Barbados in particular, having moved closer to the United States in the late 1970s, affirmed its solidly pro-West orientation in playing a leading role in the Grenada intervention. Meanwhile, Belize experienced a change of government in 1984 that brought a more conservative government into power. At the same time, for most of these countries, relationships with the Third World remained important, and support for Third World political and economic causes continued.

At the end of the 1980s, domestic changes and potential changes are producing the possibility of new configurations in international policies. In 1986 both Barbados and Trinidad and Tobago changed governments: In the first instance, a less openly pro-U.S. government was installed; in the second, a more pro-West government. Guyana's foreign (and domestic) policy after Burnham is still in the process of redefinition in the late 1980s. And in Jamaica, Manley was returned to power in 1989, and may pursue once again a more militant, albeit more moderated, foreign policy.

Table 1.3 provides a schematic representation of the broad outlines of foreign policy changes that have taken place in the region under

TABLE 1.3. Major Thrusts of Caribbean Foreign Policy

Time Period	Type of Foreign Policy	Influencing Events	Primary Orientation	Major Linkages
1962-1969	Status quo	Internal: peaceful transition to independence / External: bipolar international system	Pro-West	West/Carifta/U.N.
1970-1979	Nationalist and / Militant Nationalist	Internal: "Black Power" movements / External: U.S. in Vietnam/Civil rights unrest in U.S./detente/ strengthening of Non-Aligned movement/flexibility of Carter administration in U.S.	Third World	West/Carifta-Caricom/ Third World at U.N. and in Non-Aligned Movement / Specific attention to broadening of links with Latin America and Afro-Asia / Soviet bloc/Cuba/ Nicaragua/militant Middle East, Asia and Africa
1979-1983	Conservative/moderate	Internal: Independence of Eastern Caribbean and rise of conservative governments there/change of government in Jamaica/Grenada invasion / External: Reagan administration in U.S.	Pro-West/Moderate Third World	West/Caricom/Third World at U.N. and in Non- Aligned Movement

study. Our aim in this book is to supply some empirical data and analysis to fill out this brief descriptive outline and, in so doing, to provide a framework for theorizing about the Caribbean.

Existing Theoretical Frameworks
and Their Relevance to the Study
of Caribbean Foreign Policy

The traditional international relations literature has produced a number of frameworks that have guided researchers in the formulation and testing of foreign policy theory. Most of these can be usefully incorporated into a framework for the study of Caribbean foreign policy.

Among these frameworks or "models," is James Rosenau's pre-theory of foreign policy that posits the relevance to foreign policy outcomes of five sets of variables: individual-level factors (values, beliefs, personality of decision-makers), societal, governmental, role (roles decision-makers occupy), and systemic (external environmental) factors. Moreover, Rosenau proposed that the influence of these factors will vary according to size, level of economic development, and type of political system, to which he later added the level of "penetration" (participation of outsiders in decision-making) of the system, and the issue-area in which policy is being made.[31]

The value of Rosenau's scheme has been primarily to provide classificatory guidelines to empirically minded researchers. Comparative foreign policy specialists have focused largely on testing certain aspects of the model, especially the effects of size, development, and political system on foreign policy behavior. A substantial literature on the effects of these "national attributes" has evolved.[32] Given the prevalence of this type of testing in the comparative foreign policy field and the obvious importance of size to the foreign policy of the countries in our study, we find it useful to test here what influence Rosenau's variables have on the Caribbean. Rosenau posited that in small, developing, relatively open societies such as those of the Caribbean, the primary influences on foreign policy will be individual, followed by systemic, role, societal and governmental factors. We will apply aspects of this framework in our chapter on influences.

Rosenau's issue-areas were territorial, status, human resource, and non-human resource areas. However, most researchers have opted for more general and more easily defined categories of behavior, primarily military/security, political or diplomatic, economic, and societal or sociocultural areas.[33] We find that Caribbean foreign policy can adequately be analyzed according to three issue-areas: security (which includes some social issues), diplomatic, and economic (which also inherently involves some social concerns.) Issue-area classification is useful not only for organizing analyses of foreign policy but also for theorizing, in that the expectation is that foreign policy and foreign policy influences differ according to issue-areas. Again, this idea is worth testing in the Caribbean context.

The mainstream, primarily U.S., foreign policy literature has also relied heavily on decision-making frameworks, of which the most popular have been those of Richard Snyder, H. W. Bruck and Burton Sapin, of Michael Brecher, and of Graham T. Allison.[34] Snyder's comprehensive framework listed as influences on decision-making the internal human and non-human environment, the external environment (other societies and cultures, states, and the non-human environment), the domestic social structure and behavior, and the decision-making process itself (perceptions, characteristics of the decision-making unit, communication and information, and motivation). Brecher and colleagues' "framework for research on foreign policy behavior" presents a less complex though similar model that includes as inputs the operational environment (external systemic factors and internal capability factors), communications, the psychological environment (societal and personality factors), and the decision process (formulation and implementation of decisions).

The last framework, Allison's model, has contributed a focus on the effects of bureaucratic and organizational competition and procedures on the decisional outcome. However, scholars working on Third World countries have generally avoided this model, since it was developed specifically to describe U.S. policymaking. In fact, the psychological emphasis of Snyder and Brecher has long been considered the most applicable model for the Third World, given the dominance of individuals in Third World decision-making. Nevertheless, there has been a growing backlash against the presumption that idiosyncratic factors are overwhelmingly predominant in Third World policy. Clearly, as the decision-making process has become more technocratic to suit an increasingly more complex world environment, the role of personality is decreasing proportionately. This is why Bahgat Korany, for example, calls for more attention to be paid to the operational environment of Third World foreign policy.[35]

In the case of the Caribbean, although personalism has pervaded decision-making, there are aspects of the operational environment that are of equal, even greater, importance than individual-level factors. These include geopolitical and international systemic considerations as well as size, economic, political, and historical/cultural considerations. Any model of Caribbean external behavior must reflect these complexities.

In recent times, new contributions to the field of comparative foreign policy have been made by political economists, largely following the dependency and world systems schools, and by others researching trends toward global interdependence. The importance of the economic dimension of foreign policy has been highlighted by these theorists, as has the influence of economic interaction on patterns of compliance/consensus or resistance on the part of states.[36] The political economist's view of the state as actor in the economy, rather than simply as the

FIGURE 1.1.   Preliminary Framework for Analyzing Caribbean Foreign Policy

Influences   Processes

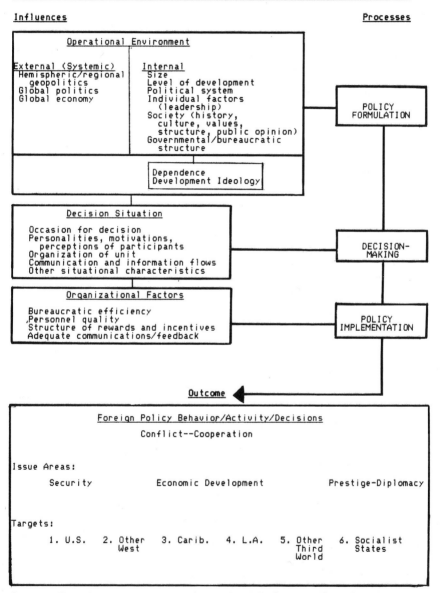

Sources: This framework draws on the works of M. Brecher, Decisions in Israel's Foreign Policy (London: Oxford University Press, 1974); Richard C. Snyder, H. W. Bruck and Burton Sapin, eds., Foreign Policy Decision-Making: An Approach to the Study of International Politics (New York: Free Press, 1962); and James Rosenau, "Pre-Theories and Theories of Foreign Policy," in R. Barry Farrell, eds., Approaches to Comparative and International Politics (Evanston, Ill.: Northwestern University Press, 1976): 27-92.

sum total of the actions of decision-makers, is also beginning to contribute a new dimension to comparative foreign policy.[37]

These contributions are relevant to the study of Caribbean foreign policy, given the fact that the Caribbean economies are intimately linked to the global capitalist economy and that Caribbean economic dependence on Western countries has in large part determined the scope and direction of their security and diplomatic activities as well. Thus the role of international economic factors, mediated through national development orientations, must be incorporated into any model of Caribbean foreign policy.

Figure 1.1 gives a schematic representation of a tentative framework for analyzing Caribbean foreign policy, based on the discussion above. The rest of the book is devoted to detailing the various aspects of this framework and, in the process, refining the model itself.

Notes

1. Bahgat Korany, "The Take-Off of Third World Studies: The Case of Foreign Policy," *World Politics* 35 (3), April 1983: 465–466.

2. Jennie K. Lincoln, "Introduction to Latin American Foreign Policy: Global and Regional Dimensions," in Elizabeth G. Ferris and Jennie K. Lincoln, eds., *Latin American Foreign Policies: Global and Regional Dimensions* (Boulder, Colo.: Westview, 1981): 3. Significant work on Latin American foreign policy, from the Latin American point of view, is currently being done in Chile by PROSPEL, which produces a review entitled *Politicas Exteriores*, and in Puerto Rico by the Social Science Council of the University of Puerto Rico (CLASCO). INTAL, associated with the Inter-American Development Bank, has also produced useful research on Latin American and Caribbean integration.

3. Ibid., p. 5.

4. Paget Henry and Carl Stone use the adjective "newer" in their edited volume *The Newer Caribbean* (Philadelphia: Institute for the Study of Human Issues, 1983). However, the use of it is never explained, and Haiti, the Dominican Republic, and Puerto Rico are included in their analyses. Here I am referring only to those independent territories that emerged in the twentieth century. See Chapter 1's section on geographical scope for details.

5. Roy Preiswerk, "The New Regional Dimensions of the Foreign Policies of Commonwealth Caribbean States," Introduction to Preiswerk, ed., *Regionalism and the Commonwealth Caribbean* (Trinidad: Institute of International Relations, 1969): 1–24.

6. See Basil Ince, "The Administration of Foreign Affairs in a Very Small Developing Country: The Case of Trinidad and Tobago," in Vaughan A. Lewis, ed., *Size, Self-Determination and International Relations: The Caribbean* (Mona, Jamaica: Institute for Social and Economic Research, 1976): 307–339; Ince, "Leadership and Foreign Policy Decision-Making in a Small State: Trinidad and Tobago's Decision to Enter the OAS," in Basil Ince, Anthony T. Bryan, Herb Addo, Ramesh Ramsaran, eds., *Issues in Caribbean International Relations* (Lanham, Md.: University Press of America, 1983); Ince, "Parliament and Foreign Policy in a Commonwealth Caribbean State: The Case of Trinidad and Tobago," in L. F. Manigat, ed., *Caribbean Yearbook of International Relations 1976* (Leyden, Neth.:

A. W. Sijthoff; Trinidad: Institute of International Relations, 1977): 325–346; and Ince, "The Information Gap and Non-Consultation: Effects on Foreign Policy-Making in Commonwealth Caribbean States," *International Journal* 34, Spring 1979: 227–250.

7. Among others, see Basil Ince, ed., *Contemporary International Relations of the Caribbean* (Trinidad: Institute of International Relations, 1979); *Issues et al.*, op. cit.; and Manigat, *Caribbean Yearbook 1976*, and *Caribbean Yearbook 1975*. The institute also publishes occasional papers.

8. Among these local scholars are Vaughan Lewis, Anthony Bryan, Henry Gill, Carl Parris, and George Danns. Among those abroad are Locksley Edmonson and Anthony Maingot.

9. Robert Crassweller, *The Caribbean Community: Changing Societies and U.S. Policy* (New York: Praeger, 1972).

10. G. Pope Atkins, *Latin America in the International Political System* (New York: Free Press, 1977); John Bartlow Martin, *U.S. Policy in the Caribbean* (Boulder, Colo.: Westview, 1978).

11. Harold Davis and Larman Wilson, eds., *Latin American Foreign Policies* (Baltimore: Johns Hopkins University Press, 1975); Ferris and Lincoln, *Latin American Foreign Policies.*

12. Richard Millett and W. Marvin Will, eds., *The Restless Caribbean: Changing Patterns of International Relations* (New York: Praeger, 1979). A second edition, *Crescents of Conflict*, is in press.

13. In particular, see H. Michael Erisman, ed., *The Caribbean Challenge: U.S. Policy in a Volatile Region* (Boulder, Colo.: Westview, 1984); and H. Michael Erisman and John D. Martz, eds., *Colossus Challenged: The Struggle for Caribbean Influence* (Boulder, Colo., Westview, 1982).

14. Georges A. Fauriol, *Foreign Policy Behavior of Caribbean States* (Lanham, Md.: University Press of America, 1984). All references to Fauriol's work in this book are from the original dissertation available from University Microfilms International, Ann Arbor, Michigan.

15. Georges A. Fauriol, *Foreign Policy Behavior and the Smaller Less Developed States* (Ph.D. dissertation. Ann Arbor, Michigan: University Microfilms International, 1983): 52, quoting from Stephen A. Salmore, Margaret G. Hermann, Charles F. Hermann, and Barbara G. Salmore, "Conclusions: Towards Integrating the Perspectives," in Maurice East, Stephen Salmore and Charles Hermann, *Why Nations Act: Theoretical Perspectives for Comparative Foreign Policy Studies* (Beverly Hills, Calif.: Sage, 1978).

16. David Vital, *The Inequality of States: A Study of the Small Powers in International Relations* (Oxford: Clarendon Press, 1967); Jacques Rapoport, Ernest Muteba, and Joseph J. Therattil, *Small States and Territories: Status and Problems,* United Nations Institute for Training and Research Series No. 3 (New York: Arno Press, 1971); Charles L. Taylor, "A Statistical Typology of Micro-States and Territories: Towards a Definition of a Micro-State," Annex to UNITAR study above; Patricia Wohlgemuth Blair, *The Ministate Dilemma* (New York: Carnegie Endowment for International Peace, 1968); Elmer Plischke, *Microstates in World Affairs: Policy, Problems and Options* (Washington, D.C.: American Enterprise Institute, 1977).

17. Plischke, *Microstates*, 24.

18. Vaughan A. Lewis, "The Commonwealth Caribbean and Self-Determination in the International System," in Lewis, *Size, Self-Determination*, 229.

19. James N. Rosenau, "Pre-Theories and Theories of Foreign Policy" in R. Barry Farrell, ed., *Approaches to Comparative and International Politics* (Evanston, Ill.: Northwestern University Press, 1976): 27–92. See especially Table 2, p. 48, and p. 65.

20. For an overview, see C. Richard Bath and Dilmus P. James, "Dependency Analysis of Latin America," *Latin American Research Review* 11 (3), 1976: 3–54.

21. For more, see my *Interpreting the Third World: Politics, Economics, and Social Issues* (New York: Praeger, 1986).

22. For more on the activity of the neutralists, see Peter Willetts, *The Non-Aligned Movement: The Origins of a Third World Alliance* (New York: Nichols, 1978).

23. Marshall R. Singer, *Weak States in a World of Powers: The Dynamics of International Relationships* (New York: Free Press, 1972): 216.

24. John Sewell and the Staff of the Overseas Development Council, *The United States and World Development, Agenda 1977* (New York: Praeger for the ODC, 1977): 2.

25. For more on the West Indies Federation, see Sir John Mordecai, *The West Indies: The Federal Negotiations* (Evanston, Ill.: Northwestern University Press, 1968).

26. See Cheddi Jagan, *The West on Trial: My Fight for Guyana's Freedom* (London: Michael Joseph, 1966); and Peter Simms, *Trouble in Guyana* (London: Allen and Unwin, 1966).

27. For more, see my "Changes in the English-speaking Caribbean: Implications for the International System," *Latin American and Caribbean Contemporary Record*, vol. 1, 1981–1982: 101–109.

28. *Declaration of Sophia*, Address by the Leader of the People's National Congress, Prime Minister Forbes Burnham at a Special Congress to Mark the 10th Anniversary of the P.N.C. in Government, December 14, 1974. (Georgetown, Government Printery).

29. United Nations General Assembly Resolutions 3201 and 3202, May 1974.

30. Eric Williams' well-known anti-Venezuela speech to his party on May 4, 1975, was published under the title *The Threat to the Caribbean Community* (Port-of-Spain: PNM Publishing Company). On Venezuela's relations with the Caribbean, see Andres Serbin, ed., *Geopolitica de las Relaciones de Venezuela con el Caribe* (Caracas: Fundacion Fondo Editorial Acta Cientifica, 1982).

31. Rosenau, "Pre-Theories," 71–91.

32. For an overview, see, for example, Michael P. Sullivan's *International Relations: Theories and Evidence* (Englewood Cliffs, N.J.: Prentice-Hall, 1976), or Patrick M. Morgan, *Theories and Approaches to International Politics* (New Brunswick, N.J.: Transaction Books, 1987).

33. See, for example, Michael Brecher, B. Steinberg, and J. Stein, "A Framework for Research on Foreign Policy Behavior," *Journal of Conflict Resolution* 13 (1), March 1969: 75–102; and Charles F. Hermann, Maurice A. East, Margaret G. Hermann, Barbara G. Salmore, and Stephen A. Salmore, *CREON: A Foreign Events Data Set* (Beverly Hills, Calif.: Sage, 1973).

34. Richard C. Snyder, H. W. Bruck and Burton Sapin, "Decision-Making as an Approach to the Study of International Politics," in Snyder, Bruck, and Sapin, eds., *Foreign Policy Decision-Making* (New York: Free Press, 1962); Michael Brecher, *Decisions in Israel's Foreign Policy* (London: Oxford University Press, 1974); Graham T. Allison, *Essence of Decision: Explaining the Cuban Missile Crisis* (Boston: Little, Brown, 1971).

35. Bahgat Korany, with contributors, *How Foreign Policy Decisions are Made in the Third World* (Boulder, Colo.: Westview, 1986): 48.

36. See, for example, Neil R. Richardson and Charles W. Kegley, Jr., "Trade Dependency and Foreign Policy Compliance," *International Studies Quarterly* 24 (2), June 1980: 191–222; Bruce E. Moon, "Consensus or Compliance? Foreign Policy Change and External Dependence," *International Organization* 39 (2), Spring 1985: 297–330; and David A. Baldwin, *Economic Statecraft* (Princeton, N.J.: Princeton University Press, 1985).

37. See James Capososo, Charles F. Hermann, Charles W. Kegley, Jr., James N. Rosenau, and Dina A. Zinnes, "The Comparative Study of Foreign Policy: Perspectives on the Future," *International Studies Notes* 13 (2), Spring 1987: 33, 38.

2. Caribbean Foreign Policy Goals and Strategies

In a pioneering attempt to devise a framework for analyzing Caribbean foreign policy, Roy Preiswerk concentrated on goals and strategies. He defined Caribbean foreign policy goals as first, fulfillment of economic needs (specifically, access to traditional markets for crops and to new markets for manufactures; securing financial and technical aid for social and infrastructural purposes and for diversification of agriculture; increased tourism; and financing of common services); second, security; and third, anti-racialism and anti-colonialism. He identified the corresponding strategies as preservation and diversification (of external ties); commitment to the Western world; and support of the United Nations.[1]

Identification of the goals of foreign policy is a difficult process. As James Rosenau has pointed out:

> Few aspects of the field are more resistant to clarifying analysis than the objectives that states pursue in their international relationships. Foreign policy goals have been the subject of extensive investigation and have been classified and conceptualized in countless ways. Peace, security, power and prosperity have been identified as long-range goals . . . [but] . . . because these concepts are so general, they fail to differentiate one type of goal-seeking action from another. . . . [I]t is [also] necessary to determine what kinds and amounts of data will constitute evidence of the existence of foreign policy goals. . . . This is not an easy task. Decisions must be made as to the reliability of official pronouncements of goals, with regard to the handling of discrepancies between past behavior and announcements of revised plans for the future, concerning the relative weight to be attached to historical, political, economic, social, geographic, and a host of other factors.[2]

While the analysis of goals is problematic, this does not mean that it should be eschewed altogether. For one, as far as the Caribbean is concerned, a look at the speeches or writings of decision-makers and former decision-makers reveals quite a few references to "goals" and "objectives," leading the researcher to conclude that goal setting is quite important to the practitioner. This is not to say that objectives are always clearly defined: clarity of definition depends on the sophistication of decision-makers and the level of organization of the foreign policy bureaucracy. It is also clear that policymakers may state different objectives at different times. Nevertheless, observation suggests that small states tend to vary less on this dimension than large states do, perhaps because they have limited scope for action and therefore limited aims. Small states also conduct much of their foreign policy rhetorically, given the limited capacity for action, so the researcher cannot ignore official pronouncements on foreign policy altogether.

The broad goals of foreign policy in the Caribbean can be stated without much controversy, based on Preiswerk's suggestions: States are concerned with *security* (survival of the system, the government, and the prevailing value system, and peace), *economic development* (economic survival and, if at all possible, "prosperity"), and *prestige* or status (achieving some level of international visibility and influence; Preiswerk's goal of "anti-racialism and anti-colonialism," with its concomitant strategy of support for the United Nations, can best be seen in this light).

It is generally accepted that Third World states place highest priority on the goal of economic development, as reflected, for example, in Preiswerk's framework. Logic suggests that the Caribbean states, with limited resource endowments and small-scale, primarily island, economies, would rank this goal first. Yet this is not always the case. In the Caribbean as elsewhere, there have been times when security issues have been the overriding or comparably important concern for governments. Examples of this have been Guyana's territorial problems with Venezuela; Grenada's concerns about the United States between 1979 and 1983; and the Eastern Caribbean's misgivings about Grenada in 1979 to 1983. Additionally, some states have searched more actively than others for prestige or status in the international system. The socialist-leaning states/governments, in particular, have stressed global status issues in their goal setting. (Interestingly, because of the uniqueness of their ideological experiments to the Caribbean, the leaders of these countries have taken some pains to enunciate their positions, with the result that more specific foreign policy statements are available for these countries/governments than for others.) For example, in describing Jamaica's foreign policy objectives in the 1970s, Michael Manley noted first that "we would seek to avoid being sucked into the East/West polarisation and play our part in the building of a third, non-aligned political force."[3] Similarly, the Minister of External Affairs of Grenada's People's Revolutionary Government offered the following as guiding "principles" of Grenada's foreign policy:

1. Anti-imperialism and Non-Alignment;
2. Achievement of a New International Economic Order;
3. Promotion of World Peace and Co-operation;

4. Pursuit of Regional Co-operation and Integration;
5. Support for National Liberation struggles.[4]

Again, non-alignment has been placed first and, except for principle 4, global participation is emphasized. Guyana, too, has consistently emphasized the priority of non-alignment.

Thus the hierarchy of goals varies depending on specific circumstances, both external (environmental events) and internal. Internal events include not only governmental changes but also societal pressures and economic changes—that is, the determination of foreign policy goals is affected by all the factors that affect the foreign policy process as a whole. To give an example, in 1975 Barbados' Minister of External Affairs confidently noted that "it is clear that national economic development is Barbados' main foreign policy goal" and that "We have neither the resources nor the desire to exercise military power."[5] But by 1983, while economic development remained a priority, security had also become a major issue, and Barbados had turned toward militarization to achieve its goals. Again, while economic development was clearly the prime goal of the larger Caribbean countries after independence in the 1960s, societal and environmental changes allowed them to become more active globally in the 1970s, leading to an elevation of the goal of prestige.

The presumption, then, is that Caribbean foreign policy is guided by a changeable hierarchy of broadly defined goals of security, development and prestige. This is confirmed in interviews with diplomats whose views were solicited on the theory that they must act according to official guidelines of some sort, either written or verbal, stated or implied. Responses were part of a larger series of responses solicited by mail and in personal interviews with diplomats at the United Nations, an organization of particular importance to small states. When asked "what are the foreign policy goals of your country?" most answered in general terms: "peace and development"; "economic development"; "to contribute to the establishment of world peace"; "regionalism, peace and defense of sovereignty"; "friendly relations with democratic countries"; "projection of image of country as that of a stable democracy; friendly relations with countries with similar philosophy." One specific answer was "to maximize official development assistance." Guyana's permanent representative to the United Nations (to 1986), Noel Sinclair, in an in-depth interview, gave a most complete answer: "maintenance of our independence and territorial integrity; friendship with those who profess our ideals; to be respected as a member of the international community; and to seek to win friends in support of Guyana's development."[6] On the whole, respondents from the smaller Eastern Caribbean states placed economic development first, while respondents from the larger countries gave broader political aims. Democracy was the concern of Grenadian diplomats, and territorial integrity was, not suprisingly, given as a priority for Guyana.

Based on the above, we can make the following assumptions about the goals of the English-speaking Caribbean states:

1. Caribbean states pursue broad goals of security, economic development and prestige/status in the international system.
2. Economic development will normally be given priority but not when threats are perceived to the security of the state.
3. Absent any perception of threat, the behavior of the Eastern Caribbean states is best analyzed in terms of their search for economic development.
4. Absent any perception of threat, the behavior of the larger states is best analyzed in terms of the search for both prestige and economic development.
5. Left-leaning states/governments have given more priority to the goal of prestige than have states with more conservative political orientations.

It is not enough, however, to describe the broad foreign policy goals of Caribbean countries. Although the goals may remain relatively constant, changes are continually taking place in the definition of the goals themselves, in the definition of specific objectives subsumed within the broader goals, and in the strategies espoused to achieve goals. First, there are the goals themselves. There have been changing definitions of the essence of security, of development, of prestige. For most of the Caribbean, security in the 1960s and early 1970s clearly meant preservation of territorial integrity and, incidentally, self-preservation on the part of the governmental elite. Most of the states were not threatened physically by any power, but just in case, given their limited military capabilities, they opted to depend on the United States and Britain (see Chapter 3). Real territorial problems only pertained to Guyana and Belize, and the latter was not yet independent. For most of the 1960s, Guyana was under siege from Venezuela, which claimed five-eighths of its territory and over a period of time annexed the Guyanese part of Ankoko Island on the disputed border, issued a decree annexing the marine borders of the disputed Essequibo, and was involved in various seditious activities within Guyana, including an attempted rebellion in the south.[7] In 1967, the Caribbean also had to cope with another threat to territorial integrity, this time Anguilla's rebellion against St. Kitts/Nevis. Anguilla decided to revert to full colonial status rather than be part of the Associated State of St. Kitts/Nevis.

It cannot be said that the conception of security was strictly territorial. Since the 1950s, as noted in Chapter 1, Guyana had been the scene of Cold War tensions with British and U.S. interference in its affairs. But after independence this threat was reduced by Prime Minister Burnham's alliance with the United States. Instead, the Caribbean conception of non-territorial (specifically, ideological) security was defined in terms of nearby Cuba. As Preiswerk then noted:

Because of Cuba, the rejection of Communism is not simply accomplished by ignoring the existence of the sources of Communist power. Jamaica, a close neighbour of Cuba, and Trinidad, aware of Castro-inspired subversive activities in Venezuela, display extreme vigilance in matters of Communist penetration. Both countries have banned the importation of Communist literature and the Jamaican government has acquired notoriety for withdrawing passports from University lecturers who visit Castro's island. One of the major elements which accounts for the close relationship between Trinidad and Venezuela is the recognition of a mutual interest in the control of Communist infiltrators using Trinidad either as a springboard or as a retreat from their activities on the continent.[8]

Venezuelan president Romulo Betancourt (1959 to 1963) was a particular target of Castro, and the newly independent Trinidad and Tobago found itself very much involved when in 1963 a Venezuelan airliner was hijacked by anti-government, Castro-inspired guerrillas of the Fuerzas Armadas de Liberacion Nacional. When Trinidad refused to give the hijackers political asylum, the residence of the Trinidadian ambassador to Caracas and the British embassy were bombed. Caribbean anti-Castroism, then, was not just prompted by the region's relationship with the United States; it also stemmed from a genuine concern about political survival in the face of Castro's revolutionary activities in the hemisphere.

In the 1970s and 1980s, in view of the environmental and internal changes already described, the goal of security in the Caribbean was redefined or expanded. The aim of territorial integrity remained: Despite the freezing of the border dispute with Venezuela in 1970, Guyana still faced problems with Suriname and with French Guyana; the Guatemala-Belize dispute threatened to prevent Belize from gaining its independence; and a secessionist attempt by St. Vincent's Union Island in 1979 was put down only with help from Barbados forces. But there were new slants to the traditional territorial emphasis. First, in 1975 the prime minister of Trinidad and Tobago raised concerns not only about Venezuelan territorial ambitions in Guyana but also in Curacao, and possibly Trinidad, and special concerns were raised in the context of the law of the sea. (See Chapter 3.) Then, in 1981 new issues were raised when an invasion of Dominica was foiled as it was about to be launched from the United States by a group affiliated with the Ku Klux Klan.

Trinidad's concern about Venezuelan ambitions also included a broader definition of security as protection against Venezuelan cultural, economic, and political expansionism or "imperialism." Moreover, some of the actions taken by Caribbean states in the 1970s can be seen as reflecting a similar concern about security from U.S. "imperialism." The economic aspect of this security concern, closely related to the goal of economic development, was in accord with the Third World programs that gained international prominence in the 1970s and 1980s. For the Third World, the goal of security was not just a military issue—an area in which the Caribbean continues to be ill-equipped—but also an economic and social issue in two senses: first, the belief that territorial security or stability depends in no small measure on economic and social development; and second, the right of all states to adopt the economic and social systems they see fit. For example, as to the first, Bahamas' Prime Mininster Lynden Pindling, speaking on behalf of the Commonwealth, noted in 1985:

> [A Commonwealth] study has emphasized the fact that security is a multifaceted issue which needs to be addressed simultaneously on a variety of fronts, thereby requiring action at the national, regional and international levels and in the economic, political and military spheres. There was a solemn recognition of the integral link between poverty and defence-lessness.[9]

Pindling went on to introduce a new social element, noting that Caribbean "peace, stability and security" are seriously threatened by the drug trafficking barons because these states "straddle the flight paths and sea lanes between the narcotics-producing countries of South America and the principal consumer markets on the North American continent."[10] Clearly, the type of concerns that now fall under "security" go well beyond simply threats to physical survival.

On the second socioeconomic definition, security came to include the right of all states to choose their economic, social, cultural, and political systems as they see fit, without outside coercion and interference. The second principle, discussed since the 1960s in the United Nations, was enshrined in the U.N.'s Charter of Economic Rights and Duties of States.[11] In a similar vein, in 1975 the concept of "collective economic security" was incorporated into the Inter-American (Rio) Treaty of Reciprocal Assistance, the security treaty of the Organization of American States.[12]

The issue of economic aggression and security was closely linked to the greatest change in the definition of security in the Caribbean in the 1970s and 1980s: the introduction of ideological criteria. The states that turned to socialism in the 1970s were all subjected to economic coercion on the part of the United States. Bilateral aid was reduced or cut off and multilateral agencies were pressured to deny loans or, in the case of the International Monetary Fund, to impose its strictest conditions. The socialist states also alleged that they were the targets of other types of destabilization attempts sponsored by the United States, and thus they defined their security in the context of "imperialism."

On the other hand, at least after the Grenada revolution, there was the perception by the non-socialist states of a security threat that was in accord with the U.S. perception. The threat perceived was not a territorial one (a physical takeover by Grenada/Cuba/Soviet Union) but a threat to governmental survival through contagion and possibly sub-version, as well as a threat to the traditional political culture. This security concern culminated in the U.S.–Eastern Caribbean intervention in Grenada in 1983.

In sum, the broad goal of security has, for the Caribbean countries as for most nations, been defined differently at different times. Redefinitions (or expansions of the goal) have taken place, so that security now involves not just issues of territorial survival but also regime survival involving economic and ideological dimensions and also issues of economic and social integrity.

The goal of economic development has also been perceived in different terms across the years, but the variation here is almost exclusively attributable to ideological differences. Andrew Kamarck's comment in 1966, made within the African context, is still very valid:

> The economic forces affecting politics and foreign policy stem from a) the structure and nature of a country's domestic economy and its external economic and financial relationships, b) the objectives of the government and people as to the kind of economy and external economic relationships they want, and c) the tension between "what is" and "what ought to be" or "what is desired to be."[13]

"What ought to be" or "what is desired to be" for most Caribbean countries has been economic growth along Western developmental lines, a choice engendered by the structure of Caribbean economies and the various dependent linkages that are in place. (Of course, "what is" has not in any way kept up with "what is desired to be.") The Western economic outlook has not at all precluded a rhetorical concern with questions of equity. Even in the 1960s, Preiswerk could say:

> The almost exclusive objective of the foreign policy devised by the Governments in the Commonwealth Caribbean is to ensure that conditions prevail on the external scene which favour the achievement of a high domestic growth rate of the economies, the *general improvement of living standards of the population and the reduction of unemployment* (emphasis added).[14]

Or again, in the mid-1970s, the Democratic Labor Party government of Barbados was defining its foreign policy thrust as geared toward national economic development seen as "improving the quality of life of Barbadian citizens."[15]

For these countries, what has changed across time is the strategies used to achieve this "growth with equity" (or growth with quality) rather than the definition of the objective itself. On the other hand, a few governments have indeed changed their definition of development in favor of "independent" or "self-reliant" development,[16] entailing the same equity objectives but with some "de-linking" from the capitalist economy.

Finally, the goal of international visibility or prestige has also undergone some redefinitions across the years in the sense that the perception of what it involves has been expanded. Even though a country may achieve status through regional activities, it is surely in the global realm that it must seek broad international repute. Initially very aware of their limitations as small states, the English-speaking Caribbean countries confined their activities in the global arena to support for anti-colonialism, anti-racialism, and human rights in the United Nations. Across the years, as Third World issues increased in global importance, Caribbean countries have expanded their objectives, seeking prestige through greater global participation in conference diplomacy and diversification of their diplomatic ties and involvements. Expectations of participation have increased, as evidenced by our interviews with U.N. diplomats, almost all of whom wanted their countries to become more active on a wider range of issues. It should also be noted that a certain amount of prestige can be achieved through having a strong relationship with the superpowers: Countries in such a position can try to gain leverage over their superpower partners as well as over their regional colleagues. Thus, for example, Israel's relationship with the United States has allowed it to gain leverage over that superpower and international influence beyond its size and resources; Saudi Arabia's similar relationship has allowed it to exercise more regional and global influence than it might otherwise have, oil wealth notwithstanding; Cuba's relationship with the Soviet Union has also allowed it to increase its regional and global influence. Recent special relationships or interactions between the United States and Jamaica and Barbados (and even, briefly, Dominica) can be viewed in this light.

So far we have been discussing the changes that have taken place in the definition of foreign policy goals over the last two decades. However, within each broad goal, countries specify particular objectives, most of which are obvious from our discussion above. For example, under security, countries have specified preservation of territorial integrity (anti-intervention, anti-secession); preservation of economic integrity (anti-economic coercion from outside); economic and social growth; anti-smuggling/marine pollution/illegal immigration/narcotics trade; and anti-imperialism (U.S., Cuba/Soviet, Venezuela). In economic development, countries have stressed preservation and expansion of markets; commodity price stabilization; preferential treatment by developed countries; access for manufactures to developed-country markets; support for the New International Economic Order and other Third World initiatives; multilateral and bilateral financial assistance for infrastructural development, agricultural and industrial projects, and balance-of-payments problems; attracting foreign investment, with the conditions varying for different countries and at different times; and increased tourism. Finally, in the area of prestige, specific objectives have included exerting influence in regional, and global forums in support of individual, regional and Third World objectives such as decolonization, elimination of racism (especially apartheid), support for human rights, non-alignment, nuclear disarmament, and so on. (This is not to suggest that activities undertaken in these spheres are undertaken solely in order to gain prestige but rather that these activities tend to bring international respect to the actors.)

From the above, it is clear that the line between objectives and strategies is a thin one. In many official documents and scholarly writings, the objectives listed above may have been listed as strategies. Here we are attempting to use the term "strategy" in its pure sense of method or means, not principle. The strategies used to pursue the various foreign policy goals can be described in a general way as the following:

For preservation of territorial and ideological (anti-socialist) integrity: defense arrangements/military agreements with external powers; membership in Rio Treaty (Trinidad and Tobago and Bahamas only) and the OAS; Organization of Eastern Caribbean States (OECS) and Eastern Caribbean security systems; peaceful relations with other countries; membership in the Non-Aligned Movement; cooperation with Third World; use of United Nations machinery; support in organizational forums for non-intervention and peaceful settlement of disputes; military intervention (in the case of Union Island and in Grenada).

For preservation of economic and ideological (anti-U.S.) integrity: Third World cooperation; non-alignment; support for United Nations and OAS; diversification of diplomatic and economic relations; security assistance from Eastern bloc and socialist Third World nations (Grenada).

For economic development (Western model): Continued trade with Western countries; some diversification of trade links, primarily with Latin America; support for regional integration; support for the "Group of 77" (Third World economic bloc); search for aid from Western and regional sources, bilateral and multilateral; search for private investment (with some nationalist conditions imposed in the 1970s and 1980s); support for the New International Economic Order and other Third World initiatives.

For economic development (self-reliant model): Diversification of trade and aid ties, including tapping socialist partners/donors; support for regional integration; support for "Group of 77," New International Economic Order and Third World economic initiatives.

For prestige: Participation in the United Nations activities, including search for elective offices; expansion of diplomatic ties; hosting of international conferences and receiving and sending important official visits; proposing initiatives at regional level; support for Commonwealth; support for Non-Aligned Movement.

Again, this list of strategies is not at all exhaustive but should capture the essence of the type of strategies Commonwealth Caribbean countries have employed. More details are given in the next few chapters as we study the way in which these strategies have been actualized.

In Chapter 1, we referred to the concept of "issue-areas" and its usefulness both as an organizing framework and as a handle by which to compare behavior on different dimensions and to compare behavior with goals. In keeping with the categorization of goals given in this chapter, we can also categorize the output of Caribbean foreign policy in terms of the issue-areas of security, economic development, and prestige. The relationship between the first two clusters of activities and the relevant goals is quite self-evident. The last cluster involves general diplomatic activities that are primarily but not exclusively related to the goals of international influence. These diplomatic activities include such actions as the establishment of diplomatic relations, state visits, and participation in international organizations and conferences. Given the limited resources of very small states, activities such as these are carefully selected not only for prestige reasons but also to achieve other goals such as security or socioeconomic benefits. For example, Guyana's diplomatic initiatives toward the non-aligned countries can be seen as a diplomatic activity that has been undertaken both for prestige and for security against Venezuela. The assumption is that respect for and peaceful relations with a large number of nations reduce the likelihood of external aggression. Or again, Caribbean diplomatic initiatives with respect to a receptive Venezuela, including the signing of several cultural agreements, have been undertaken primarily to achieve economic goals. Thus it should be clear that what is described in this book as "prestige" activities are in most cases also joined to other goals.

Two facets of Caribbean foreign policy behavior are of particular concern as we move on to detailing Caribbean activities: the geographical direction of Caribbean activities and the cooperative and conflictive trends in such activity. Geographically, the broadest categorization is by regional and global dimensions. Within the region, we can assume that the English-speaking Caribbean countries interact first, with one another within the Caribbean Community; second, with other Caribbean and circum-Caribbean (Basin) states, especially Venezuela; and third, with Latin America as a whole. Outside the immediate region, the Commonwealth Caribbean states interact, first, with the United States, their hemispheric neighbor; second, with Europe (including the United Kingdom); third, with Afro-Asia; and fourth and selectively, with the socialist states.

In analyzing the relations of the Caribbean with each of these geographical areas, we will use an inductive approach, considering first the more general and common patterns of cooperative interaction in each of the issue-areas posited: for the security area, the level of military assistance from external sources; for the economic area, trade and aid patterns; and for the diplomatic area, changes in the Caribbean's diplomatic relationships, state visits, and voting in the United Nations. All of these are considered across time from the 1960s to the present. Finally, we will describe the patterns of conflict activity that Caribbean territories have demonstrated up to the present in each of the defined issue-areas.

Notes

1. Roy Preiswerk, "The New Regional Dimensions of the Foreign Policies of Comonwealth Caribbean States," in Preiswerk, ed., *Regionalism and the Commonwealth Caribbean* (Trinidad: Institute of International Relations, 1969): 1–24.

2. James N. Rosenau, "The Actions of States: Theories and Approaches," in Rosenau, ed., *International Politics and Foreign Policy* (New York: Free Press, 1969): 167–1969.

3. Michael Manley, *Jamaica: Struggle in the Periphery* (London: Third World Media Limited in association with Writers and Readers Publishing Cooperative Society Limited, 1982): 66.

4. *Grenada Is Not Alone*, Speeches by the People's Revolutionary Government at the First International Conference in Solidarity with Grenada, November 1981 (St. George's, Grenada: Fedon Publishers, 1982): 108.

5. "The Role of The Foreign Policy in Barbados Development Strategy," Address delivered by Senator the Honorable George C. R. Moe, Q. C., Minister of External Affairs at a Special Meeting of the Barbadian Chamber of Commerce on Thursday, November 27, 1975, *Barbados Bulletin* 1 (3), October–December 1975: 22.

6. Interview with Ambassador Noel Sinclair, December 23, 1986.

7. See my *The Venezuela-Guyana Border Dispute: Britain's Colonial Legacy in Latin America* (Boulder, Colo.: Westview, 1984).

8. Preiswerk, "New Regional Dimensions," 9.

9. Address of Sir Lynden O. Pindling, Prime Minister of the Bahamas, to the 40th session of the U.N. General Assembly, October 23, 1985. (U.N. Doc. A/40/PV. 47, October 24, 1985).

10. Ibid.

11. Originally proposed by the president of Mexico, Luis Echeverria, the charter was drafted over a two-year period under the auspices of the United Nations Conference on Trade and Development by a working group of representatives of U.N. member states. See UNGA Res. 3281(XXIX), December 12, 1974.

12. For details, see *Draft Report of the Permanent Council on the Study of the Texts Proposed by CEESI on the Subjects of Collective Economic Security and Cooperation for Development* (OAS, Washington, D.C., April 28, 1977).

13. Andrew Kamarck, "Economic Determinants," in Vernon McKay, ed., *African Diplomacy: Studies in the Determinants of Foreign Policy* (New York: Praeger, 1966): 56.

14. Preiswerk, "New Regional Dimensions,"2.

15. Address of George Moe, p. 23.

16. See, for example, Michael Manley, *Struggle in the Periphery*, 59–71, especially 65; and *Grenada Is Not Alone*, 116-7 (speech of Unison Whiteman, Minister for Foreign Affairs). For a relatively deep treatment of Guyana's search for self-reliant development, see Robert Manley, *Guyana Emergent: Guyana's Search for Non-Dependent Development* (Boston, Mass.: G. K. Hall; and Cambridge, Mass.: Schenkman, 1979).

3. Patterns and Directions in Policy: Security

General Patterns of Interaction

Given their small size, Caribbean states have not engaged, and have not been inclined to engage, in the external military adventures common to their larger colleagues. As a former Barbadian Minister of External Affairs noted: "We have neither the resources nor the desire to exercise military power. We have little land but we do not (like some with even more than they can properly handle) want to acquire others. We have no quarrels to pursue and do not regard any state as a natural opponent."[1] Although this statement was made in 1975, it continues to apply to Caribbean foreign policy. Thus in 1985, Trinidad and Tobago's Minister of External Affairs reiterated that "Trinidad and Tobago is a small nation that can threaten no one, and for that matter could hardly resist the least sophisticated attack by the powerful."[2] In other words, the security posture of the countries in our survey has been defensive. None of these countries has demonstrated any territorial ambition nor has the military means to promote its influence over others the way that the United States, for example, can promote its influence through military sales and training programs. Nevertheless, in the late 1970s and 1980s, military-security issues attained an important place in Caribbean foreign policy, and some analysts may be tempted to describe Caribbean participation in events in Grenada in offensive terms rather than the defensive explanations given by the participants.

The Caribbean nations have had traditional small-state security concerns, focused on possible, albeit unlikely (except in a world war situation), threats to Caribbean survival coming from outside the core region. This situation has translated into policies of formal or informal alliance with larger powers and the development of peaceful ties with as many countries as feasible, within economic and financial constraints. On the other hand, more likely threats have long been perceived from the domestic rather than external sphere, and external alliances that are apparently entered into for defense purposes are usually also oriented toward preserving internal security. Thus the British defined the functions of the British-imposed armies of Jamaica, Trinidad and Tobago, and Guyana as not just ceremonial and "symbolically" defensive—resisting until help should arrive from the U.N., the United States, or the Commonwealth—but also as providing help to the government in internal security matters.[3] In the 1970s the concern with internal security intensified in two ways: The Caribbean socialist governments feared destabilization by the United States, while the non-socialists feared destabilization by the left-wing states and their allies, specifically Cuba and the Soviet Union. These fears led to the increasing emphasis on military-security issues referred to earlier. In this chapter, we attempt to describe some of the more important activities and linkages of the Caribbean states in the various dimensions of security.

Territorial Security

Guyana and Belize. Two states have had to deal with the very basic security issue of threats to physical survival: Guyana and Belize have unsolved territorial disputes with Venezuela and Guatemala respectively. Venezuela claims almost two-thirds of Guyanese territory, a claim rooted in alleged British expansionism and irregularities in the arbitral procedure of 1899. Guatemala's claim to Belize is rooted in British non-compliance with the terms of a treaty by which Guatemala formally recognized the existence of the British settlement on its eastern coast. Mexico had also claimed part of Belize on historical grounds but dropped its claim in the mid-1970s. Additionally, Guyana has a border dispute with its eastern neighbor, Suriname, over the true course of the river that defines the frontier. However, although this dispute has been periodically troublesome, it has not presented the threat to national security that the dispute with Venezuela has.

The responses of Guyana and Belize to their territorial problems have been both similar and different. Both disputes delayed independence for the countries involved, but the Belize-Guatemala dispute proved to be the more problematic. In the period immediately preceding independence, Guyana, Britain, and Venezuela signed the Geneva Agreement setting up a mixed commission to seek solutions to their dispute.[4] This allowed Guyana to move into independence with a breathing space of four years to devote to the tasks of nation-building, although, as it turned out, there was a high level of conflict between the parties during these four years. Subsequently, in 1970, the parties met in Trinidad and Tobago and agreed to freeze the dispute for twelve years. In 1982, Venezuela refused to renew the 1970 Protocol of Port-of-Spain; the refusal brought back into effect the terms of the Geneva Agreement, specifically the terms calling for the parties to resort to various methods of peaceful settlement. At the time of writing, the United Nations secretary-general's office was trying to mediate the dispute.

The deferral of the dispute between 1970 and 1982 allowed Guyana to become independent without the necessity of security guarantees from Britain, except through continuing Guyanese membership in the Commonwealth. It should be noted that on the Suriname front, that dispute was also minimized in late 1970 by the establishment of a mixed commission to seek a peaceful settlement. Although Britain trained the Guyanese army, as well as the armies and police forces of all the other Caribbean countries before independence, no defense agreement was signed between Guyana and Britain after independence. Instead, Guyana expanded its diplomatic linkages with the Third World, working hard to gain support and prestige at the United Nations and in the Non-Aligned Movement, which it joined in 1970. Guyana's non-aligned activity produced direct results, insofar as the border dispute is concerned, when Venezuela submitted its application for admission to the Non-Aligned Movement in 1983. Guyana objected on the grounds that Venezuela had not renounced the use of force as required by the movement. Guyana's objections delayed action on the Venezuelan request for admission and Venezuela eventually withdrew its application.[5] To Venezuela's chagrin—since Venezuela would like to be considered a leader of the Third World—the non-aligned countries have consistently supported Guyana's position in the dispute.

At the United Nations, Guyana has also used the members' stated opposition to (neo)colonialism and external intervention to its advantage by bringing up the dispute before the General Assembly and the Security Council and portraying Venezuela as imperialistic and aggressive. This was done in the difficult period of the late 1960s, before the Protocol of Port-of-Spain was signed, and in the early 1980s when Venezuela refused to renew the Protocol.[6] Guyana has also relied heavily on regional support. Despite closer relations with Venezuela in the 1970s and 1980s, Caribbean Community nations have fully supported Guyana on this issue. Finally, Guyana has developed stronger functional relations with Venezuela itself both bilaterally and multilaterally through such agencies as the Latin American Economic System (SELA), and the Latin American Energy Organization (OLADE), and the Treaty of Amazonian Cooperation signed in 1978.

In the case of Belize, the dispute with Guatemala delayed independence until 1981, well into the twilight of the global decolonization movement. As in Guyana, the parties sought an agreement that would allow the small state to survive without external pressure after independence, but unlike the Guyanese case, efforts were unsuccessful. The Heads of Agreement of 1981, which gave Guatemala access to the sea through Belizean territorial waters, free port facilities, and the use of the seabeds around two cays,[7] was scuttled by popular opposition in Belize and by new Guatemalan claims. As a result, Belize needed security guarantees in order to gain its independence; these have been provided by Britain, which stationed a garrison in Belize of almost 2,000 men.

Like Guyana, Belize has benefited from "internationalizing" its border problem. In the 1970s, a diplomatic offensive was launched that succeeded in gaining Belize firm support from the Caribbean Community (Caricom), the Commonwealth, and the Non-Aligned Movement in Belize's quest for independence. Caricom support was especially helpful in fragmenting the Latin American bloc and in promoting the issue in international forums. Belize also reached out to Central America, gaining the support of Panama and Nicaragua (after the revolution). By 1981, both the U.N. and the OAS were endorsing independence for Belize, with security guarantees. The United States, which had abstained on U.N. resolutions on Belize since the first one in 1975, now supported independence.[8]

Thus Belize's strategy prior to independence (and activity used to operationalize it) was similar to Guyana's after independence. On the other hand, although Belize was quick to join the Non-Aligned Movement after independence in 1981, it has, unlike Guyana, depended less on sustained international visibility—in which area Belize is constrained by its very small size and lack of resources and skills—and more on its bilateral military arrangement with Britain for its security needs.

Both Guyana and Belize have also concentrated on building up their own militaries for external defense, although in both cases the military is also being used for internal purposes, primarily drug control in Belize's case and, in the case of Guyana, for the self-preservation of the regime. In the 1970s, the Burnham government became increasingly more authoritarian and there was a high level of spending not just on the army but on the paramilitary and police units. Within this context, the border dispute has often been used simply as a pretext for justifying military spending.[9]

Conforming to their different political orientations, Guyana and Belize have sought military assistance, for both their territorial disputes and for other security problems, from quite different sources. Britain has borne primary responsibility for training and equipping the Belize Defense Force and its small naval and air wings. However, the United States, in view of its ideological and anti-narcotics interests, has been playing an increasing role in this area since 1982, training Belizeans under its International Military Education and Training Program (IMET) and providing equipment under the Military Assistance Program (MAP). (Under the IMET program, foreign military personnel are trained in military schools in and outside the United States. Under the MAP program, loans or grants are made to foreign countries for military equipment, technical and administrative support, maintenance of facilities, and other operational support.) Table 3.1 gives the level of this assistance for Belize as well as for other Caribbean countries. Commercial arms sales by the United States to Belize have also been increasing since 1979, and especially after independence (Table 3.2). Moreover, the United States has been negotiating with Belize for the establishment of a military base there.[10] Other countries mentioned as involved in the training of the small Belize Defense Force under bilateral agreements are Canada, Panama, and Jamaica.[11]

Guyana's relatively large military acquisitions across the years have come from more diverse sources. United States Arms Control and Disarmament Agency figures (Table 3.3) show that since 1967 Britain has been Guyana's major supplier of arms, despite curbs supposedly initiated against the Burnham regime in the early 1980s.[12] But there have also been purchases from France, and half of Guyana's arms comes from "unidentified sources." Among these, observers have placed Cuba and North Korea. Note that the ACDA figures show no significant exports of arms to Guyana from the traditional socialist suppliers, most of which have diplomatic relations with Guyana. Guyana has, however, received some military support from these nations.[13] Guyana's military relationship with Cuba has included a limited Cuban military presence in Guyana and Guyanese assistance in ferrying Cuban troops to Angola in 1975. Apart from Cuba and North Korea, Canada, which has Commonwealth ties with the Caribbean, and Brazil, which has a geopolitical interest in Guyana, have to be included in the "unidentified" category of arms sources.

Guyana's military relationship with Brazil was first established in 1969 when Guyana Defense Force personnel participated in a jungle warfare course in Brazil not long after a military cooperation agreement was signed. Brazil extended various lines of credit to Guyana from 1971 on, some of which may have been used for military purchases. However, Brazil's role as arms supplier was only clearly established in 1982 at the height of renewed conflict between Venezuela and Guyana. Brazil extended a $17 million line of credit for military purchases to Guyana, agreeing to sell equipment including troop carriers and reconnaissance planes for patrolling the disputed frontiers.[14]

Finally, although Guyana's security relationship with the United States has not been close,[15] the United States began to assist Guyana in training its military forces in the early 1980s (Table 3.1). During World War II, the United States had established bases, with British agreement, in Guyana as well as in other areas of the Caribbean, including Trinidad and Tobago, Jamaica, Antigua, St. Lucia and the Bahamas. In 1966, the new government renogotiated the base lease agreement of 1941, but the United States maintained the right to use temporary military facilities in Guyana and to overfly Guyana's territory. After independence, Guyana did not sign a defense treaty with the United States, and its army received no U.S. help. However, the Agency for International Development provided counterinsurgency communications and transportation equipment to the police.

Guyana does not appear to have received any government-to-government arms transfers from the United States, although relatively small commercial purchases were made across the years, peaking in 1977 (see Table 3.3). During these years, the Guyana government was attempting

TABLE 3.1. U.S. Military FY(s) Assistance to the Caribbean (dollars in thousands)

Country	FY(s)	FMS[a]	MAP[a]	IMET[a]	IMET Students[b]
Jamaica	1950-1976	157	1,057	13	11
	1977-1980	-[c]	--	--	--
	1981	1,633.-[d]	--	49	8
	1982	--	1,000	73	20
	1983	3,275	2,250	168	73
	1984	2,921	4,000	201	60
	1985	5,687	7,360	281	72
	1986	9,079	7,656	295	59
Guyana	1950-1981	--	--	--	--
	1982	--	--	14	22
	1983	--	--	25	10
	1984-1986	--	--	--	--
Trinidad and Tobago	1950-1976	85	--	--	--
	1977-1980	--	--	--	--
	1981	15	--	--	--
	1982	--	--	--	--
	1983	5	--	--	--
	1984	--	--	--	11
	1985	--	--	39	11
	1986	--	--	50	10
Barbados	1950-1978	--	--	--	--
	1979	--	--	6	1
	1980	--	--	30	13
	1981	13	--	17	12
	1982	--	100	56	10
	1983	3	--	52	22
	1984	--	275	69	22
	1985	132	--	69	18
	1986	355	1,097	69	15
Grenada	1950-1983	--	--	--	--
	1984	2,877	3,750	63	18
	1985	4,615	2,514	63	18
	1986	591	546	75	
Antigua/Barbuda	1950-1982	--	--	--	--
	1983	1,033	633	14	9
	1984	353	377	30	9
	1985	1,559	445	45	11
	1986	615	1,813	45	10

Country	Year	FMS	MAP	IMET ($000)	IMET (students)
Dominica	1950–1980	--	--	--	--
	1981	--	--	8	7
	1982	--	--	4	1
	1983	1,033	300	11	6
	1984	377	733	43	16
	1985	1,359	399	44	8
	1986	548	420	46	10
St. Kitts/Nevis	1950–1983	--	--	--	--
	1984	3,933	1,800	32	10
	1985	388	862	26	7
	1986	--	408	27	8
Saint Lucia	1950–1980	--	--	--	--
	1981	--	--	2	2
	1982	--	--	8	3
	1983	1,033	300	14	6
	1984	377	733	42	15
	1985	1,362	420	48	12
	1986	385	341	48	13
St. Vincent	1950–1980	--	--	--	--
	1981	--	--	1	1
	1982	--	--	--	--
	1983	--	300	31	8
	1984	--	399	44	12
	1985	40	341	51	13
	1986	4,632	2,637	51	13
Bahamas	1950–1984	--	--	--	--
	1985	--	--	44	24
	1986	--	--	46	29
Belize	1950–1981	--	--	--	--
	1982	--	--	20	16
	1983	--	--	48	19
	1984	178	500	50	23
	1985	876	500	100	79
	1986	524	479	72	23

a FMS = Foreign Military Sales; MAP = Military Assistance Program; and IMET = International Military Education and Traning Program. MAP funds include MAP Merger and Excess Defense Articles funds, both applicable for Jamaica only. FMS are agreements, not deliveries (which are naturally less).

b This column gives the absolute number of students trained under the IMET program.

c Less than $500.

d Includes $1,587 from the Foreign Military Sales Financing Program.

Source: U.S. Department of Defense, Foreign Military Sales, Foreign Military Construction Sales and Military Assistance Facts as of September 30, 1986 (Washington, D.C.: Data Management Division, Comptroller, DSAA, 1986).

TABLE 3.2. U.S. Commercial Exports Under Arms Export Act (by fiscal years, dollars in thousands)

	1950-1972	1950-1976	1977	1978	1979	1980	1981	1982	1983	1984	1985	1986
Antigua and Barbuda	35	40	2	2	5	9	1	15	a	--	2	1
Bahamas	30	69	8	10	21	124	46	150	100	47	91	5,088
Barbados	14	51	8	5	26	10	13	15	18	7	69	10
Belize	12	62	12	16	55	73	186	100	7	26	16	181
Dominica	1	11	a	--	--	10	--	--	2	a	11	1
Grenada	5	12	2	1	7	--	--	1	--	--	--	19
Guyana	12	64	113	4	5	7	707	20	5	368	9	32
Jamaica	186	381	216	157	87	48	443	200	175	120	265	206
Saint Kitts/Nevis	--	1	1	--	1	--	--	--	--	--	--	a
Saint Lucia	2	7	3	2	4	1	--	2	--	7	2	3
St. Vincent and Grenadines	3	4	--	--	--	2	--	--	--	1	a	4
Trinidad and Tobago	8	255	27	85	61	368	138	500	659	708	253	182

a Less than $500.

Source: U.S. Department of Defense, Foreign Military Sales, Foreign Military Construction Sales and Military Assistance Facts as of September 30, 1986 (Washington, D.C.: Data Management Division, Comptroller, DSAA, 1986).

TABLE 3.3. Arms Transfers by Major Supplier and Recipient Country (millions current U.S. dollars)[a]

	1967-1976	1976-1980	1978-1982	1979-1983
Recipient				
Barbados	--	--	10 (U.K.)	10 (U.K.)
Guyana	5 (U.K.) 1 (France)	10 (U.K.)	5 (U.K.) 5 (others)	10 (U.K.) 10 (others)
Jamaica	1 (U.S.)	--	--	--
Trinidad and Tobago	1 (U.K.)	20 (others)	20 (others)	20 (others)

[a] Supplier in parenthesis.

Sources: United States Arms Control and Disarmament Agency, World Military Expenditures and Arms Transfers 1967-1976, 1971-1980, 1972-1982, 1985, Washington, D.C., July 1978, p. 160; March 1983, p. 119; April 1984, p. 97; April 1985, p. 133.

to develop a socialist and self-reliant economy. In the early 1980s, Guyana, plagued by economic and political difficulties, turned back to the West for assistance. In the military area, this was reflected in an increase in commercial arms purchases from the United States. The figures show that 86 percent of Guyana's purchases across the years 1950–1986 were made during the period 1981–1986, specifically during 1981 and 1984. Guyana's participation in IMET (discontinued, at least temporarily, in 1988) began in 1982 and reflected the first time since the early post-independence period that Guyana had looked to the United States to meet training needs. (Guyana had benefited in 1966–1970 from police training organized under a program, now defunct, called the U.S. Public Safety Program.)[16]

To sum up the external policy/activities of Guyana and Belize on the issue of territorial security, both have adopted similar strategies in promoting peaceful settlement of the disputes, in searching for international support, and in building up their military capacities through external arrangements. However, Guyana has depended more heavily on international visibility as a strategy to win friends and raise the costs to Venezuela of continuing to press its claim, while Belize has relied on bilateral relationships with Britain and, increasingly, with the United States. Although Guyana has also sought military assistance from outside, its sources of aid have been more diverse than Belize's.

Jamaica and Trinidad and Tobago. The other Caribbean countries, though not in any immediate danger of territorial disintegration, have sought to preserve their physical integrity from threats without and within through a variety of strategies. Among the larger islands, Jamaican policy from the beginning involved heavy reliance on the United States. In 1963 Jamaica signed a military assistance agreement with the United States, under which it received counterinsurgency equipment, primarily for the coast guard and police. Also in the 1960s, the Agency for International Development lent money for the modernization of Jamaica's army and police forces and, like Guyana, Jamaica received assistance under AID's Public Safety Program.[17] At this time and into the 1970s, Britain and Canada appear to have provided most of the training of the military, while the U.S. provided training for other security forces under IMET. A military training agreement had been signed with Canada in 1965, and Britain maintained responsibility for training the army of its former colony.

In terms of arms transfers in the early period of Jamaica's independence, the USACDA reports no data for Jamaica. However, Jamaica was a beneficiary under the U.S. Foreign Military Sales Program under which buyers receive credit for purchases of defense articles. Also, as shown in Table 4.2, Jamaica's commercial arms purchases were high by Caribbean standards ($186,000) between 1950 and 1972.

Jamaica did not only rely on the United States, Britain, and Canada. It also joined the Organization of American States in 1968 and in so doing came under the general security umbrella of the organization. However, the fact that it did not adhere to the Inter-American Treaty of Reciprocal Assistance (Rio Treaty) can be taken as indication not only of its wariness of involvement in Latin American security matters but also of its intention to rely less on OAS mechanisms than on bilateral arrangements for its own security.

Jamaica's military relationship with the United States declined in the late 1970s under the Manley administration at the same time as Jamaica's predominant security concerns were redefined. Internal security became the major issue, seen in terms of U.S. "destabilization" as well as keeping socioeconomic unrest in check. In the 1980s, the issue of internal security, including ideological (now anti-socialist) security, has remained important, this time redefined to reflect the coincidence of interest with the United States.

For Trinidad and Tobago, security concerns have played a relatively minor role in policymaking across the years, although domestic distur-bances in 1970 led to a period of obsession with internal security in the early 1970s. These concerns faded with the advent of unexpected oil wealth in 1973. In the early years of independence, Trinidad's security concerns were probably minimized by the continuing, if not very welcome, U.S. presence at the naval base at Chaguaramas. In any event, there is no evidence of Trinidad's receiving military or police help from the United States until the 1980s.[18] The base was closed in 1967 by agreement of the U.S. and Trinidad governments, and in that year Trinidad and Tobago joined the Organization of American States and adhered to the Rio Treaty. Until 1982 when the Bahamas joined, Trinidad remained the only English-speaking Caribbean country to have adhered to the Rio agreement.

Trinidad's military training needs appear to have been met primarily by Britain and, to a lesser extent. by Canada. In the 1970s, Venezuela also lent some support.[19] Informal security collaboration between the two countries can be said to have existed at least since Trinidad and Tobago extradited the hijackers of a Venezuelan airliner in 1963. Military assistance arrangements in the 1970s can be viewed in terms of both countries' wariness of Cuba. Significantly, in 1970 when civil instability threatened the Trinidad government, Venezuela and the United States provided it with arms and military equipment. Both the United States and the U.K. demonstrated their concern for the island's security, the first by sending a shipload of marines to the area and the other by putting frigates in the region on alert.

Despite this U.S. help in crisis, Trinidad did not receive military aid from the United States in the 1970s. USACDA figures indicate that Trinidad purchased its arms from Great Britain in the 1960s and 1970s and from unidentified suppliers in the late 1970s and early 1980s. These unidentified countries can be assumed to include Canada and Venezuela. Data on commercial sales show that in the 1970s a relatively small amount of arms was purchased from the United States, except in 1975, a time of industrial unrest. The highest purchases have taken place in the 1980s, again attributable to internal events and to the general regional political climate. A significant change in orientation toward the United States has taken place in the second half of the 1980s: Small purchases of arms have been made under the Foreign Military Sales (FMS) program, and IMET training was begun in 1985.

Trinidad's external linkages have been less concentrated than Jamaica's. Distance has been maintained, at least up to the mid-1980s, from the United States and even from Britain. Trinidad also differs from Jamaica in having sought stronger security linkages with the OAS and in having received aid from Venezuela.

Barbados and the Eastern Caribbean. For the Eastern Caribbean, including Barbados, military-security issues have been placed on the agenda only since the late 1970s, when the smaller islands became independent. Although Barbados became independent earlier (1966), security issues were not considered vital, given the island's smallness, and Barbados chose not to enter into any formal alliances with the U.K. or the United States. However, the presence of a U.S. submarine base at St. Lucy, a remnant of World War II, provided an element of security, as did Britain's lingering sense of responsibility. (The base was closed in 1979 in a dispute over payments.) Moreover, Barbados joined the OAS in 1967, assuring itself of another security umbrella. It was only after 1979 that Barbados transformed its largely ceremonial regiment into an army and created an airforce and coast guard. This took place in accordance with a redefinition of security in the wake of the overthrow of Gairy in Grenada, an attempt by mercenaries to overthrow the Barbados government, and the sabotage of a Cuban airline over Barbados. The redefinition was in large measure ideological, but it also focused on "traditional" security concerns of states such as defense of the nation's borders and control of smuggling, piracy, and other activity. Table 3.3. shows that Barbados purchased all its arms during this time from Britain, which gave help primarily for developing the coast guard. The United States also provided assistance in training customs agents and narcotics officers,[20] as well as other ideologically grounded security assistance. Britain too has provided considerable assistance in training the army and police in Barbados.

Meanwhile, as the Eastern Caribbean islands emerged to independence, they formed the Organization of Eastern Caribbean States (OECS) in 1981 to replace the Associated States Council (WISA) and the Eastern Caribbean Common Market. Too small to deal with defense matters alone—which until then were left to Britain—these former Associated States joined the OAS and also provided for defense in the OECS treaty (Article 8). This agreement called for collective defense and the preservation of peace and security against external aggression and cooperation in matters such as combating mercenary activity, Dominica having recently been the target of just such an attack.[21] Except for Antigua and Grenada, the OECS countries had no army per se, only police forces. In 1982, a separate security accord was signed by Barbados, Antigua, Dominica, St. Lucia, and St. Vincent. This one called for mutual aid in several areas, including national emergencies, prevention of smuggling, control of immigration and pollution, and threats to national security.[22] However, in excluding Grenada, this agreement was clear in giving priority to ideological security concerns.

In meeting their defense needs, the Eastern Caribbean states have been assisted by Britain and Canada, as well as by the United States. Because U.S. assistance is closely tied to ideological considerations, it is discussed in the next section. Britain has been training the region's security forces since 1980 and has given technical assistance and other help under its Military Loan Service Personnel program. Canada's aid has also been for training of police forces and the regional coast guard under the 1982 security system.

Among the Eastern Caribbean states, Antigua deserves special mention. It has had a stronger link with the United States than have the other British-oriented Eastern Caribbean states. This stronger link has resulted from the continued presence of a U.S. base established since World War II. In 1977, an agreement was signed allowing the U.S. to continue to use the area for research and testing. In 1985, it was announced that a training center for the regional security system would be established at these facilities. Antigua's external military links have also been somewhat controversial not just because of the relationship with the United States, but also because among those training the Antiguan army was a Canadian company that was subsequently forced to close its Antiguan operations because of charges that it was sending arms to South Africa.

Overall, then, the Eastern Caribbean and Barbados have defined their security in terms of national defense in several areas beyond (but related to) the more well-known ideological area. Their strategies have been to seek military assistance both bilaterally and regionally, and this they have received from the traditional sectors, Britain and Canada. However, as common defense needs have become redefined in ideological terms, major relationships have been developed with the United States.

The Bahamas. Although pro-West in its foreign policy (see economic and diplomatic acvitity in Chapters 4 and 5), the Bahamas has not become embroiled in the ideological concerns of the Caribbean, at least in part because of its relative geographic distance from its more southern neighbors. Rather, Bahamian security concerns have been defined in broad, quite traditional terms—that is, small-power vulnerability—as well as in socioeconomic terms, specifically, issues of smuggling, drug trafficking, fishing rights (vis-à-vis Cuba, the United States, and Dominican Republic), and illegal immigration of Haitians.

Like some of the other Caribbean territories, independent Bahamas inherited several U.S. military bases, a naval base, an oceanographic research center, an airforce missile tracking station, and a Coast Guard navigational radar station. The United States has managed to retain these bases despite some financial conflicts with the Bahamas over the years. Again, as in other Caribbean territories, the presence of these bases provides some security assurance to the hosts. And again, although the Bahamas has only recently taken advantage of allocations under the IMET program, commercial arms purchases from the United States have been increasing substantially in the 1980s. In addition, as part of a new 1980s thrust for increased visibility in foreign affairs, the Bahamas joined the OAS in March 1982, signing the Rio Treaty nine months later. This is significant in that only Trinidad among the Caribbean states had adhered to the treaty until then. Finally, as in the other countries, Britain has continued to be the Bahamas' traditional partner in security matters.

Ideological Security

The strategies the Caribbean countries have adopted in order to meet the perceived needs of ideological security in the 1970s and 1980s have depended, of course, on whether the security threat has been seen as emanating from the United States or the Soviet Union (or Cuba). That perception has in turn depended on the political and economic orientation of the particular country. In the case of Guyana, Jamaica to 1980, and Grenada to 1983, the threat has been one of "destabilization" by the United States. For other countries and regimes, the threat has been from the Soviet Union and its allies. In the former case, security activities have focused on strengthening alternative diplomatic alliances to ensure broad international support and on acquiring some security assistance from socialist allies. In the second case, Caribbean activity has been geared toward cooperation with the United States.

In the diplomatic realm, which is elaborated in Chapter 5, the left-leaning governments of the Caribbean have apparently wholeheartedly endorsed the sentiment of Grenada's People's Revolutionary Government (PRG) that "as a small country Grenada requires extensive and intensive international support to combat successfully U.S. imperialism . . . Grenada's foreign relations must be the front line of the defence of the . . . Revolution."[23] Guyana, Jamaica, and Grenada are or have been very active among the non-aligned and in other Third World forums. Jamaica and Grenada also joined the Socialist International, garnering much global, including European, support there. In addition, all three expanded their political links with socialist nations in Europe as well as in the Third World.

In point of fact, Guyana's security activity in the ideological area has not differed from the activities already described in the priority territorial sphere. The same strategies have served many different purposes. Indeed, although Guyana has periodically complained of destabilization by the United States, ideological concerns have been muted by U.S. distaste for the Marxist and radical opposition. In the circumstances, Guyana has maintained its U.S. links—albeit somewhat shaky links—to the point of participating in the IMET program in the 1980s.

On the other hand, in the 1970s, Jamaica's decision to seek a more self-reliant development led to U.S. antagonism and the downgrading of its traditional military relationship with the United States. As indicated in Table 3.1, U.S. Department of Defense data note no training costs for Jamaica between 1974 and 1981 and Foreign Military Sales tapered off after peaking at $78,000 in 1975. (However, commercial arms purchases from the U.S. were at their highest in 1976–1978, a period of great instability in Jamaica [see Table 3.2].) Garcia notes that training linkages were maintained with Great Britain and Canada,[24] but data on other military linkages are scarce. Although Jamaican foreign policy was reoriented toward the Third World and Cuba and the Soviet bloc, this orientation seems to have been more in the diplomatic, economic, and technical fields than in the military. Official U.S. figures, for example, do not show the presence of Cuban military advisers in Jamaica in the crucial period of the late 1970s,[25] although, as seen in Grenada, many of Cuba's technical advisers are trained in military techniques. Despite Jamaican instability, military expenditures increased only slightly in Jamaica across the years, with somewhat higher increases occurring after 1980.[26] In the period 1976 to 1980, U.S. military assistance to Jamaica ended altogether.

In the 1980s, with the redefinition of ideological security by a new Jamaican government, the United States again became the focus of Jamaican military assistance. As shown in Table 3.1, Jamaica renewed its purchase of equipment under the Foreign Military Sales Financing Program, its receipt of funds from MAP, and IMET assistance, all at far higher levels than previously. Commercial arms purchases also increased.

Grenada represented a special case in the Caribbean since the People's Revolutionary Government chose to pursue an anti-U.S. foreign policy that was stronger than Jamaica's democratic socialist thrust but without the environmental flexibility built into the Guyanese situation. The ensuing pressure from the United States coupled with domestic factors led to major increases in domestic military spending and a diversification of the country's external security links. After independence in 1974, these links had centered primarily on Britain, although a minor but controversial training link was also developed with Chile. After the coup of 1979, Grenada turned almost exclusively to the Eastern bloc. In 1980, there were some 100 military advisers from Cuba in Grenada, along with about 1,000 technical assistance personnel,[27] many of whom, as events proved, had some basic military training. Moreover, members of the Grenadian army were being trained in Cuba and in the Soviet Union, and according to information made public after the invasion, Grenada had military transfer agreements with the Soviet Union, Cuba, and North Korea.[28] After the removal of the PRG in 1983, Grenada moved again to the West, with the difference that the prime focus of activity has been the United States as well as regional cooperation under U.S. auspices.

For the non-socialist Caribbean states, the issue of ideological security against socialist contagion was not a major one prior to the Grenada revolution. Guyana was viewed as a unique aberration, and Jamaica was not only maintaining its democratic structure but has historically been perceived as sufficiently remote from the Caribbean heartland to be viewed with a certain detachment. Grenada's radicalization, however, pushed its conservative neighbors into the regional Eastern Caribbean–Barbadian security arrangement that became established after the invasion as a cooperative venture with the United States. The venture includes U.S. military training of military and police units and Eastern Caribbean participation in periodic U.S. military maneuvers.

The data in Table 3.1 show that Barbados and the Eastern Caribbean islands as a security grouping have been benefiting rather handsomely under the various U.S. military assistance programs since 1982. In addition, Dominica, Saint Lucia, and St. Vincent (and, as previously noted, Barbados) have been individually allocated funds under IMET. Grenada received a separate $15 million in military aid from the United States after the invasion for the maintenance and training of the Caribbean troops stationed there. It also joined the Regional Security System (RSS) in 1984.

Although the Eastern Caribbean and Jamaica have been the core of U.S. efforts to preserve its own and the Caribbean's ideological security, the other countries—Guyana, Trinidad and Tobago, Bahamas, and Belize—have, as we have seen, also been recipients of U.S. assistance. The first three have benefited mainly from the IMET program, whereas Belize has received larger amounts of assistance, primarily because of its vulnerability in the Central American ideological context, and also because of its territorial problems.

While the United States has clearly been given the prime responsibility for Caribbean security needs in the ideological area, Britain and Canada have provided a second tier of assistance. Britain has trained the region's security forces at an estimated cost of about $1.3 million through the mid-1980s.[29] It has also given special assistance to Grenada in training and equipping the police and army. As noted earlier, Canada has contributed to the training of police forces, including individual assistance to Grenada, but not to the more controversial army or special service units of the Regional Security System.[30]

In sum, then, Caribbean activity in this ideological area has been geared either toward the Eastern bloc and diplomatic initiatives in the Third World, or toward the United States. This is to be expected, given the nature of the global ideological competition. The traditional partners, Britain and Canada, have been relegated to a clearly secondary role in these security issues.

Social Threats

The geographical characteristics of Caribbean countries have opened them to social problems that have an external dimension, among them narcotics trafficking, refugee-immigration problems, smuggling, and piracy. We have already noted that the defense arrangements established within the Eastern Caribbean (OECS and RSS) were intended to confront some of these issues. Of those problems mentioned, the narcotics issue has been the most salient in recent times. Here again, circumstances have required the Caribbean to collaborate closely with the United States, given active U.S. prodding of Caribbean governments to act to halt the flow of drugs into North America. As a foreign policy problem, the issue of drug trafficking has particularly involved the Bahamas, Jamaica, and Belize.

The Bahamas, with its approximately 700 or so islands and limited resources, has simply been unable to successfully patrol its borders. In 1985, Prime Minister Pindling stressed that difficulty to the United Nations General Assembly:

The peace, stability and security of small island States have been seriously threatened by the drug trafficking barons. . . . The islands of the Caribbean and the Bahamas straddle the flight paths and sea lanes between the narcotics-producing countries of South America and the principal consumer markets on the North American continent and have found themselves, by these geographic circumstances, especially vulnerable to exploitation as transhipment centres for international drug trafficking operations. Archipelagic nations like the Bahamas have been pressed to the outer limits of their financial and security resources in the attempt to sustain effective interdiction and law enforcement measures against this nefarious scourge.[31]

Similarly, the importance of the issue in Belize's foreign policy was stressed by Foreign Minister Dean Barrow at the United Nations in 1985. He noted:

On another aspect of security concerns . . . my government has been greatly exercised by, and absolutely condemns the blot on our society that is the production and trafficking of drugs.

Over the past five years, and spurred by the phenomenal and continually expanding consumer market provided by the United States, Belize has become a large scale producer and trafficker of marijuana. We do not need anyone to tell us of the insidious nature of the threat posed by this aberrant activity—to our institutions, to the moral and ethical dimensions of our national life, to the very rule of law and democracy in our country. Within the limits of our resources, we have made herculean efforts to stamp out the trade and defeat the danger of destabilization which it presents.[32]

While the narcotics issue has only attained major proportions for Belize in recent times, Jamaica has long been attempting to curb the illegal export of marijuana and other drugs. For all three countries, the drug issue has been intimately linked with the maintenance of good relations with the United States, which has at times attempted to link this cooperation with economic assistance.

In terms of responses, the Bahamas created an overburdened coast guard to deal with this and other problems. In addition, Prime Minister Pindling estimated that expenditure on law enforcement, "as a direct result of drug trafficking," increased by more than 100 percent between 1975 and 1980.[33] The U.S. role has been to assist the Bahamas in the training of narcotics agents and in the interception of drug shipments. IMET training costs presumably reflect some of this cooperation. Jamaica and Belize, too, have benefited from U.S. help, through the Drug Enforcement Agency, in eliminating marijuana fields. Mexico has also assisted Belize in this area.[34] Finally, as in the Bahamas, the United States has been training narcotics officers in these countries. In fact, the figures show that Jamaica has far outdistanced the rest of the Caribbean in the numbers of agents trained in the United States.[35]

Another important security issue for the Bahamas and for Belize has been the influx of refugees from troubled Caribbean and Central American areas. In the case of the Bahamas, Haitian refugees have slipped in, again highlighting the fact that the coast guard is poorly equipped. Although the problem has been handled domestically and bilaterally (with Haiti), U.S. security training has also been helpful in this area.

The situation in Belize has been more complex because it has had to be viewed in terms of a larger issue of East-West confrontations in Central America. Belize perceives a threat to its socioeconomic resources coming from the influx of refugees fleeing from its Central American neighbors. In response, refugees from El Salvador have been resettled under an official resettlement scheme, but others from Guatemala and Honduras have reportedly been slipping in illegally.[36] Again, the perception of threat was outlined, somewhat ambiguously, in an important foreign policy speech given by Foreign Minister Barrow at the United Nations in 1985:

> My government has a particular concern in this matter [of violence in Central America] because the trans-border migration of those fleeing the conflicts has produced an influx of refugees into Belize which strains our already thinly-stretched social and economic resources, and threatens to produce serious ethnic and demographic tensions.
>
> Furthermore, Belizeans with our history of peaceful and stable development, cannot forever remain immune to the inherent hostility and mistrust that characterise the evolution of the conflict in the region. We cannot ignore the attempts being made by outside powers to exploit historical and prevailing conditions in an effort to gain advantage in the global East/West confrontation.[37]

The response of Belize to this situation—apart from spending more on security, with British and U.S. help—has been to seek a peaceful settlement of the larger political problem. Belize ministers have held discussions with the "Contadora" governments of Mexico, Venezuela, Colombia, and Panama involved in Central American peace initiatives, and Belize has participated in U.S.-sponsored initiatives intended to contribute to the search for solutions to Central American problems. Belize has strongly endorsed the Contadora process.

To sum up, in the area of "social" security, specifically the drug problem, Caribbean activity has centered on cooperating with the United States and facilitating training for security forces with U.S. help. Refugee problems have been handled diplomatically, although the ability to protect borders has again been linked to general military assistance provided by the United States and Britain.

A Note on Economic Security

In the last chapter, it was mentioned that security for the Caribbean has also been defined in the Third World sense of economic security. Thus it is that, primarily through the work of the United Nations, economic development has come to be viewed as an essential component of peace and security. The Commonwealth recognized this in its study of the security problems of small states made after the invasion of Grenada. The study "emphasized the fact that security is a multifaceted issue which needs to be addressed simultaneously on a variety of fronts, thereby requiring action at the national, regional and international levels and in the economic, political and military spheres. There was a solemn recognition of the integral link between poverty and defencelessness."[38]

As noted earlier, there are two facets to the question of security as defined in economic terms. On the one hand, there is the development issue, the recognition that economic growth is required to maintain internal and external stability. Related to this is the issue of economic non-intervention, the right of all states to adopt appropriate development measures without interference or pressure from the outside. Both these facets have concerned Caribbean policymakers in the decades of the 1970s and 1980s. The second issue is included in the last section of this chapter. However, since these questions are not primarily military but rather economic issues with implications for security, they are also referred to and implied in our discussions in Chapter 4.

It can simply be noted here that although all development assistance can be viewed as having security implications, the United States has a special program directly related to peace and security—the Economic Support Fund (ESF), which is used to "promote economic or political stability in regions which affect U.S. interests, national security, and achievement of foreign policy objectives."[39] Not unexpectedly, Jamaica and the Eastern Caribbean have been the prime beneficiaries of such funding, which includes appropriations for the Caribbean Basin Initiative (see Chapter 4). Two countries received aid prior to 1981 but not after: Trinidad and Tobago ($32.1 million) and Guyana ($9.7 million). The

Bahamas has received no aid under this fund. Jamaica received only $11 million in the pre-1981 period, but assistance jumped to $41 million (1981), $90.5 million in 1982, $59.4 million in 1983, $55 million in 1984, $81 million in 1985, and $58 million in 1986. The Eastern Caribbean received only $4 million between 1946 and 1980, but $20 million in 1982, $35 million in 1983, $45.8 million in 1984, $20 million in 1985 and $35 million in 1986. Since 1983, Barbados has been included in the Eastern Caribbean allocation, and since 1986, Grenada has also been included. Grenada received $47 million in ESF funds in 1984 and $11.1 million in 1985. Finally, Belize received $14 million in 1985 and $1.9 million in 1986.[40] As with other forms of aid from the United States, Jamaica has consistently received the most assistance over the years.

Bilateral and Multilateral, Regional and Global Comparisons

The above presentation has stressed the importance of bilateral security arrangements for the Caribbean. Both quantitative and qualitative analyses suggest that the United States has increasingly been replacing, or for certain countries equaling, Britain as the main partner for the English-speaking countries in security matters. The other consistent partner has been Canada which continues to play a tertiary role in training and equipping the military and police forces of the Caribbean. Other countries noted as being or having been involved in bilateral arrangements with the Caribbean—although comparative figures are not available—are Brazil, Mexico, Venezuela, France, Cuba, the Soviet Union, North Korea, and some nations of Eastern Europe. At the multilateral level, the two organizations that have been targeted by the Caribbean for security assistance are the OAS and the Commonwealth. All the countries in our study, with the exception of Belize and Guyana, are members of the OAS; two, Trinidad/Tobago and Bahamas, have joined the Rio Treaty. Although assistance under this organization has not yet been requested by the Caribbean countries, participation in it forms an integral part of the security network relied on by the group. As to the Commonwealth, informal security links exist among the governments of its members, including the English-speaking Caribbean. Often this has resulted in practical cooperation, especially in the exchange of training opportunities for security forces. Membership in the Commonwealth contributes to Caribbean security needs not only by virtue of the possibility of collective military assistance in times of crisis but also because the organization serves as a useful forum for garnering international support on security issues.

In this diplomatic multilateral sphere, Caribbean activity within the Non-Aligned Movement and the United Nations must also be considered as having security implications. Strong Third World activity has been viewed by small states as needed to preserve their independence in the face of threats from larger powers. This multilateral global activity has, however, been secondary to the bilateral and regional relationships.

Regionally, prior to the 1980s, there was some low-level cooperation among the military and police organizations of the Caribbean. Thus, Trinidad and Tobago helped train the Guyanese coast guard and the Antiguan army. Nationals of the Bahamas and Trinidad and Tobago served in the high command of the Jamaican army, and Trinidad lent its second-in-command to the new Barbadian army in 1980. Similar informal linkages existed among the Eastern Caribbean islands and between these islands and Trinidad. More importantly, the Caribbean countries attempted to cooperate in solving some major disputes.

In 1963, Trinidad and Tobago, Barbados, and Jamaica offered to mediate during racial and political disturbances in British Guiana, but the Guiana government refused to comply with suggestions for a high-level, four-power meeting to discuss various proposals. These proposals, it must be noted, included a Trinidadian proposal for U.N. peacekeeping forces, if necessary, to supervise upcoming elections.[41] In 1967, Jamaica, Trinidad and Tobago, Barbados, and Guyana sent a fact-finding commission of civil servants to St. Kitts/Nevis/Anguilla to investigate Anguilla's dispute with St. Kitts. They subsequently agreed to various proposals for peaceful settlement, including the sending in of a peacekeeping force composed of police units from the four countries. However, their attempt failed when Anguilla refused to accept the agreement and Jamaica changed its position on participation in a peacekeeping force.[42]

In reality, the only successful Caribbean action in the security area prior to 1979 was Trinidad's peaceful intervention in 1970 in the dispute between Venezuela and Guyana. Trinidad was used as a meeting site for discussions between the opposing sides; the result was the Protocol of Port-of-Spain, which froze the dispute for twelve years. In other areas, Caribbean countries tended to be sidelined. For example, in 1969 the army chiefs of Trinidad, Jamaica, and Guyana met in Georgetown to discuss questions of security in the wake of disturbances in Jamaica. However, this was their only meeting and no substantive results were produced. Again, during disturbances in Trinidad in 1970, the commander in chief of the Jamaican army visited Trinidad, but nothing concrete came of the visit. (Trinidad is also said to have unsuccessfully sought arms from Jamaica and Guyana at that time.)[43]

In 1974, the Big Four Caribbean countries offered to mediate Grenada's internal disturbances, and in the late 1970s and early 1980s, Barbados, Jamaica, and Guyana offered to participate in a multilateral force for Belize. Replacement of the British garrison in Belize by a multilateral force, possibly including Caribbean membership, is still being considered. In 1979, Barbados and Trinidad agreed to consult from time to time on security matters. By this time, events in Grenada and elsewhere in the Caribbean were catalyzing Caribbean action. In 1979, Barbados sent some fifty soldiers to St. Vincent to help quell a rebellion on Union

Island. In the words of Prime Minister Milton Cato, this was "the first time one of these islands has looked to one of its own for help."[44] The 1979 action can therefore be viewed as the second successful cooperative effort of the Caribbean states in security matters.

In 1981, during an attempted coup in Dominica, the second against Eugenia Charles' government, a small detachment of Barbados security forces was sent to Dominica; in 1982 the Barbados coast guard stayed around the St. Lucia coast during elections, which were won by John Compton.[45] Thus by 1982, when the Regional Security System was established, a tradition of security cooperation between Barbados and the Eastern Caribbean was already somewhat in place. Furthermore, the OECS, created in 1981, included, as noted earlier, a mechanism for cooperation in defense matters.

The 1982 Regional Security System (RSS) took cooperation further along the lines of institutionalization. Barbados contributes 49 percent of the funding, and the rest is divided equally among the other islands. The Barbadian army chief is the RSS coordinator and adviser on security matters, and the coast guard is also centered in Barbados. The other islands contribute security (military or police) forces and handle their training individually, but rely on a collective program for arms and equipment acquisitions.[46] We can therefore say that Caribbean security cooperation reached its zenith with the creation of this system.

In practice, the first concerted collective security action the English-speaking Caribbean has taken was the 1983 decision by Jamaica, Barbados, and the Eastern Caribbean countries to invite U.S. intervention in Grenada and to provide troops for a Caribbean peace force. Note that even here cooperation was only partial because several Caribbean countries dissented, as discussed later in this chapter. It must also be noted that participation in the RSS is uneven, with Barbados and St. Vincent displaying limited enthusiasm under the Barrow/Sandiford and Mitchell governments. Nevertheless, the arrangement is signifcant for Caribbean military-security interaction, especially as Jamaica is associated informally with the system and Trinidad and Tobago, despite official wariness, has sent units to participate in a few training sessions.

Conflict Behavior on Security Issues

So far we have been dealing with general cooperative patterns of activity and behavior, the most common kind of foreign policy interaction. The other dimension of general concern to foreign policy theorists is the dimension of conflict. Conflict behavior can be plotted on a graph by using events data, a methodological technique popularized in the 1970s.[47] For example, in his study of three Caribbean countries, Guyana, Jamaica, and Haiti, between 1967 and 1975, Georges Fauriol used this technique and found that conflict accounted for only a fifth of all estimated interactions of the selected countries during that time.[48] Even when broken down into verbal and non-verbal activity and political and economic categories, conflict was still very low, with the highest areas being 10 percent verbal political conflict for Guyana and 6 percent for Jamaica. Overall, Guyana had 20 percent conflict activity and Jamaica only 9.4 percent.[49] Obviously the results here reflect the characteristics of the time period used, with Guyana having a relatively high amount of conflict with Venezuela in 1967–1969 and Jamaica enjoying a period of relative calm before the second Manley era of 1976–1980. However, the results also reflect a general finding in international relations: The vast majority of interactions among states are cooperative, although conflict issues tend to be more salient.[50]

The issue of conflict is traditionally very much a military-security one. The crises that have occurred in the Caribbean have come in the very security areas we have already discussed: territorial, ideological, and socioeconomic areas. In the territorial area, the peak periods of conflict in the Venezuela-Guyana dispute were in 1966–1969 and in 1982–1983. Various incidents initiated by Venezuela increased the levels of tension between the countries:[51] In 1966, Venezuelan troops occupied what the Guyanese regarded as their side of Ankoko Island, an island in the Cuyuni river along the disputed frontier; in 1968, the then Venezuelan president Raul Leoni issued a decree annexing the marine areas bordering the disputed Essequibo zone; and in 1969, Venezuela was implicated in an unsuccessful rebellion of ranchers in the southern region of Guyana. In addition, during this period Venezuela publicly tried to dissuade international companies from investing in the disputed zone.

In 1982, when the Protocol of Port-of-Spain ended, conflict again intensified between the parties to the dispute. Venezuela refused to include Guyana in an oil-purchase scheme in which it was a partner with Mexico and made strenuous efforts to dissuade the World Bank from giving Guyana a much-needed loan for development of the hydroelectric potential of the Essequibo. Venezuelan aircraft frequently violated Guyanese airspace, and there were various incidents involving Venezuelans crossing the frontier. Ultranationalists in Venezuela began calling for a seizure of the disputed territory by force. The atmosphere was not improved when Guyana detained some Venezuelan fishing boats in late 1983 and the Venezuelan ambassador to Georgetown was shot during a robbery early in 1984.

While the Guyana-Venezuela dispute has produced some physical conflicts, Guyana-Suriname hostilities have been more muted. Peak periods of hostility have, not entirely fortuitously, paralleled periods of conflict on the Venezuelan border. Between 1967 and 1970, as Guyana attempted to reinforce its territorial sovereignty, there were incidents arising out of Guyanese expulsion of some Surinamese from the disputed area. In the mid-1970s, in the wake of Suriname's independence and charges of Guyanese military collaboration with Cuba, and in the early

1980s when Guyana blocked a Surinamese hydroelectric project in the disputed area, reports of troop mobilizations and border violations heightened tensions between the countries.

In the other major dispute, between Belize and Guatemala, there have been periodic reports of Guatemala mobilizing its troops along the border. In 1975, Guatemala was rumored to be preparing for an invasion, and in 1977 the Barbadian government intercepted a planeload of arms bound for Guatemala.[52] Tensions have continued to be high at various times, including in 1982 when Guatemalan army officials allegedly ventured across the border.[53] However, the dispute has primarily been manifested in verbal hostility, and the conflict engendered has been internal more than interstate. Thus in 1968, when a U.S. mediator suggested that Belize be granted independence in return for certain Guatemalan rights over defense, foreign affairs, and Belize's economy, there were riots in Belize. Similarly, when in 1981 a Heads of Agreement plan gave Guatemala access to certain marine territory of Belize, there were widespread civil disturbances in Belize.[54]

Other territorial conflicts have included Anguilla's secession from St. Kitts/Nevis, Union Island's attempt to secede from St. Vincent, and external attempts to overthrow regimes in Dominica and Barbados. These have already been discussed in the context of Caribbean cooperation. More important here have been marine conflicts existing between some Caribbean territories and other nations. The most significant have been fishing disputes between Venezuela and Trinidad and Tobago and between the Bahamas and a number of countries. Despite various attempts to agree on the delimitation of fishing zones in the Gulf of Paria separating the two countries, Trinidadian fishermen continue to encounter difficulties with the Venezuelan authorities. Major fishing disputes have also arisen between the Bahamas and the United States, Cuba, and the Dominican Republic. In the case of the United States, in 1979 Bahamian patrol boats intercepted thirty-five U.S.-based boats; in the ensuing gunfire, one Cuban-American was shot and other Americans were captured.[55] Longstanding problems of Cubans fishing in Bahamian waters came to a head in 1980, when Cuban fighter aircraft fired on a Bahamian patrol boat that had apprehended Cuban fishermen for poaching in the waters between Cuba and the Bahamas. Cuba later apologized for "involuntary violation" of Bahamian sovereignty and agreed to pay the Bahamas compensation of $5.4 million.[56] Finally, problems with Dominicans fishing in Bahamian waters led in 1983 to an incident in which the Bahamian coast guard, which had arrested a large number of Dominicans for illegal fishing, was accused by the Dominican Republic of firing on a Dominican fishing boat. This accusation was later proved to be without substance.[57]

A major dispute that can be described as territorial was Trinidad's well-known conflict with Venezuela in the 1970s over the issue of the latter's "expansionism." At that time, Venezuela had begun to define the Caribbean as an area of crucial strategic interest and, given the vacuum left by the pullout of Britain, had begun to engage in various economic initiatives in the Caribbean. Although this was viewed with equanimity by most Caribbean leaders, Trinidad's Dr. Eric Williams was less enthusiastic. His suspicions of Venezuelan imperialism were based on a variety of factors, primarily economic, with an emphasis on Venezuelan "oil politics" and on then-ongoing discussions on marine limits. However, his concerns also contained an element of territoriality. In various speeches made at the time, Dr. Williams pointed to the Venezuelan history of claims against Guyana, Trinidad (its offshore islands) and the Dutch Antilles, and Venezuela's claim to Bird Island, an uninhabited island off Dominica. He related these claims to law-of-the-sea considerations and to Venezuelan redefinition of the Caribbean as the Caribbean Basin, then a new concept, as well as to the exclusion of Belize from a Venezuelan agreement to sell oil to Central American countries and to Venezuelan intransigence in deciding the fishing disputes with Trinidad and Tobago. He concluded that the bilateralism being pushed by Venezuela in the Caribbean "has all the hallmarks of the colonialism implicit in all the statements of Venezuelan publicists—the new Venezuela they preach of in the context of the old colonialism of the Caribbean."[58] Venezuela reacted by emphatically denying any expansionist ambition in the Caribbean, and the verbal dispute diminished in importance over time.

In the ideological arena, the major Caribbean conflict has been the polarization caused by the advent of political pluralism. The central concern was Grenada, and Caricom countries were antagonized by two factors: one, the unconstitutionality of the government, which refused to hold elections; and two, its close ties with Cuba and the Eastern bloc and the fear of contagion engendered by these ties. The reaction of the more conservative Caribbean countries to events in Grenada ranged from a refusal to deal with the new regime (Trinidad and Tobago) through verbal onslaughts (between Grenada's and Dominica's prime ministers) to open hostility (Barbados). Although the region moved in 1982 toward acceptance of political pluralism, events in Grenada led to the U.S.-Caribbean intervention of 1983.

From the conflict perspective, what is significant about the invasion is the fact that the Caribbean was not united: Trinidad and Tobago, Guyana, Bahamas, and Belize all refused to agree to the use of force. As is well known, this intraregional dispute threatened to destroy the already teetering Caribbean Community. In particular, the dispute between Trinidad and Barbados is often cited. While Barbados Prime Minister Tom Adams maintained that he had informed Trinidad's ambassador of the decision of the OECS to invade, the ambassador categorically denied that this was so. The ensuing bitterness led to the reassignment of the ambassador and to a high level of hostile verbal interchanges. Adams also engaged in verbal sallies against Guyana's Prime Minister Forbes Burnham. After Burnham criticized the U.S.

invasion at the Commonwealth summit in New Delhi in late 1983, Adams was quoted as saying: "Mr. Burnham is regarded in the Caribbean not only as a cross that Guyana has to bear, but a cross that many of us have to bear . . . a figure of fun and his speeches are entertained as light relief."[59] For her part, Dominica's Prime Minister Charles stated at the time that she had never viewed Caricom as anything other than a trading organization. "I have refused to ever attend a meeting of ministers of foreign affairs of Caricom. I think it is unnecessary."[60] Fortunately, Caricom was saved from complete disintegration by a determined attempt, particularly on the part of Trinidad and Tobago's Prime Minister George Chambers, to refocus attention on regional economic integration at the next summit meeting in July 1984 in the Bahamas.

While the larger Caribbean community was attempting to recover from the ideological problems of the 1970s, the new security community engendered by the Grenada events developed some small cracks of its own. St. Vincent and the Grenadines, while remaining in the Regional Security System, declined to participate in military exercises. Prime Minister James Mitchell, whose government came to power in mid-1984, has stated often that his government is more concerned with meeting the people's basic necessities than with security questions.[61] Moreover, electoral changes in Barbados returned the Democratic Labor Party of Errol Barrow to power in 1986. Barrow also expressed reservations about the Regional Security System and its close links with Washington. Barbados downgraded its participation in military exercises to observer status, and Barrow's successor, Erskine Sandiford, is making no changes in the late prime minister's policy. Finally, a Barbados proposal made in 1984 for the creation of a Caribbean defense force, a permanent regional army that could be called on if local units and the special service units trained under the RSS failed to put down disturbances, did not elicit any support from Caribbean governments, including Eastern Caribbean governments. Not only was the necessity and desirability of having such a force unclear, but also no one was willing to bear the cost. Prime Minister Adams had envisaged that the army would be heavily subsidized by the United States but the latter appears to have found the cost prohibitive and in any event preferred bilateral to multilateral security arrangements.[62]

Ideological conflict must also be viewed from the perspective of the "embattled" socialist states. Guyana, Jamaica, and Grenada perceived threats of destabilization from the United States, not without foundation. Guyana, of course, was an early object of Western intervention in the 1950s and 1960s, first when the British landed troops after Prime Minister Cheddi Jagan's government passed some socialist-sounding laws and second when the Central Intelligence Agency became involved in sugar-belt agitation in 1964. Despite the fact that the United States helped Forbes Burnham come to power, the ruling party has sometimes accused the United States of destabilizing Guyana. In the 1970s, as discussed in Chapter 1, Burnham moved toward socialism, nationalizing all major foreign firms and generally increasing the role of the public sector. U.S. aid and investment in Guyana were considerably reduced, and Burnham charged that the United States was engaged in a destabilization campaign. In the early 1980s, before Burnham's death, the charge was again made. This time the United States was responding to the deterioration of the economy and the neglect of human rights in Guyana. International Monetary Fund loans, renewed in 1979, were suspended because the country did not meet its economic performance criteria,[63] and the United States worked to deny Guyana loans from the Inter-American Development Bank. The Grenada invasion, strongly opposed by Guyana, increased fears of destabilization: The Guyanese vice president told a rally that "any internal disturbance in Guyana can now be used as an opportunity to intervene militarily."[64] In the next few months, Burnham expelled two U.S. embassy employees and rejected the American appointee as ambassador. However, given economic realities, Burnham's tone became more conciliatory by the mid-1980s.

Under Michael Manley, Jamaica too was placed under intense U.S. pressure. This came primarily in economic form, first through the lack of cooperation of the bauxite multinationals after Manley imposed increased taxes on them, then through the decline in U.S. economic aid and in multilateral assistance from the U.S.-dominated international agencies, and finally through the tough terms imposed by the International Monetary Fund. Moreover, there were allegations of CIA involvement in internal violence in Jamaica, which in turn affected the tourist sector. In the final analysis, U.S. support for the opposition was quite openly given. When the Edward Seaga government came to power, it quickly broke relations with Cuba and returned Jamaica to a close relationship with the United States.

Finally, in Grenada, destabilization took essentially the same forms: denial of economic assistance, including participation in the Caribbean Basin Initiative; pressure on multilateral agencies to deny aid; and charges of intervention in counterrevolutionary activities. In addition, there were stepped-up U.S. military maneuvers in the Caribbean region, including at least one that the Grenada government assumed to be aimed particularly at its country—a rehearsal for the invasion of a fictitious country called "Amber and the Amberdines," a name presumed to be a code for Grenada and (its dependencies) the Grenadines.

A final category of security conflicts is the one loosely described as socioeconomic, centering, as we have seen, on issues of smuggling, illegal immigration, and in particular, drug trafficking. The problems of Belize and the Bahamas in terms of Central American and Haitian immigration respectively have involved primarily internal solutions. Belize has been attempting to resettle legal immigrants and the Bahamas has sought to repatriate Haitian immigrants. (In an interesting link-up of issues, in the early 1980s, Belize agreed to allow Haitians detained in the United States or Puerto Rico to resettle in Belize.)[65] On the salient drug issue, Jamaica, Belize, and the Bahamas have been in constant conflict with the United States on the issue of drug enforcement. The United States has tended to assume that these countries are not doing enough to halt drug trafficking and has imposed fines on airlines on which drugs have been transported. A more antagonistic move has been the attempt by the United States to force cooperation through threats of cutoffs of economic aid. Thus the Belizean Minister of Foreign Affairs noted in 1985:

> We find it . . . distressing when the claim is advanced that Belize has failed to eradicate any of its drug crop. To say that is to propagate disinformation of the most malicious sort.
>
> To be sure, we have had differences of opinion with others who are engaged in the war against drugs, over the methodology to be used in our own eradication campaign. Aerial spraying of marijuana plantations, using chemical herbicides, has been pressed upon us. But we have so far preferred to employ manual eradication methods, until we can assure ourselves and our people that the aerial spraying exercise would involve no unacceptable health or environmental risks. . . .
>
> This position has not proved satisfactory to some which is regrettable. But power disequilibria cannot be allowed to defeat the sovereign right of small states to act in what they consider to be their national interests. We must, therefore, . . . reject the threat of coercion implied in the possibility (which has been held out to us) of an aid cut-off or other measures designed to force us to move prematurely and in a way we consider undesirable.[66]

The Bahamian problem with the United States has produced an even higher level of conflict. The U.S. Drug Enforcement Agency and the Federal Bureau of Investigation engaged in clandestine drug operations in the Bahamas in the 1970s. When the Bahamian government learned of this, it demanded that the United States cease its operations and, in the future, obtain prior permission for any activity carried on inside Bahamian waters. Sometime later, the U.S. media alleged that Bahamian nervousness was attributable to the fact that top-level government officials, including the prime minister, were involved in the illegal drug business. Angry denials from the prime minister and minister of external affairs followed, with the latter accusing the U.S. "imperialist" communications media of conspiracy to destabilize the Bahamas. In the end, a commission of inquiry appointed in 1983 by the Bahamian government to investigate the charges implicated several officials in the drug trade, leading to the resignation or firing of several top cabinet ministers, including the deputy prime minister.[67] But the drug scandal and its suggestion of U.S. interference in the Bahamas' internal affairs continued to affect U.S.-Bahamian relations well through the Bahamian national elections of 1987 (see Chapter 5).

In sum, there have been a number of security conflicts involving Caribbean states: territorial problems that have erupted at times in intense verbal and/or moderate levels of physical conflict; regional tensions based on ideological differences; and differences with the United States on the handling of economic and social issues. All of these problems have been handled by negotiation and diplomacy so that essentially, even in the absence of quantitative data, it can safely be said that patterns of cooperation have been much more dominant than those of conflict.

For the Caribbean, except for the boundary disputes, military matters were secondary in foreign policy until very recently. Because their salience has been tied primarily to ideology, the decline of ideology has reemphasized the importance of issues in another area—economic development. Therefore, we turn in the next chapter to a discussion of Caribbean action and interaction in the economic areas of trade and aid.

Notes

1. "The Role of the Foreign Policy in Barbados Development Strategy," Address by Senator the Hon. George C. R. Moe, Q. C., Minister of External Affairs, at a Special Meeting of the Barbadian Chamber of Commerce on Thursday, November 27, 1975, *Barbados Bulletin* 1 (3), October–December 1975: 24.

2. Speech of Trinidad and Tobago's Minister of External Affairs, Errol Mahabir, to the Security Council September 26, 1985, U.N. Doc. S/PV. 2608, p. 33.

3. This was so defined by Admiral Mountbatten in 1962 during a visit to Trinidad and Tobago. See S. Hylton Edwards, *Lengthening Shadows: Birth and Revolt of the Trinidad Army* (Port-of-Spain: Inprint Caribbean Limited, 1982): 23, 27–28. I am indebted to Humberto Garcia Muniz for this and other references and information indicated in other footnotes.

4. On the Venezuela-Guyana dispute, see my book *The Venezuela-Guyana Border Dispute: Britain's Colonial Legacy in Latin America* (Boulder, Colo.: Westview, 1984).

5. For details, see ibid., pp. 223–224, 239–240.

6. For details, see ibid., pp. 167–173 and 237–238.

7. For text of Heads of Agreement, see Jack Hopkins, ed., *Latin America and Caribbean Contemporary Record*, vol. 1, 1981–1982 (New York: Holmes and Meier, 1983: 667–681.

8. See Anthony T. Bryan, "The Islands and the Littoral: New Relationships," in R. Millett and W. Marvin Will, eds., *The Restless Caribbean: Changing Patterns of International Relations* (New York: Praeger, 1979): 240–245; and Alma H. Young and J. Braveboy-Wagner, "Territorial Disputes in the Caribbean Basin," in W. Marvin Will and Richard Millett, eds., *Crescents of Conflict* (New York: Praeger, forthcoming).

9. Military spending was 7.2 percent of central government expenditures in 1967, declining to between 3 percent and 4 percent in 1969–1973. It rose to 10 percent–12 percent in 1975–1977, significantly not a period of high border conflict in Guyana. In 1981 and 1982, spending was 5.4 percent and 6.5 percent respectively. See United States Arms Control and Disarmament Agency, *World*

Military Expenditures and Arms Transfers, 1967–1976, 1985 (Washington, D.C.: July 1978): 46; and Washington, April 1985, p. 65.

10. Alma H. Young, "Belize," in *Latin America and Caribbean Contemporary Record* (LACCR), vol. 2, 1982–1983: 452.

11. Young, *LACCR*, vol. 3, 1983–1984: 490.

12. *Latin America Weekly Report*, August 29, 1980: 12.

13. For example, in 1985 President Hoyte got a gift of three combat helicopters from the U.S.S.R. See *Caribbean Insight*, November 1985: 8.

14. *Latin America Weekly Report*, October 29, 1982: 6.

15. I am indebted to Humberto Garcia Muniz of the Institute of Caribbean Studies, University of Puerto Rico, for the historical background on the military in the Caribbean. I have made generous use of his excellent unpublished work, *El Caribe Angloparlante: Del "SMLE" al "M-16": Ensayo sobre el Desarrollo Historico de la Presencia Militar de Estados Unidos en el Caribe*, 1985, hereafter referred to as "*Ensayo*." Information on Guyana is at 190–213.

16. This program was discontinued in the mid-1970s after Congress declared that the training of police forces was illegal. Various changes were made in the 1980s to accommodate the fact that Caribbean countries have no armies. See Garcia, *Ensayo*, 302–310.

17. Garcia, "Jamaica: las fuerzas de seguridad, fiel de la balanza en el futuro?" *Secuencia* (Mexico), September/December 1986: 120, 121; and "La Estrategia Military en el Caribe Angloparlante," in *El Caribe Contemporaneo* (Mexico), no. 11, December 1985: 32, 34.

18. Garcia, *Ensayo*, 350.

19. Ibid., p. 236. Venezuela gave scholarships in return for language training for army officers and agriculture courses for university students.

20. For figures for 1969–1978, see Michael T. Klare and Cynthia Arnson, with Delia Miller and Daniel Vollman, *Supplying Repression: U.S. Support for Authoritarian Regimes Abroad* (Washington, D.C.: Institute for Policy Studies, 1981): 35–36.

21. For text of the OECS treaty, see *LACCR*, vol. 1, 1981–1982, 685–697.

22. For text of the Memorandum of Understanding, see *Caribbean Monthly Bulletin* 17 (11–12), November–December 1983, Supplement.

23. *Grenada Documents: An Overview and Selection* (Washington, D.C.: Departments of State and Defense, September 1984): 106–112.

24. Garcia, "Jamaica," 125.

25. See H. Michael Erisman and John D. Martz, ed., *Colossus Challenged: The Struggle for Caribbean Influence* (Boulder, Colo.: Westview, 1982): 91, Table 3.1.

26. Jamaica spent 4.9 percent of central government expenditures on the military in 1973, rising to 5.5 percent in 1974. Spending then declined to 3 percent in 1977 and 3.1 percent in 1979 before rising slightly to 4 percent in 1981 and 5 percent in 1982. See USACDA, *World Military Expenditures and Arms Transfers 1985*, 68.

27. Erisman and Martz, *Colossus Challenged*, 91.

28. The Grenada documents are available in the United States National Archives. For major excerpts, see *Grenada Documents*.

29. Garcia, *Ensayo*, 396. Figure was given in Barbados dollars at $2.5 million.

30. Ibid., p. 397.

31. Statement by The Right Honorable Sir Lynden O. Pindling, Bahamian Prime Minister, to the 40th General Assembly of the United Nations, October 24, 1985, U.N. Doc. A/40/PV. 47, pp. 51–52.

32. Statement by Honorable Dean Oliver Barrow, Minister for Foreign Affairs and Economic Development of Belize, to the 40th General Assembly of the United Nations, October 8, 1985 (original), p. 6.

33. Ibid.

34. Alma H. Young in *LACCR*, vol. 3, 1983–1984: 490.

35. See Klare and Arnson, *Supplying Repression*. We can assume that the trends for the 1970s have continued into the 1980s.

36. Young in *LACCR*, vol. 2, 1098–1983: 452.

37. Dean Barrow's statement to the U.N., p. 4.

38. Pindling's statement to the U.N., p. 51. For the actual Commonwealth study, see Commonwealth Secretariat, *Vulnerability: Small States in the Global Society*, Report of Consultative Group (London, 1985).

39. Tom Barry, Beth Wood, and Deb Preusch, *The Other Side of Paradise: Foreign Control in the Caribbean* (New York: Grove Press, 1984): 159. The authors are critical of the use of this fund and of foreign aid in general.

40. Figures are actual appropriations. See U.S. Congress, House of Representatives, *Foreign Assistance and Related Appropriations for 1986, 1987*. For pre-1984 data, see Barry et al., *Other Side of Paradise*, 161–2.

41. Government of Trinidad and Tobago, Trinidad and Tobago and the British Guiana Question, Speech by the Prime Minister of Trinidad and Tobago, The Honorable Eric Williams, in the House of Representatives, November 22 and 27, 1963 (Port-of-Spain: Government Printery, 1963). See Roy Preiswerk, ed., *Documents on International Relations in the Caribbean* (Trinidad: Institute of International Relations; Rio Piedras, Puerto Rico: Institute of Caribbean Studies, 1969): 820–825.

42. For excerpts of the report of the investigatory commission, see Preiswerk, ibid., pp. 825–829.

43. Garcia, *Ensayo*, 245.

44. Quoted by W. Marvin Will in *LACCR*, vol. 1, 1981–1982, 506.

45. Garcia, *Ensayo*, 281, quoting from Dion Phillips, "Barbados and the Militarization of the Eastern Caribbean, 1979–1985," *Bulletin of Eastern Caribbean Affairs* 11 (6), January–February 1986. St. Vincent's Cato also reportedly called for help from Barbados during the 1984 election won by James "Son" Mitchell.

46. See Memo of Understanding, *Caribbean Monthly Bulletin* 17 (11–12), Supplement.

47. In events data research, interactions among nations are treated as discrete events suitable for rigorous quantitative analysis. See Edward E. Azar and Joseph D. Ben-Dak, eds., *Theory and Practice of Events Research: Studies in Inter-Nation Actions and Interactions* (New York: Gordon and Breach, 1975) for an overview.

48. Georges A. Fauriol, *Foreign Policy Behavior and the Smaller Less Developed States: Guyana, Haiti, and Jamaica* (Ph.D. dissertation. Ann Arbor, Michigan: University Microfilms International, 1981): 289. Fauriol actually notes the inverse— that cooperative events constituted only 79.59 percent of all events.

49. Fauriol, *Foreign Policy*, 326, Table 8-14, also 289–290.

50. Using data for 1966, Charles McClelland, one of the pioneers of events research, discovered that only 31.5 percent of interstate interaction was conflictual. See Charles A. McClelland and Gary D. Hoggard, "Conflict Patterns in the Interactions Among Nations," in James N. Rosenau, ed., *International Politics and Foreign Policy* (New York: Free Press, 1969): 715.

51. For details, see my *Venezuela-Guyana Border Dispute*.

52. Anthony Bryan, "The Islands and the Littoral," 242–243.

53. Alma H. Young in *LACCR*, vol. 2, 1982–1983, 454.

54. See Young and Braveboy-Wagner, "Territorial Disputes in the Caribbean Basin."

55. Incident cited in Steve Dodge and Dean W. Collinwood, "Foreign Policy Making in the Bahamas: A Case Study of Nassau's Anti-U.S. Reaction to the Invasion of Grenada," paper presented at the Caribbean Studies Association Annual Conference, San Juan, Puerto Rico, May 1985, 9–10.

56. Arthur Banks, ed., *Political Handbook of the World 1986* (Binghamton, N.Y.: Center for Social Analysis of the State University of New York, and Council on Foreign Relations, 1986): 468.

57. Dean Collinwood in *LACCR*, vol. 3, 1983–1984, 662. The incident was said to have occurred in an area where Bahamian boats were not likely to have been.

58. Speech to Special Convention of the People's National Movement, Sunday, June 15, 1975, Chaguaramas, Trinidad. See also, *The Threat to the Caribbean Community*, Speech of Dr. Williams to the PNM General Council, May 4, 1975 (Port-of-Spain: PNM Publishing, 1975).

59. Foreign Broadcast Information Service, Daily Report, November 30, 1983.

60. Ibid., January 16, 1984.

61. See, for example, Rickey Singh, "Caribbean Turnabout," *Caribbean Contact*, September 1985: 1.

62. Garcia, *Ensayo*, 407–411.

63. William Ratliff, "Guyana," in *LACCR*, vol. 3, 1983–1984: 377.

64. Quoted ibid., p. 416.

65. Alma Young in *LACCR*, vol. 2, 1982–1983: 452.

66. Statement by Honorable Dean Oliver Barrow to the United Nations General Assembly, 1985, p. 6.

67. Dean Collinwood, "Bahamas," in *LACCR*, vol. 4, 1984–1985: 617–625.

4. Patterns and Directions in Policy: Economics

As in the last chapter, we are again primarily concerned with two aspects of foreign policy activity: cooperation (or at least general interaction) and conflict; and the targets or direction of Caribbean activity. In the economic field, the fact of Caribbean dependence is not in question, given the region's historical role as supplier of primary products to the industrial countries. Analysis of the direction of foreign policy activity is undertaken primarily to ask the key question: What is the extent of Caribbean dependence? Implied in the answer is an evaluative issue (discussed in Chapter 9) of whether this dependence is facilitating or undermining Caribbean achievement of stated goals. Also we are interested in determining the extent to which some level of diversification is being achieved. As is traditional, we consider Caribbean foreign policy activity and behavior in the economic areas of trade and aid and investment.

General Patterns of Interaction

Trade

A quick view of the trading activity of the states in our study can be gleaned by looking at the International Monetary Fund/United Nations percentages given in Tables 4.1 and 4.2. In exports, Caribbean countries have concentrated and continue to concentrate on the industrial countries—the United States and the European Economic Community (EEC), with most EEC trade directed at the U.K. The secondary concentration is on the Caribbean community itself. There is quite some variation, with the Bahamas having the highest concentration on the United States and the Eastern Caribbean very few exports to that country. For the Eastern Caribbean, the U.K. and the Caribbean countries have been the steadiest partners. In imports, the general pattern is the same, but trade is more evenly distributed and the EEC is most important overall. A growing trade with Japan is noticeable, especially for imports. Finally,

TABLE 4.1. Exports of Caribbean Countries, by Region, 1967, 1974, and Latest Year Available (percentages)

	U.S.	Canada	U.K.	EEC[a]	USSR[b] East Europe	Caribbean[c]	Latin[d] America	Africa	Asia[e]
Bahamas									
1967	74.7	6.6	8.9	3.5	--	0.6	4.1	0.1[f]	0.4
1974	90.3	2.0	1.4	2.2	--	0.7	0.6	0.6[f]	0.5
1985	57.9	2.8	7.3	16.9	--	0.1	8.0	--	10.8
Barbados									
1967	15.1	6.6	40.8	0.1	--	8.5	8.0	--	0.2
1974	26.0	5.7	15.9	16.9	--	14.8	9.8	4.4	0.1
1985	52.8	1.4	5.9	7.1	0.0	18.1	6.3	0.0	1.9
Belize									
1967	35.0	10.8	45.0	0.8	--	11.1	1.7	--	0.0
1974	78.9	1.7	9.8	10.7	--	0.8	1.3	--	--
1985	57.9	5.0	22.7	24.6	--	5.9	4.4	0.0	1.9
Guyana									
1967	20.5	20.5	19.2	3.7	--	14.7	0.9	--	1.2
1974	25.4	4.6	20.9	26.8	5.0	9.2	9.9	9.3	2.7
1985	21.1	7.4	26.7	47.0	3.2	9.0	5.5	0.0	5.5
Jamaica									
1967	39.8	13.6	26.9	1.5	--	3.6	2.4	0.0	0.3
1974	46.4	5.3	15.4	16.4	4.4	4.3	3.6	2.2	1.3
1985	33.7	16.4	16.7	24.2	5.3	8.6	2.9	3.1	1.4
Trinidad /Tobago									
1967	42.8	4.4	12.7	5.5	--	5.3	8.7	0.8	1.2
1974	67.3	2.4	2.2	6.3	--	7.4	10.9	0.3	1.5
1985	62.6	1.5	3.9	13.8	--	8.5	10.0	0.3	1.2
Eastern Caribbean[g]									
1967	5.7	3.5	82.7	--	--	3.0	--	--	0.3
1966[h]	4.8	1.7	69.0	--	--	11.3	6.9	0.4	3.6
Antigua[i]									
1974	36.4	0.1	5.7	5.8	--	9.2	4.4	0.0	0.0
1984[j]	17.9	1.7	3.4	3.4	--	38.2	21.0	--	--

Dominica[j]									
1974	1.9	0.1	80.0	80.3	--	14.1	2.4	--	--
1984[j]	1.8	0.1	45.8	46.2	--	50.7	0.9	0.0	--
Grenada									
1974	2.0	2.5	42.7	81.9	6.0	4.8	1.2	0.1[f]	--
1982	2.3	2.3	30.7	54.8	3.9	30.6	0.4	0.8	0.2
1985	--	--	42.2	63.1	--	23.5	1.1	0.6	0.6
St. Kitts/Nevis									
1982[j,k]	28.1	--	45.5	45.5	--	22.7	0.5	--	--
St. Lucia									
1974[i]	1.9	0.3	67.3	68.3	--	26.9	2.5	0.0	0.0
1981[i,j]	10.6	0.2	37.0	37.9	--	47.4	3.7	0.0	0.0
St. Vincent									
1974[i]	3.2	1.6	66.2	66.2	--	27.8	0.5	--	--
1980[i,j]	4.2	0.6	50.4	50.6	--	44.0	0.6	--	0.0
1985	--	--	86.0	86.4	--	10.7	2.9	--	--

-- No trade reported; 0.0 means less than 0.1 percent but more than 0.

[a] Includes the U.K. after 1973.

[b] Includes China in 1967 and 1974. U.N. data exclude Cuba.

[c] Refers to Carifta/Caricom area only, except when U.N. data are used.

[d] "Other Western Hemisphere" in IMF data. U.N. data include Cuba.

[e] Includes the Middle East but not North Africa. Most Caribbean exports to Asia are to Japan and Hong Kong.

[f] Includes exports to South Africa.

[g] Windward/Leeward Is. IMF data for 1967 are not disaggregated.

[h] Included because the data for 1966 are more representative.

[i] U.N. data.

[j] Latest year for which complete data are available.

[k] No data are available for St. Kitts prior to 1978 or after 1982.

Sources: International Monetary Fund, Direction of Trade Statistics Annual/Yearbook, 1970, 1980, 1981, 1979-1985 (Washington, D.C.: 1971, 1981, 1982, 1986), supplemented by data from United Nations, International Trade Statistics Yearbook, 1977, 1980, 1985 (New York: United Nations, 1979, 1983, 1987).

70

TABLE 4.2. Imports of Caribbean Countries, by Region, 1967, 1974, and Latest Year Available (percentages)

	U.S.	Canada	U.K.	EEC[a]	USSR[b] East Europe	Caribbean[c]	Latin[d] America	Africa	Asia[e]
Bahamas									
1967	69.4	4.9	10.6	4.3	0.0	3.3	1.7	0.1[f]	0.9
1974	12.2	0.5	2.4	4.5	0.0	1.5	8.5	29.7	45.2
1985	43.4	1.1	4.9	8.8	0.0	1.0	6.6	13.8	23.1
Barbados									
1967	19.1	12.3	28.0	7.8	0.5	8.9	8.6	0.1	3.8
1974	19.5	9.1	20.6	29.7	0.3	16.5	15.7	0.1	3.3
1985	41.4	5.1	9.1	16.1	0.1	0.5	24.7	0.5	7.1
Belize									
1967	34.8	4.4	30.8	8.8	0.2	9.2	2.8	–	4.4
1974	35.4	2.9	17.6	23.5	0.2	0.0	11.3	–	4.0
1985	48.1	2.7	9.3	18.7	0.0	2.2	20.3[f]	0.2	5.2
Guyana									
1967	27.6	9.9	26.1	13.4	0.9	10.9	0.5	–	5.4
1974	25.9	5.0	20.6	31.0	1.6	26.4	27.9	0.1	5.8
1985	17.6	1.3	9.8	16.0	0.7	43.3	17.2	–	3.2
Jamaica									
1967	38.7	11.4	20.0	8.2	–	1.2	8.2	–	0.9
1974	35.5	5.4	12.4	20.7	0.4	7.5	20.2	0.2	4.6
1985	42.3	3.6	5.2	10.3	0.4	3.8	28.0	0.0	8.1
Trinidad /Tobago									
1967	15.3	5.2	14.5	4.3	–	4.5	43.5	0.0	3.2
1974	10.8	2.2	5.5	8.2	–	1.5	10.7	0.2	64.6
1985	37.7	7.2	9.2	17.9	0.1	4.2	13.7	0.6	12.0
Eastern Caribbean[g]									
1967	28.9	14.5	37.5	–	–	11.5	4.4	–	2.2
Antigua									
1974[h]	13.6	4.4	11.7	15.3	0.1	10.1	32.9	0.0	22.5
1984[h,i]	37.8	3.4	10.6	10.6	–	7.4	5.3	–	–

Dominica								
1974[h]	10.2	9.8	29.3	29.3	–	22.3	2.7	–	–
1984[h,i]	28.6	7.7	12.8	19.1	0.0	28.6	1.7	0.2	12.5
Grenada								
1974	8.3	8.8	26.5	34.3	–	30.9	6.1	–	2.4
1982[h]	21.2	5.4	15.1	23.3	5.2	30.0	5.3	0.1	7.3
1985	–	–	30.0	40.1	–	32.0	8.3	0.2	17.1
St. Kitts/Nevis								
1982[i,j]	36.3	5.6	17.0	19.8	–	19.3	0.4	–	3.8
St. Lucia								
1974[i]	18.5	8.7	26.2	34.7	0.0	23.6	7.5	0.3	4.6
1981[h,i]	38.9	4.0	14.3	20.5	0.3	22.3	4.8	0.1	6.7
St. Vincent								
1974[h]	9.0	13.1	30.4	35.9	–	25.9	2.3	–	–
1980[h,i]	26.4	7.8	18.4	23.9	0.4	27.5	7.5	0.1	5.1
1985	–	–	26.3	66.2	1.3	12.3	7.9	0.1	8.4

– No trade reported; 0.0 means less than 0.1 percent but more than 0.

a Includes the U.K. after 1973.

b Includes China in 1967 and 1974. U.N. data exclude Cuba.

c Refers to Carifta/Caricom area only, except when U.N. data are used.

d "Other Western Hemisphere" in IMF data. U.N. data include Cuba.

e Includes the Middle East but not North Africa.

f Includes imports from South Africa.

g Windward/Leeward Is. IMF data for 1967 are not disaggregated.

h U.N. data.

i Latest year for which complete data are available.

j No data are available for St. Kitts prior to 1978 or after 1982.

Sources: International Monetary Fund, Direction of Trade Statistics Annual/Yearbook, 1970, 1980, 1981, 1979-1985 (Washington, D.C., 1971, 1981, 1982, 1986), supplemented by data from United Nations, International Trade Statistics Yearbook, 1977, 1980, 1985 (New York: United Nations, 1979, 1983, 1987).

there is a notable absence of really significant trade with socialist countries, even for Guyana, Jamaica in the Manley period, and Grenada under the PRG. Almost all countries show a tiny amount of imports from Eastern Europe and China.

These percentages give us a general outline from which we can expand the discussion. The data analyzed were from the International Monetary Fund (IMF)* for the years 1967 (after the independence of the four more developed Commonwealth Caribbean countries), 1974 (after the increase in oil prices and also the creation of Caricom, as described below), and the 1980s up to 1985, the latest data available at the time of writing. Before the findings of each country are outlined, we will briefly consider two important foci of Caribbean cooperation; the regional integration movement and the Lomé agreement with the European Community.

Regional Integration and ACP-Lomé: General. The Caribbean Community began as the Caribbean Free Trade Area (Carifta) in 1968. Although the British-imposed West Indies Federation, which lasted from 1958–1962, had left Caribbean countries unwilling to attempt another political union, there was a strong sentiment that economic integration was a necessity, given the inherently small markets of these countries. In fact, the 1960s was the heyday of regional integration attempts among Third World countries, sanctioned by the United Nations as one solution to the economic problems of small states. Like many other Third World countries, the Caribbean nations were finding the markets of the developed countries closed to their commodities, especially their incipient manufactures. Within this context, the idea of integration was promoted by Antigua, Guyana, and Barbados and became a reality in 1968. In 1973 the free trade area was upgraded to a community, a move that included the harmonization of fiscal incentives, a common external tariff, greater functional cooperation, and a level of foreign policy coordination.

The smaller islands of the Eastern Caribbean, while part of the larger community, have created their own instruments of economic, functional, and political cooperation. After the achievement by most (the exceptions were Montserrat and Anguilla) of Associated Statehood with Britain in 1967, these islands formed their own Eastern Caribbean Common Market (ECCM). Functional cooperation was already being promoted through the Council of Ministers of the West Indies Associated States (WISA), formed in 1966. Both the ECCM and WISA were absorbed into the Organization of Eastern Caribbean States, established in 1981 with responsibilities in both socioeconomic and foreign policy and defense areas.[1]

The second major external economic thrust of the region has been the achievement of an association with the European Community. As

---

*This source had the most complete and recent data up to 1985 at the time of writing. However, it did not at the time include data for Antigua, Dominica, Saint Lucia, and St. Christopher/Nevis. Having determined that the data in the IMF and U.N. sources are highly comparable, we decided to use U.N. sources for information on these islands.

former colonies of Britain, the Caribbean states were beneficiaries of preferential economic treatment for their major exports, especially sugar, on the British market. After Britain joined the EEC in 1971, the concern to preserve these preferences, especially in the face of competition from the EEC's strong beet sugar market, led to Caribbean cooperation with African and Pacific commodity producers in the negotiation of an accord with the expanded EEC. African producers already had accords with the EEC under the Yaoundé and Arusha conventions, so in essence the broader association built on this foundation. The first Lomé convention was signed in 1975 and a second and third in 1981 and 1984 respectively. Negotiations on a fourth convention were underway in 1988/1989. Under the conventions, the African, Caribbean, and Pacific (ACP) countries receive duty-free access on a non-reciprocal basis for all their industrial and most of their agricultural products. They also receive increased development assistance and are beneficiaries of the community's STABEX (export stabilization) scheme under which funds are set aside to help stabilize earnings from exports of certain agricultural products.[2]

The importance of these arrangements explains why the external economic foci of the Caribbean in trade would be the EEC and Caricom, along with the traditional metropole the U.K., and the hemispheric power, the United States. As noted in our earlier chapter on strategies, Caribbean states are concerned with preserving and expanding their traditional links, but they have also (at least in theory) been engaged in a search for new markets.

While regional trade increased in the first few years after the formation of Carifta (from 8 percent in 1967 to 11 percent in 1973),[3] there were precipitous declines in the 1970s and early 1980s. This was attributable in part to problems specific to the community, but it also reflects the experience of most integration movements in the Third World where the regional market proves to be insufficient. The call for a New International Economic Order, espoused by developing nations in 1974 and strongly endorsed by the Caribbean nations, recognizes these limitations by promoting broader international cooperation among developing countries. This is the principle of collective self-reliance or, in more general U.N. parlance, ECDC—economic cooperation among developing countries.[4] Moreover, in the 1960s and early 1970s, inward-looking import substitution was the main strategy espoused by developing countries, including the Caribbean countries, for managing the industrialization process. However, the tide turned in the 1970s towards export promotion in the search for wider markets.[5] Given all this, it is not surprising that one analyst from the Ministry of External Affairs in Trinidad and Tobago should define the country's export thrust in terms including the following:

> An examination of the geographical structure of Trinidad and Tobago's foreign trade would reveal a pattern that is highly skewed in favor of developed market-economy countries. With the exception of petroleum there is comparatively minimal trade with Africa, Latin America and Asia

(excluding Japan, Taiwan, South Korea, Singapore, Hong Kong) and the socialist countries of Eastern Europe.

Granted that lack of transportation may be an important factor responsible for the under-development of trade with these countries. It is felt that in the context of the acknowledged need for greater economic co-operation among developing countries and the trend towards counter-trade, more can be done to develop trade with these areas. It may well be that the success of efforts to diversify the commodity structure of our exports would be contingent on the success of attempts to diversify the geographical structure of our foreign trade.[6]

This linkage between a diversified export structure and diversification of trading partners is an important one. In the following discussion, then, we are primarily interested in the extent to which Caribbean countries have diversified their export direction as well as in any changes that there might be in the shares of trade directed at the traditional and regional partners.

Bahamas. The export trade of the Bahamas was highly concentrated just after independence on the United States (90.3 percent in 1974 and 79 percent in 1975), with the U.K., Netherlands, and Canada as very secondary partners. Among developing countries, the only exports of any significance went to Panama. Exports to the English-speaking Caribbean, focused on Jamaica, were minimal. The figures for 1979–1985 show that dependence remains high, especially given the fact that the data given are extrapoplated and therefore artificially low. (This is borne out by comparing the data with U.N. figures, which go up to 1983.) Nevertheless, there have been some changes: Italy and the Netherlands have become major partners, and trade with Japan has increased. Trade with the EEC as a whole not unexpectedly increased after 1975 until the declines in commodity prices of the early 1980s. Among developing countries, there were exports of some significance to French Polynesia, the Netherlands Antilles (figures for which are generally inflated due to the petroleum trade), Brazil, and Panama. Exports to the Caribbean have been diversified to include other countries, particularly Trinidad and Tobago, although they remain proportionally small. It may be noted that the Bahamas formally joined Caricom only in 1983, although it was loosely allied with it before then. The noticeable absences in terms of the Bahamas' export thrust are in exports to the socialist countries and to non-Western Hemisphere developing countries.

As to the import structure, in the period after independence, the most significant import partners for the Bahamas were the United States and the U.K., although the largest partners were the oil exporting countries as a whole. There was a large increase in Caricom imports in the 1970s, with Trinidad as the major partner. Imports from Venezuela not un-expectedly tapered off after 1981. Over the years, the basic import structure has held: the major partners, other than the oil exporters, are the United States, the U.K., and the EEC as a whole. Japan, however, has replaced Canada in importance. Also, there has been some diversification in import trade with Latin America in terms of expansion of relations with Brazil and Mexico. The Bahamas had some small imports from socialist countries, primarily the U.S.S.R. in the 1970s and Cuba in the 1980s.

Barbados. A year after its independence, Barbados had a very simple structure: the U.K. was its main trading partner in both exports and imports, followed by the United States and Canada. Its only other important export partner was the Caribbean, especially Trinidad and the Leewards as a bloc. The same applied to imports, except that Venezuela was also a major supplier (presumably of oil) in Latin America and the European Common Market was also a relatively significant source of imports.

By the mid-1970s, the U.K. had declined in importance, especially as an export market, and the United States had increased in importance proportionally; Caricom trade increased substantially, with Trinidad remaining the major partner. Some imports from Cuba appeared by 1977 and were sustained through 1982. Imports from Venezuela rose, reflecting various oil arrangements, and exports to Venezuela, although small, rose through 1979. In the 1980s, the United States has become the major export partner and has overtaken the U.K. as import supplier as well. Trade with the U.K. has continued to decline. Canada remains the third most important partner, and imports from Japan are increasing.

The data for Barbados show that Caricom trade has played a relatively major role in the Barbadian economy compared with the role it has played in other countries. Although the IMF individual figures probably underestimate the intra-regional trade, our calculations point to an increase in the percentage of total Barbados trade shared by Caricom: In 1967, the percentages for exports and imports were 8.5 percent and 8.9 percent respectively. This rose to 14.8 percent and 16.5 percent in 1974 and 31.4 percent (exports) and 16 percent (imports) at the peak in 1981. Most of this trade was conducted with Trinidad, followed not very closely by Jamaica and Guyana.

Through the years, Barbadian trade with Africa and Asia has remained negligible, and there have been no significant exports to socialist countries, although a wide range of socialist countries have been low-level import partners. The largest of these has been Cuba, at least from 1978 to 1983.

Belize. Although Belize only became independent in 1981, it was a member of Caricom (Carifta) from 1971. At that time, the United States and the U.K. shared evenly in the export and import trade of Belize, and there were a variety of other partners, especially West Germany, Italy and Canada. Trade with the Caribbean was very small and primarily focused on Jamaica.

By 1974, the United States had become Belize's major trading partner (79 percent exports, 35 percent imports): the U.S. percentage was unusually high in 1974. In the 1970s and 1980s, the more typical export percentages range from 40 percent to 57 percent. Despite the entry into Carifta, trade with the Caribbean did not improve substantially. Jamaica remained the major Caribbean partner, even though in 1974 only the Bahamas is indicated in the IMF figures. More interesting is the small but important amount of trade conducted by Belize with its Central American neighbors, in particular Guatemala (despite the border dispute) and Mexico.

After its independence, Belize continued to concentrate its trade on the United States and the U.K., with a scattering of other partners among the industrial countries, including Japan. However, its most important partner in this secondary group has been Mexico. According to one analyst, Belize's close ties with Mexico are attributable to three factors: "The first is that Mexico has dropped its claim to the northern portion of Belize and backs Belize against the Guatemalan claim. The second reason is the use of Belize as the major port of entry for Quintana Roo, Mexico's southernmost province. . . . Finally, the social and ethnic ties are close between the residents of Belize's northern provinces and the people of Quintana Roo."[7]

However, the trade figures also show as much or more trade betwen Belize and Guatemala as between Belize and its best Caribbean partner, Jamaica. There are also small amounts of exports and imports with Panama, El Salvador, Honduras, and Costa Rica. In the 1980s, Belize's trade with Caricom improved. Jamaica remained the best partner overall, but Trinidad and Tobago was the best export partner. Although no complete figures for 1986 were available at the time of writing, we can assume that under the new government that came in in 1985, Belize's trade orientation—close ties with the United States, expansion of ties with Central America and with the Caribbean—has not changed substantially, although its political orientation appears to be somewhat more toward the Caribbean (rather than Central America) than in the past. It should be noted that Belize's trade with the developing world other than Latin America and the Caribbean is minimal, as is its trade with socialist countries. There are very small amounts of imports from Eastern Europe and China.

Guyana. Immediately after independence, Guyana's trade was evenly distributed between the United States and the U.K. and Canada (exports). Trinidad and Tobago was the next most significant partner. By 1974, trade with China and the U.S.S.R. had increased and there were small amounts of imports from Eastern Europe. Some small trade with Cuba was initiated in the late 1970s, primarily imports. Caricom trade, already a very important part of Guyana's economic links, increased in importance in terms of imports. Our calculations from the IMF figures show that the share of the Caribbean in Guyana's exports and imports went from 14.7 percent and 10.9 percent respectively in 1967 to 9.2 percent and 26.4 percent in 1974, and then to between 9 percent and 16 percent for exports 1979–1985 and between 27 percent and 43 percent for imports

1979–1985. Throughout this time, Trinidad has continued as the major partner.

In the 1980s, Guyana's trade structure remains remarkably unchanged. The United States and the U.K. continue to be the main partners, with Canada third. West Germany and Japan have been increasing in importance across the years. However, there have been some interesting subsidiary linkages: First, there has been an expansion of trade with Venezuela, Brazil, and Mexico, primarily in exports. Venezuela is actually Guyana's second major Western Hemisphere partner after Trinidad. The figures for Venezuela reflect increased Guyanese sales of bauxite and alumina to Venezuela in the 1970s and 1980s, especially between 1979 and 1981, although even during the tense period after the border dispute was renewed in 1982, the two countries continued their bauxite arrangements.

Guyana has had relatively strong links with the socialist countries. China was the best partner in the 1970s and East Germany the best for 1980–85. Exports to the U.S.S.R. were also significant in the 1970s. Imports from Cuba peaked in 1979. Finally, despite Guyana's non-aligned commitment, its trade with developing African and Asian countries is small. Morocco is the only consistent partner in Africa, and India the only significant (minimally so) partner, especially in imports, in Asia.

Jamaica. As with Guyana, Jamaica's trading structure after independence was quite simple. The United States was the major partner but not overwhelmingly so, followed by the U.K. and Canada. Most of the rest of Jamaica's trade was with the Caribbean, the European Economic Community (imports especially), and Venezuela (imports, presumably oil).

By 1974, there were signs of greater diversification. The U.K. and Canada had declined in importance, especially as export partners. Trade with the United States had increased but exports were also being sent to Norway, Ghana, and the U.S.S.R., and imports were increasing from West Germany and Japan. The volume of trade with Caricom increased, as did the volume of trade with the EEC in 1974.

Jamaica's exports to Venezuela rose in 1972 and more so from 1976 but declined after 1981. No exports are reported in the IMF data for 1984–1985. Imports from Venezuela increased in the 1970s, making Venezuela Jamaica's second largest import partner after the United States, primarily due to various energy concessions. During the 1970s, under the Manley administration, trade with the U.S.S.R. also rose, reaching its peak in 1980. However, this trade has continued to be quite healthy in the 1980s, with the 1984 volume of exports comparable to the 1980 level. Imports from socialist countries peaked in 1983, with this trade evenly divided between East Germany and the U.S.S.R. There was a steady amount of trade with Cuba in the 1970s up to 1982.

Trade with the United States has remained stable in the 1980s: Exports to the United States have been between 34 percent and 48 percent of

Jamaica's exports, the last percentage representing the figure for 1984. There are peaks and valleys in Jamaica's U.S. trade and the figures show a trend toward decline in exports. The same level of variation holds for imports from the United States, which in the 1980s ranged from 31 percent to 46 percent (1984) of Jamaica's total imports, but the trend here is toward an increase. In the 1980s Japan, France, and West Germany improved as import partners. Trade with Africa remains confined to Ghana. Trade with developing Asia has always been weak, the major import partner in that region being Hong Kong. (Figures for Taiwan are not included in the IMF data but may be significant.)

At their peak in 1983, according to the IMF data, Jamaica's exports to Caricom represented some 12.6 percent of its total trade. For imports, the peak occurred in 1982 at 6.6 percent of Jamaica's total trade. Overall, Caricom trade has not been as significant to Jamaica as it has been to Barbados and Guyana. Trinidad has consistently been Jamaica's best Caribbean partner. In sum, Jamaica's closest trading relationship since independence has been with the United States, followed by the EEC (the U.K. in particular), Canada, and Caricom, Trinidad in particular. Venezuela has been extremely important in terms of Jamaica's imports. Although Jamaica's links with developing Africa and Asia remain weak, its trade with socialist countries is comparatively strong, although centered mainly on one country, the U.S.S.R.

Trinidad and Tobago. By 1967, Trinidad's exports were already centered on the United States, followed not very closely by the U.K. Imports were more evenly distributed between the two traditional suppliers. However, by far the most important source of imports was Venezuela, providing Trinidad with crude petroleum for refining. Despite the concentration on the United States and the U.K., Trinidad's trade structure was relatively diversified: Exports were sent to Switzerland, Canada, Spain, and Japan, among others, while imports were obtained from Canada, Japan, and Colombia. The Caribbean market was not as important to Trinidad as it was to Guyana or Barbados, but it was more important than it was in 1967 for Jamaica: 5.3 percent of exports and 4.5 percent of imports went to or came from the specific Carifta area. Guyana was Trinidad's best partner.

By 1974, the importance of the U.S. market had increased to 67.3 percent of exports. The rest was spread among Canada, the U.K., various European partners, and Japan. Exports to Africa increased in 1975, but because they were primarily to "Africa not specified" and to Spanish Africa, their importance is difficult to assess. For the rest, there was a diversification of Western Hemisphere partners to include Suriname, Ecuador, and Brazil. As to the Caribbean, exports from Trinidad to Caricom increased but imports declined in importance. (Guyana and Jamaica remained the best Caribbean partners for Trinidad.) In fact, Trinidad's import partners were diverse: The U.S. share was only 10.8 percent in 1974 while the largest share was assigned to Saudi Arabia, which dislodged Venezuela as a source of crude oil. The U.K. and Canada remained important as import partners, with increasing competition from Japan. EEC trade, both exports and imports, increased in the late 1970s and early 1980s before declining, especially exports.

Other interesting developments in the 1970s were the improvement in links with South and Southeast Asia and the development of ties to socialist states. Asian linkages were primarily focused on Hong Kong and India and were very limited. Some trade with the People's Republic of China (PRC) began in the late 1970s. Cuban imports appeared by 1975 and, more significantly, exports to Cuba began in 1978. A trickle of trade with other socialist states (imports only) began in 1975.

In the 1980s, Trinidad's dependence on the U.S. market has continued. From 42.8 percent of exports in 1967, the U.S. share had climbed to 67.3 percent in 1974 and averaged 58.6 percent between 1979 and 1985. The Netherlands exceeded the U.K. in the late 1970s to become the second major market for Trinidad. Caricom imports increased in importance, reaching 6.4 percent of total imports compared with only 1.5 percent in 1974, but this was still not very high. There was more diversification in Western Hemisphere trading partners to include Colombia and Honduras, as well as Suriname, Brazil, Venezuela and Panama as before. Finally, the import trade with China has persisted, though Hong Kong is a better supplier. (Imports from Korea and Singapore are also increasing.) Trade with Cuba has declined, and the import trade with the U.S.S.R. and Eastern Europe remains sluggish.

Overall, Trinidad's trade structure displays a strong reliance on the United States, which has probably deepened since a new government came to power in 1986. On the other hand, it is also somewhat diversified, especially in terms of import partners. Relations with non-Western countries—socialist and developing countries of Africa and Asia—remain limited.

Eastern Caribbean. Because these countries (except Grenada) only gained their independence between 1978 and 1984, they were technically not responsible for decisions with respect to trade made in the late 1960s and 1970s. Yet, with the agreement of the United Kingdom, they negotiated full membership in Carifta and Caricom, and therefore their trade linkages should be discussed with some reference to the pre-independence era.

At the time they gained Associated Status, the Eastern Caribbean countries as a group not surprisingly were exporting primarily to the U.K. (82.7 percent of all exports, calculated from IMF data) and importing primarily from the U.K. and the United States (37.5 percent and 28.9 percent). Canada was the third major trading partner. Caribbean/Carifta trade, centered on Trinidad and Tobago, Barbados, and to a lesser extent, Bahamas, was highly important, representing about 11 percent of exports and imports. The only other significant partner was Venezuela, for both imports and exports.[8]

Although this was the overall picture, the structure of each country differed. Thus Grenada, for example, has not relied very heavily on the

United States for its imports. As Grenada moved toward independence in 1974, its trade structure was still highly focused on the U.K. (42.7 percent of exports; 26.4 percent imports) but its spice exports were also sent to the Netherlands and other non-EEC areas of Europe. The United States trailed the Netherlands, W. Germany, Belgium and Canada. Grenada's second most important import partner after the U.K. was Trinidad and Tobago, followed by the United States and Canada. After independence, Grenada continued to export primarily to the U.K., although West Germany became the second most important partner, followed closely by the Netherlands. Altogether, in 1974 over 80 percent of Grenada's exports went to Europe. Rather surprisingly, exports to the Caribbean amounted to only 4.8 percent of the total. Imports presented a slightly different picture: The U.K. and Trinidad and Tobago remained the two most important partners and were followed by Canada and the United States.

We might expect that by the late 1970s and 1980s, Grenada would have diversified its trade structure somewhat. But the figures show that the U.K. remained the largest export partner, followed by the same group of EEC countries as before. Exports to the Caribbean improved considerably from 1980, rising to 30.6 percent in 1982. Trinidad and Tobago remained the best partner. The import data show more variation, primarily in the U.S. position. While the U.K. continued its importance, the United States grew as a major partner until it surpassed the U.K. in 1980. Although no trade with the United States is reported for 1983–1985, we can expect that it increased during this time. The Caribbean as a whole, and Trinidad in particular, held its position as a major source of Grenada's imports. (In 1982, the latest year in which data for the United States are included, Trinidad was the second major partner after the United States. In 1983–1985, the U.K. improved its position.)

Apart from the improved U.S. position and an increase in exports to Caricom, the other differences noted in Grenada's trade structure are relatively minor. Japan increased its importance as an import partner in the late 1970s. Also the small amount of trade (imports) with socialist countries, specifically Poland, Czechoslovakia, the U.S.S.R., and China, initiated in the 1970s, increased after 1979 primarily because of the addition of trade with Cuba. Cuba was a relatively important import partner through 1983. It may be added that imports from Hong Kong at all times has exceeded those from the PRC. The former increased after 1983, while no data for the PRC are reported after that year.

St. Vincent is the only other country for which IMF data on balance of payments are available. Its post-independence trading structure is simple and almost the same as it was in, say, the early 1970s. The U.K. remains the major partner, taking 50.4 percent of exports and sending 18.4 percent of imports in 1980, the last year for which complete data were available at the time of writing. (No IMF trade data are given for the U.S. or Trinidad [to St. Vincent] after 1979 and no U.N. data after

1980.) Most of the rest of the country's exports go to Caricom, with Trinidad and Barbados being the major partners. U.N. figures indicate that Caricom exports represented 44 percent of St. Vincent's exports in 1980. Caricom also is St. Vincent's second largest import partner, sending 27.5 percent of total imports in 1980. Despite the fact that no post-1980 data are reported for two crucial partners, the United States and Trinidad, an analysis of the data given for the other trade partners shows that few changes in the trade structure can be discerned. The most significant change is the same as was found for Grenada: The United States has increased in importance as an import partner over the years. The U.N. data in fact indicated that the United States surpassed the U.K. as an import partner in 1980. Other significant import partners include Canada and, in 1984 and 1985, West Germany, the Netherlands and France.

St. Vincent's trade with developing countries other than Caricom countries is very weak. Only Martinique shows up as a small but significant export partner. The Dominican Republic is the only major import partner. Interestingly, Cuba is a relatively significant supplier, its exports increasing after St. Vincent's independence. Other than Cuba and a tiny amount of imports from the Soviet Union, St. Vincent shows no trade with socialist countries.

The pattern of the increasing importance of the United States can also be seen for the other Eastern Caribbean countries. According to U.N. data, Antigua and Barbuda in the 1960s sent 19.7 percent of their exports to the United States and 27.3 percent to the Caribbean, with Barbados the largest partner. This trade pattern is unusual in that the U.K. was not a significant export partner. By independence, Antigua's exports to the U.S. had grown to 35.1 percent (1978) of all exports and exports to the Caribbean to 53.8 percent. Trinidad and Tobago had replaced Barbados as the best export partner. In 1984, the latest year for which data were available, there were real changes, although the data are not yet sufficiently disaggregated to allow for elaboration. The United States' share of Antigua's export market had declined to 17.9 percent. The Caribbean was the largest market, at 38.2 percent of exports, and most other exports went to "other America," that is, countries beyond the Latin American Integration Association and the Central American Common Market. In imports, the U.S. position, 20.2 percent in 1969, grew to 34.5 percent in 1978 and to 37.8 percent in 1984. The U.K., which until the 1970s more or less equaled the U.S. position, increased its share of imports to 29–30 percent by the end of the 1970s, but registered declines in the 1980s. Venezuela was Antigua's third most significant import partner in the 1960s and early 1970s, but its share declined considerably from 1975. Imports from the Caribbean peaked at 28.2 percent in 1975, but decreased to 13.4 percent in 1978 and to 7.4 percent in 1984. Trinidad and Tobago has been the best Caribbean partner. Overall, we can note that post-independence Antigua has been attempting to change the traditional trading structure.

Dominica's trade structure has been the traditional one, with 80 percent of exports going to the U.K. in the early 1970s and the rest to the Caribbean. In a deviation from the norm, most Caribbean exports have gone to Jamaica. Although the U.K. remains Dominica's major export partner, its share of exports has declined considerably over the years, especially after independence, and Jamaica's share has risen proportionally. For imports, the U.K. has been replaced by the United States since Dominica's independence as the country's major trading partner. The Caribbean share increased in the late 1970s to 33 percent (1982 and 1983), spread over a number of countries, with Trinidad the best partner. An interesting addition to the roster of significant import partners here is Guadeloupe. Also, imports from Japan have been growing since the late 1970s. Imports from Canada, a relatively steady fourth or fifth partner for most of the Eastern Caribbean, have been declining.

The pattern for Saint Lucia is almost identical to that of Dominica: The U.K. remains the largest export partner but its shares have been declining. The largest percentage of exports now goes to the Caribbean bloc, a percentage that has increased considerably since the late 1970s. Again, the best export partner has been Jamaica. In imports, again the United States has surpassed the U.K. since independence, and Trinidad has maintained its position as the best import partner. Imports from Japan have grown whereas those from Canada have declined. The Netherlands is a source of a small percentage of Saint Lucia's imports, and a smaller percentage of imports have also come from Venezuela.

Finally, the pattern is again similar for the newest nation, St. Christopher/Nevis. Exports are sent to the U.K., the United States, and the Caribbean, with the United States surpassing the U.K. since 1980 (except for 1982). Imports come primarily from the U.S., followed by the U.K. and Caricom. Trinidad and Tobago is the best Caribbean partner for both exports and imports. In St. Kitts' case, imports from Canada have held steady. Japan and the Netherlands are also included as import partners. None of the Eastern Caribbean nations show significant trade with socialist nations or with African and Asian nations, although most have some trade with Hong Kong, and Saint Lucia and Grenada have some minor but relatively strong (that is, compared with the other Eastern Caribbean nations) contacts with other Southeast Asian nations and India as well.

Overall, what stands out in the trade structure of these smaller Caribbean states, excluding Grenada, is the relative simplicity and continuity of their trade linkages. The importance of Caricom trade is highlighted, as is the continuing importance of the U.K. and the growth in trade, primarily imports, with the United States. It is also noteworthy that despite Eastern Caribbean membership in the ACP, trade with the EEC is almost exclusively trade with the U.K. rather than with the broader organization. The exception here is Grenada, which continues as in the past to have more diverse linkages with EEC countries other than the U.K. In addition, its trade with Caricom (exports) and with the United States has been less central than has been the case for the other Eastern Caribbean countries. Still, it is important to add that Grenada's trade linkages, like those of the other islands, have shown surprisingly little change across the years.

Aid and Investment

Specialists in the Caribbean would readily agree that the main sources of bilateral foreign aid and investment to the Caribbean have been the United States, the U.K., and Canada. Subsidiary sources of aid and technical assistance have been numerous but minor compared to the traditional sources. These subsidiary sources include EEC countries, Venezuela, Japan, China, Republic of Korea, several Eastern bloc countries, Libya, Syria, OPEC countries, Taiwan, Singapore, Israel, Brazil, Panama, Mexico, Nicaragua, India, Philippines, and a number of smaller countries. The main multilateral sources of assistance have been the International Monetary Fund, the World Bank (IBRD), the Inter-American Development Bank (for the larger countries), and the Caribbean Development Bank, all of which are heavily funded by the traditional bilateral sources mentioned above. To analyze all the aid and investment relationships of the Caribbean, we would have to undertake a lengthy and in-depth survey that is beyond the scope of this book. For our analysis, a consideration of the general flows of financial aid to the Caribbean should suffice to give us an idea of the geographical distribution of foreign aid.

The figures in Table 4.3 confirm the existence of two trends in external aid to the Caribbean: one, the dominance of bilateral over multilateral assistance and two, the general concentration of bilateral donors. As in trade, so in aid the Caribbean gets most help from the United States, the U.K., and Canada. It can be noted, however, that these trends are sharper for the larger countries. The smaller the country, the more it appears to rely on multilateral sources of aid. Also to be noted is the fact that as time goes on, the sources of aid are becoming more diversified.

The data on net financial flows are drawn from information supplied to the Organization for Economic Cooperation and Development (OECD) by the Development Assistance Committee (DAC) countries. They include private and public flows, excluding IMF loans other than from the IMF Trust Fund set up from the proceeds of gold sales between 1976 and 1981. They show that of the larger countries, Barbados had the most concentrated aid structure a few years after independence (1969), with the U.K. and Canada providing most aid and the U.N. the rest. Germany and Japan provided negligible amounts of aid as well. In contrast, Jamaica received assistance from the United States and Germany, along with the U.K. and Canada, and negligible amounts from Australia, Belgium, Japan, and Switzerland. At the multilateral level, it received aid from the

TABLE 4.3. Net Aid, Private and Public to the Independent Caribbean: Main Bilateral and Main Multilateral Donors (millions U.S. $)

		Total	Bi	Multi	Main Bi Donor[a]	Main Multi Donor[b]
Belize	1982	13.3	7.7	5.6	8.6 (U.K.)	3.4 (CDB)
					1.0 (U.S.)	1.4 (EEC)
	1985	29.1	23.6	5.5	13.0 (U.S.)	1.3 (CDB)
					5.0 (U.K.)	0.7 (EEC)
Bahamas	1975	274.5	274.0	0.5	166.1 (FRG)	0.5 (U.N.)
					104.0 (U.S.)	
	1982	250.7	243.4	7.3	229.0 (U.S.)	4.1 (IBRD)
					12.6 (Belgium)	1.5 (IDB)
	1985	477.4	477.4	0.0	220.0 (U.S.)	1.2 (IBRD)
					114.5 (Japan)	0.3 (UNDP)
Barbados	1969	1.2	1.0	0.2	0.7 (U.K.)	0.2 (U.N.)
					0.3 (Canada)	- -
	1975	-11.4	-14.2	2.8	5.4 (Canada)	1.7 (U.N.)
					1.0 (U.S.)	1.0 (IDB)
	1982	52.3	26.6	25.8	8.9 (Sweden)	8.7 (CDB)
					6.4 (U.K.)	8.2 (IBRD)
	1985	24.7	15.6	9.1	22.7 (Japan)	6.1 (IBRD)
					4.1 (France)	1.6 (IDB)
Guyana	1969	19.0	18.1	0.9	10.0 (U.S.)	0.9 (U.N.)
					5.8 (U.K.)	0.1 (IDA)
	1975	26.9	21.8	5.1	16.0 (U.S.)	2.4 (U.N.)
					5.4 (Canada)	2.3 (CDB)
	1982	56.9	14.4	42.5	5.8 (U.K.)	16.6 (IDB)
					5.0 (U.S.)	13.2 (IBRD)
	1985	30.0	1.9	28.1	3.6 (Japan)	23.8 (IDB)
					0.4 (Neth.)	2.3 (EEC)

Country	Year				Major donors			
Jamaica[c]	1969	15.8	10.6	5.2	3.1 (U.K.)	3.0 (U.S.)	3.5 (IBRD)	1.5 (U.N.)
	1975	83.1	67.0	16.1	73.0 (U.S.)	6.9 (France)	6.4 (IDB)	6.3 (IBRD)
	1982	398.0	245.3	152.7	154.0 (U.S.)	51.1 (OPEC)	110.0 (IBRD)	22.3 (IDB)
	1985	275.4	169.0	106.4	58.0 (U.S.)	31.8 (OPEC)	56.9 (IBRD)	34.9 (IDB)
Trinidad/Tobago	1969	9.5	7.3	2.2	5.7 (U.K.)	1.4 (Canada)	1.3 (IBRD)	0.7 (U.N.)
	1975	16.0	8.6	7.4	6.5 (U.K.)	1.7 (Canada)	4.8 (IBRD)	1.1 (IDB)
	1982	45.6	44.8	0.8	26.0 (U.S.)	25.4 (France)	1.1 (U.N.)	2.6 (UNDP)
	1985	-313.1[d]	-314.2	1.1	65.4 (Japan)	13.8 (France)	0.6 (EEC)	3.6 (EEC) 2.2 (UNDP)
Eastern Caribbean[e]								
Antigua	1982	6.4	3.3	3.1	--		--	
	1985	23.6	22.5	1.1	--		--	
Dominica	1982	20.4	9.1	11.3[f]	--		--	
	1985	25.8	18.1	7.7	--		--	
Grenada	1975	3.1	1.9[g]	1.2[h]	--		--	
	1982	-2.3	-7.3	5.0[h]	--		--	
	1985	33.6	29.5	4.1	--		--	
St. Kitts	1985	4.7	2.5	2.2	--		--	
St. Lucia	1982	9.7	4.2	5.5	--		--	
	1985	7.1	2.4	4.8	--		--	
St Vincent	1982	7.8	2.8	5.0[f]	--		--	
	1985	7.8	3.7	4.1	--		--	

(continues)

TABLE 4.3. (continued)

Abbreviations: CBD = Caribbean Development Bank; IBRD = International Bank for Reconstruction and Development (World Bank); IDB - Inter-American Development Bank; IDA - International Development Association; UNDP = United Nations Development Program; OPEC = Organization of Petroleum Exporting Countries.

a Due to net outflows from other donors, the figures for main bilateral donors are sometimes greater than the total bilateral aid.

b Due to net outflows from other agencies, the figures for main multilateral donors are sometimes greater than the total multilateral aid.

c In 1979, just before major electoral changes, Jamaica's total receipts net were $90.4 million, of which $58.5 million was bilateral. By far the major bilateral donor was the Netherlands ($28 million net inflow), and the major multilateral donor was the World Bank ($49.8 million). See OECD, Geographical Distribution 1977/80 (Paris, 1981).

d In this year, there was a net outflow of -$384 million to the U.S. on private investment.

e The OECD does not provide disaggregated data on donors for these countries.

f Includes 0.5 million from OPEC agencies.

g Includes 0.4 million from OPEC countries.

h Includes 2.0 million from OPEC agencies. These agencies also disbursed aid to Grenada in 1977-1981 and in 1983.

Sources: Organization for Economic Cooperation and Development, Geographical Distribution of Financial Flows to Developing Countries, 1969-1976 (Paris, 1977), 1982-1985 (Paris, 1987); United Nations Conference on Trade and Development, Handbook of International Trade and Development Statistics, Supplement 1985 (New York: U.N., 1987).

International Finance Corporation and the U.N. as well as the World Bank.

Guyana and Trinidad and Tobago fell somewhere in between Barbados and Jamaica in terms of diversity of sources. Guyana received most of its aid from the United States, the U.K. and Canada, with small amounts from U.N. and World Bank sources, while Trinidad's main sources were the U.K., Canada, the U.N., and World Bank. Interestingly, Trinidad was already drawing from the Inter-American Development Bank. The distribution of aid at this early time is compatible with our previous findings on Caribbean external policies in military and trade areas. Trinidad, for example, the most eager to join the Organization of American States, was also the first to draw on IDB resources. It also kept some distance from the United States in the early post-independence years. On the other hand, Jamaica's relationship with the United States was as strong as its relationship with the U.K. Barbados remained U.K.-oriented for quite some time after independence. Meanwhile, it is significant that of the four countries, Guyana received the largest net inflow of aid from the United States in 1969. In all cases, bilateral aid far exceeded multilateral, and in Guyana's case, the difference was especially acute.

Data for 1975 show few changes in the post-independence structure. Notably, on the multilateral side, all countries were by then drawing from the Caribbean Development Bank, established in 1970, and all but Guyana (which was admitted to the bank only in 1976) were drawing relatively large amounts from the IDB. At the bilateral level, Canada remained a big donor for Barbados but payments to the U.K. slightly exceeded inflows. U.S. aid increased considerably for Jamaica, and outflows to the U.K. again exceeded inflows in 1975. However, the continuing importance of the U.K. as a donor was reflected in relatively large inflows in 1973 and 1974. Despite Guyana's socialist thrust, U.S. aid remained of primary importance.

Larger changes are noticeable in the 1980s. For all countries, there has been a notable diversification of sources of aid. This is especially true for Barbados, given its earlier high concentration. Sweden (1982) and Japan and France (1985) surpassed the traditional suppliers (U.K. and Canada) in net inflows. Multilateral sources tapped grew to include large inflows from the CDB, the World Bank, and the IDB, as well as smaller flows from the EEC (after the Lomé agreement) and the Arab oil producers (OAPEC). Apart from the increased diversity of sources, aid to Barbados in the 1980s has been characterized by increased multilateralism—so much so that in 1982 multilateral aid equaled bilateral. Finally, given Barbados' increased closeness to the United States in the early 1980s, we might have expected more U.S. inflows, but they remained at pre-1980 levels.

Similar increases in multilateralism can be seen in the data for Guyana and Jamaica. In the 1980s, bilateral inflows to Guyana have dwindled, showing negative totals in 1983 and 1984 because of outlows to the

United States and the U.K. Multilateral aid has far exceeded bilateral aid: The major sources of funding have been the IDB, the World Bank, the EEC, the CDB, and the United Nations Development Program. Ironically, Guyana's dependence on multilateral assistance increased its vulnerability to attempts by the United States and Venezuela to block assistance from these sources (discussed in the last section of this chapter).

The data for Jamaica point to major changes in the level and sources of aid in the 1980s. Aid flows increased considerably in the 1980s in both the bilateral and multilateral spheres. Although bilateral aid flows still predominated, multilateral aid has been increasing. Bilaterally, Italy, Japan, the Netherlands, Norway, Sweden, and OPEC countries joined the U.S., U.K., and Canada in aid to Jamaica. The United States in particular increased its inflows through 1984. Multilaterally, World Bank and IDB aid continued to be most important, but funding from the IDB and IFC increased.

The picture for Trinidad and Tobago in the 1980s is somewhat different from the others. Multilateral aid to Trinidad dwindled after the oil boom, and still in the 1980s multilateral flows consisted mainly of repayments on previous loans. At the bilateral level, France and Japan joined the traditional financial contributors. U.S. aid has increased over the years, but in 1985 there was an exceptionally large outflow on direct investment (-$384 million), presumably attributable to the pullout of Texaco, Inc. under arrangements concluded with the government in that year.

Overall, for these larger countries, the trends for aid and investment can be summed up as follows: There is a continued reliance on financial flows from the United States, the U.K., and Canada, with the U.S. role increasing over the years. At the same time, there has been an increase in aid from multilateral sources (except for Trinidad) and an increase in the diversity of sources of financial assistance.

OECD data are also available for the Bahamas and Belize. These data indicate that the Bahamas has had and continues to have a very high level of financial flows, almost all due to private sector, direct and portfolio, investment flows. (Although the direct investment net was reduced in 1984–1985, the portfolio investment net climbed in 1985.) The United States has played a central and almost exclusive role in the financial affairs of the Bahamas, but Germany has also been important and Japan is increasing in importance. Other flows are relatively minor. At the multilateral level, change is more evident: In 1975, the only multilateral aid the Bahamas received was $500,000 from the U.N. By the 1980s, it was receiving aid from the World Bank, the IDB, the CDB, and the UNDP and smaller amounts from EEC and UN sources. However, multilateral aid remains small. Independent Belize displays a relative diversity in financial helpers, but the flows are small except for a few: The U.K is most important overall, while U.S. flows are almost all Official Development Assistance (ODA). Canada has also provided official loans and grants. At the multilateral level, CDB assistance is most important.

The OECD does not disaggregate flows for the Eastern Caribbean countries, so supplementary data must be found elsewhere. First, however, at the aggregate level, the data show a different trend from that observed in the larger countries: Aid to the Eastern Caribbean has been primarily multilateral until recently; however, a trend toward bilateralism is noticeable in 1984 and 1985 for some countries. Thus for Antigua, multilateral assistance exceeded bilateral aid in 1983–1984 and equaled it in 1982, but in 1985 the bilateral total net disbursements amounted to $22.5 million while the multilateral was only $1.1 million. In Dominica, bilateral assistance, which was less than multilateral in 1982 and 1983, was double the amount of multilateral assistance received in 1984 and 1985. Grenada's special circumstances are also reflected in its aid structure: In 1975, it received equal shares of bilateral (ODA) and multilateral assistance. By 1979, bilateral aid had dwindled and multilateral aid increased proportionally. In 1982 there was a relatively large negative financial inflow in bilateral assistance, but from 1983–1985, the bilateral flow not only resumed but increased considerably while multilateral aid is declining. Nevertheless, the increase in bilateralism is not universal in the Eastern Caribbean. The figures show that Saint Lucia and St. Vincent still draw most of their external funding from multilateral sources. And even though it is impossible to compare trends across time for St. Kitts, which became independent in 1984, multilateral aid almost equaled bilateral assistance in 1985.

Eastern Caribbean aid has come from a variety of sources in the years after independence. The U.K. has continued to be a major bilateral source (Table 4.4), but U.S. aid has far exceeded U.K. assistance in the 1980s. Other bilateral assistance has come from Canada, Venezuela, and the EEC and from such non-traditional sources as Taiwan and South Korea. OPEC has contributed some bilateral funds to Grenada and to Dominica. Unlike the larger countries, the small Eastern Caribbean states have been heavily dependent on official development aid rather than on non-concessional and private assistance. As to multilateral assistance, the Caribbean Development Bank has been perhaps the major donor, with other assistance coming from the World Bank, U.N. agencies, and the European Development Fund. Small amounts have gone from OPEC agencies to Antigua, Dominica, and St. Vincent. Grenada received the greatest OPEC funding over a period from 1977 to 1983. A large increase in OPEC aid can be noted in 1979 and the highest levels of aid were in 1981 and 1982. OPEC aid thus helped reduce Grenada's dependence on DAC-financed agencies until 1983.

As noted earlier, the OECD data used are aggregate statistics that include both public and private financial flows. Among the private flows are flows of private direct investment, an area of concern to many who have analyzed the Caribbean's dependence on the United States. In foreign policy, these investment flows have often provided an additional constraint under which Caribbean decision-makers have had to operate.

90

TABLE 4.4. Selected Data on Official Aid to the Eastern Caribbean in the 1980s (gross disbursements, U.S. $ million)

		Bilateral			
	1981	1982	1983	1984	1985
Grenada					
U.S. (ESF)	--	--	--	47.0	11.1
U.K.[a]	0.06	0.06	0.07	0.53	1.1
Eastern Caribbean[b] U.S.	27.0	66.7	53.2	56.0	46.5
DA	27.0	30.1	18.2	25.2	26.5
PL 480	--	16.6	--	--	--
ESF	--	20.0	35.0	30.8	20.0
U.K.[a]	5.0	4.7	4.7	2.7	3.7
of which					
Antigua	0.7	0.4	0.3	0.3	0.4
Dominica	1.2	1.5	1.3	0.9	1.2
St. Kitts	0.4	0.7	0.6	0.7	0.7
Saint Lucia	1.7	1.2	2.0	0.4	0.4
St. Vincent	1.0	0.9	0.5	0.4	1.0

| | Multilateral | |
	Caribbean Development Bank cumulative 1970-1986[b]	World Bank cumulative to 6/1985[c]
Antigua	14.4	--
Dominica	30.4	5.0 (IDA)
Grenada	18.0	5.0 (IDA)
St. Kitts	15.1	--
Saint Lucia	31.5	--
St. Vincent	27.1	5.0 (IDA)

Abbreviations: ESF = Economic Support Funds (security assistance); DA - Development Assistance; PL480 = Food for Peace Program; IDA = International Development Association (World Bank's long-term loan program).

[a] British data include technical assistance. U.K.£ sterling has been converted into U.S. $s at the rate of £1 = $1.3.
[b] Eastern Caribbean figures are not disaggregated in the U.S. data.
[c] Excludes loans to "Caribbean Region" amounting to $43 million (IBRD) and $14 million (IDA).

Sources: United States Congress, House of Representatives, Foreign Assistance and Related Programs Appropriations 1986, 1987 (Washington, D.C.: Government Printing Office, 1985, 1986); United Kingdom, Overseas Development Administration, British Aid Statistics 1981-1985 (London: Government Statistical Service, 1986); Caribbean Development Bank, Annual Report 1986 (Barbados: CDB, 1987); World Bank, Annual Report 1985 (Washington, D.C.: World Bank, 1986); and Tom Barry, Beth Wood, and Deb Preusch, The Other Side of Paradise (New York: Grove, 1984): 161.

According to the OECD data, the Bahamas received by far the largest amount of investment activity, followed by Jamaica and Trinidad and Tobago, although Trinidad had negative net inflows in most of the 1980s. Without dissagregating investment data by the sending country, it suffices to note that U.S. transnational corporations (TNCs) occupy a dominant position in the Caribbean, as shown in Table 4.5. Note that the U.S. dominance is much less sharp in St. Lucia and St. Vincent; as with aid, these two countries seem to follow their own trend. Among the non-U.S. multinationals operating in the English-speaking Caribbean are British, Canadian, and German enterprises.

Finally, it should be mentioned that although the Caribbean receives almost all of its aid from DAC sources, there has been a small amount of development assistance from the Communist bloc to the left-wing Caribbean regimes. Not surprisingly, Guyana has been the main recipient of such assistance, receiving first $36 million from China between 1972 and 1975 and later $35 million from the Eastern European bloc through 1981, with unspecified amounts coming from the U.S.S.R. After it established relations with China in 1974, Jamaica received $10 million from that country and, through 1979, $285 million from Eastern Europe and $30 million from the Soviet Union. Grenada also received small amounts of aid from the U.S.S.R. and Eastern Europe.[9] Our OECD source also reports sporadically on assistance from the Committee for Mutual Economic Assistance (CMEA) to developing countries: Guyana is noted as receiving gross aid of $13.7 million in 1982 and $2.7 million in 1984 from CMEA sources. Apart from these financial flows, it should be noted that other Caribbean countries have received very small amounts of aid and technical assistance from Eastern bloc countries and from Yugoslavia and Romania.

Regional Financial Flows. The Caribbean region benefits from its own multilateral bank, the Caribbean Development Bank, and from the Inter-American Development Bank, agencies whose lending activities have been incorporated in the preceding discussion. These banks are regional in their lending but not in their membership and contributors. Britain, France, Canada, Colombia, and Venezuela are members of the CDB, and the U.S. is its largest contributor. Sixteen industrial nations and the United States are members of the IDB. Thus bank lending is not regional lending in the pure sense. On the other hand, exclusively intraregional assistance has had a place in the Caribbean at the bilateral level. Specifically, this took the form of aid disbursed by Trinidad and Tobago to the rest of the Caribbean during the years of the oil boom, and, using an extended concept of regionalism, similar aid given by Venezuela to the Caribbean countries. Our analysis can benefit from a brief look at these regional dimensions of aid.

In the 1970s and early 1980s Trinidad gave various types of support to Caricom countries, including balance-of-payments support, project aid, technical assistance, the purchasing of bonds and debentures of

TABLE 4.5. Transnational Corporations in the Caribbean

	U.S.	Non-U.S.
Antigua-Barbuda	31	9
Bahamas	169	29
Barbados	103	48
Dominica	16	7
Grenada	15	4
Guyana	23	27
Jamaica	280	143
St. Kitts/Nevis	14	7
St. Lucia	25	19
St. Vincent	16	11
Trinidad and Tobago	246	61

Source: Tom Barry, Beth Wood, and Deb Preusch, The Other Side of Paradise: Foreign Control in the Caribbean (New York: Grove, 1984): 24.

other member countries, granting access to its domestic capital market, and allowing the floating of CDB and IDB issues in the domestic market with proceeds going to Caricom countries.[10] Trinidad disbursed about TT$451 million in aid to Caricom between 1970 and 1976 and between 1974 and 1976, TT$340.8 million as balance of payments support loans. (TT$2.40 equaled U.S.$1 until 1986, when the Trinidad dollar was devalued to $3.60 for U.S.$1. A further 15 percent devaluation took place in 1988.) In 1978, the Caribbean Aid Project was created under the Caribbean Aid Council to assist Caricom members by providing concessionary financing for development-oriented projects. The CAC was disbanded in 1984, having disbursed TT$31 million out of a total allocation of $54 million. CAC's functions were then reassigned to the Finance and External Affairs ministries. In 1980, the Caricom Oil Facility was established to help Caricom countries finance purchases of petroleum products. About TT$200 million was disbursed from this facility through 1983. Because of the decline in the price of oil, only small amounts of aid have been disbursed since then, but altogether, Trinidad disbursed more than TT$1 billion to Caricom during the years of the oil boom.

Venezuela's assistance to the Caribbean was the result of two factors: the emergence of a perception of the Caribbean as a Venezuelan "sphere of influence," occasioned by the pullout of Britain from the region; and the financial bounty generated by the rise in oil prices. The latter provided the means to carry out policies based on the former; the Venezuelan concern about stability and influence in the Caribbean was heightened in the late 1970s by the ideological changes and problems experienced by some of the countries of the region.[11]

Beginning in 1974, Venezuela assisted the Caribbean through contributions to the Caribbean Development Bank and through bilateral aid targeted mainly at the Eastern Caribbean countries under the Programa de Cooperacion con el Caribe (PROCA). Venezuela's contribution to the CDB included loans to the bank's Special Development Fund as well as the establishment in 1975 of a trust fund to be used for development projects. Jamaica, Barbados, Bahamas, Guyana, and St. Vincent have been the major beneficiaries under the trust fund. In addition, in 1980 Venezuela and Mexico agreed to sell oil at preferential prices to Caribbean Basin countries and to underwrite part of the cost of oil imports through loans that could be converted into development loans. However, only Barbados, Belize, and Jamaica were designated beneficiaries of this program. Also in 1980 a fund was established to finance balance-of-payments deficits and development projects in the Caribbean.[12]

Table 4.6 gives data on these regional aid projects. In the 1980s, Venezuelan aid has declined as its internal economic situation has worsened. The Venezuelan thrust has turned toward investment and trade projects that might provide more benefit to the Venezuelan private sector as well as the government.[13]

Other Financial Flows. The International Monetary Fund has over the years increased its lending for balance-of-payments difficulties, partic-

TABLE 4.6. Selected Data on Assistance by Trinidad and Tobago and Venezuela to the Caribbean, cumulative through 1985/1986 (U.S. dollars in thousands)

	Trinidad and Tobago[a]	Venezuela[b]
Antigua	9,141	--
Bahamas	--	1,924
Barbados	1,821.[c]	2,168
Belize	--	441
Dominica	156	--
Grenada	--	--
Guyana	87,934.[d]	971
Jamaica	198	2,615
St. Kitts	1,099	154
St. Lucia	320	404
St. Vincent	1,105	954
Total	93,565	9,631

[a] Under Caribbean Aid Project (CAP) for development assistance, established in 1978, and the Caricom Oil Facility, established in 1980. Data are disbursements through 1985. CAP was disbanded in 1984, and aid through the Oil Facility was reduced.

[b] Disbursements from the Caribbean Development Bank's Venezuelan Trust Fund only. Data are cumulative 1975-1986.

[c] All but $833 was disbursed under the Oil Facility.

[d] All of this amount was given through the Oil Facility.

Sources: Republic of Trinidad and Tobago, Ministry of Finance, Review of the Economy 1982 (Port-of-Spain, Trinidad: Government Printery, 1983): 57; Review 1983 (Port-of-Spain, 1984): 54; Review 1984 (Port-of-Spain, 1985): 63; Review 1985 (Port-of-Spain, 1986): 66; Caribbean Development Bank, Annual Report 1986 (Barbados: CDB, 1987): 91. The data for Trinidad and Tobago has been converted into U.S. $ at the then-prevailing rate of U.S. $1 = TT $2.40.

ularly through the compensatory financing facility, extended facility, and enlarged access policy. Several Caribbean states have borrowed generously from the IMF, in particular Jamaica and Guyana. In 1980 Jamaica was the fund's largest borrower, drawing 360 percent of its quota; in the same year, Guyana drew more than 100 percent of its quota. The IMF has drawn much criticism for the conditionality of its loans, which includes cutbacks in government spending and social programs, reduction of imports and other terms that often most affect the poor of developing countries and tend to be politically difficult. Thus Caribbean nations, like many others, have had rather rocky relationships with the IMF. Attracted by need, they often find the conditions difficut to live with. Guyana and Jamaica, as the largest Caribbean borrowers, have had the most problems in this respect. As is well known, the Manley government's refusal to continue to deal with the IMF became an issue in the 1980 elections which Manley lost.

In terms of our analysis, a look at drawings from the IMF can tell us something about the foreign policy orientation of various countries even though the motivating factor behind the borrowings is need rather than ideology. Since the United States exerts much influence over the IMF's lending, countries that are closely tied financially to the U.S. or are very pro-West in development orientation are more likely to be heavy borrowers. Table 4.7 lists the borrowing of Caribbean countries across the years. As can be seen, Guyana and Jamaica have been the most frequent borrowers, and Jamaica the largest borrower. It is interesting to note that Dominica has also borrowed relatively heavily. Others making good use of the various IMF resources have been Barbados, Grenada and Belize. In the 1970s, Grenada borrowed under the Oil Facility as well as under Standby Arrangements, and these have been resumed after a hiatus under the revolutionary government.

Economic Conflict

In Chapter 3 on security, we discussed the conflicts that have often arisen between the United States and Caribbean countries that have not conformed to U.S. ideals of friendship, democracy and development. The United States has often threatened, or carried out threats, to reduce economic aid in such circumstances. For example, we noted that U.S. economic aid to Jamaica in the latter half of the Manley tenure declined to almost nothing, and there have also been reductions at various times for Guyana. With the declination by Maurice Bishop of the limited amount of aid offered by the United States after the coup of 1979, Grenada was excluded from U.S. aid allocations until 1983 and from the 1982 Caribbean Basin Initiative which was designed to give preferential treatment to various products coming into the United States from the Caribbean. In addition to bilateral reductions, the U.S. at various times has pressured the international lending agencies and other countries

TABLE 4.7. Selected Data on IMF Drawings of Caribbean Countries

	Use of Fund's Resources as of April 30, 1986: Fund's Holding of Currencies (percent of quota)[a]	Extended Fund Facility Arrangements July 7, 1975 - April 20, 1986[b] Total Amt. of Arrangement[c] (SDR millions)	Total No. of Standby Arrangements Approved 1953-1986, With Years of Last Arrangements
Antigua	100.0	--	--
Barbados	206.6	--	1 (1982-1984)
Bahamas	83.6	--	--
Belize	180.5	--	1 (1984-1986)
Dominica	317.1	8.55 (1981-1984)[d]	1 (1984-1985)
Grenada	128.6	13.50 (1983-1986)	3 (1979-1980)
Guyana	245.8	62.75 (1979-1982)[e] 150.00 (1980-1983)[f]	11 (1978-1979)
Jamaica	515.3	200.00 (1978-1981)[g] 260.00 (1979-1981)[h] 477.00 (1981-1984)[i]	5 (1984-1985, 1985-1987)
St. Kitts	99.8	--	--
Saint Lucia	100.0	--	--
St. Vincent	100.0	--	--
Trinidad	40.5	--	--

a Not all of these resources were borrowed before expiration or cancellation or before April 30, 1986.
b Includes some arrangements under the Supplementary Financing Facility and the Enlarged Access Policy. Most Caribbean countries have also borrowed under the Compensatory Financing Facility and Oil facilities.
c Countries deposit their own currencies in exchange for an equivalent amount of borrowed currency or SDRs.
d Arrangement canceled as of January 23, 1984.
e Arrangement canceled as of June 24, 1980.
f Arrangement augmented to SDR50 million in July, 1981 to a total of SDR150 million. Arrangement canceled as of July 22, 1982.
g Canceled as of June 10, 1979.
h Canceled as of April 12, 1981.
i Arrangement augmented by SDR241.3 million in June, 1981 to a total of SDR477.7 million.

Sources: International Monetary Fund, Annual Report 1986 (Washington, D.C., 1986): 79, 138-141; 1984, p. 109; 1981, p. 120; 1979, p. 110.

as well to deny aid to countries it does not favor. Thus it tried to pressure the EEC, the IMF, the IDA and the CDB—unsuccessfully, in the case of the EEC and the CDB—to deny aid to Grenada, and its disfavor led the IMF to apply rigid conditionality on loans to Jamaica and Guyana.

Taking a page from the U.S. book, Venezuela has also engaged in economic pressure, this time with reference to Guyana. Since the 1960s, prospective investors in the disputed Essequibo zone have been deterred by Venezuelan warnings of non-recognition of their investment, and in the early 1980s, Venezuela put pressure on the World Bank to deny aid to Guyana for a major hydroelectric project. Pressure was also exerted on the Inter-American Development Bank and on the EEC countries in the effort to deny aid to Guyana. Taken in conjunction with other technical consideration, Venezuelan pressure generally proved successful.

We also noted in Chapter 3 that some Caribbean countries have been resentful of U.S. threats to reduce aid for what it sees as insufficient effort to control drug trafficking. Belize, Bahamas, and Jamaica have been particularly vulnerable in this regard. But even for countries that have not attracted U.S. disfavor on any particular issue, there have still been tensions. Like the developing countries as a whole, the Caribbean states have felt that developed countries have not provided them with enough financial assistance. And like the Latin American countries, most have naturally looked toward their northern neighbor for the bulk of this assistance, especially after their security importance was affirmed in the late 1970s and early 1980s. The U.S. reaction to ideological problems in the Caribbean was indeed to step up its economic as well as military assistance, but the amount and the results were not nearly as much as expected.

Half of the increase in economic aid, targeted mainly at Jamaica and the Eastern Caribbean, came from Caribbean allotments under the Economic Support Fund program, a flexible fund used for strategically important countries. The Caribbean Basin Initiative (Caribbean Basin Economic Recovery Act), financed from these funds, was the special trade and aid program formulated by President Reagan in 1982 in response to Caribbean instability. Under this, $350 million in emergency economic aid was allocated to Caribbean Basin countries. But of this, the English-speaking Caribbean received only $75 million, and of that amount, $50 million was for Jamaica, the country selected by President Reagan to be the showcase of the private enterprise model. The remaining $25 million went to the Eastern Caribbean and Guyana ($15 million) and Belize ($10 million). Note that the funding program was a bilateral one, so that full control over eligibility and other criteria lay with the donor.

Under the program, U.S. businesses were encouraged to invest in the Caribbean, although the 10 percent tax credit originally proposed was not included in the act signed into law in 1983. However, business is unlikely to invest in countries that do not have the necessary infrastructure and incentives. Meanwhile, the centerpiece trade provisions—duty-free entry into the United States for Caribbean products—proved to be inadequate because exclusions were granted for textiles and apparel, canned tuna, petroleum and petroleum products, footwear, and certain leather goods, all of which were highly important to the Caribbean export effort. Even more crucial was the fact that duty-free exports of sugar to the United States were limited by the competitive-need criteria of the Generalized System of Preferences (GSP). Apart from the technical inadequacy of the program, the U.S. exclusion of then-socialist Grenada was opposed as undue politicization by many Caribbean policymakers.

Overall, the aid given under the CBI and under other U.S. programs barely begins to address the problems of the Caribbean countries. The figures show that Barbados (electronics), Trinidad (sugar), Jamaica (rum and citrus), and Belize (citrus) have made relatively substantial use of CBI benefits but that the smaller islands have had limited access.[14] In fact, throughout the 1980s the leaders of the Eastern Caribbean complained about various aspects of U.S. economic policy. Thus in 1981, Antigua and Barbuda's Vere Bird criticized U.S. promotion of the private business "pull-yourself-up-by-your-bootstraps" model, noting: "First we have to have the straps with which to pull up the boots. And we will never have the straps if the order of priority does not place the required aid at the forefront."[15] In 1986, Dominica closed its mission at the United Nations because of lack of funds, an action partly designed, according to some observers, to protest the insufficiency of U.S. aid to Dominica.[16] In addition, St. Vincent's Prime Minister Mitchell, later joined by the late Errol Barrow of Barbados, publicly expressed concern about the diversion of economic resources into the military as a result of U.S. military funding and programs that have been offered in tandem with U.S. economic assistance.[17] Another area of U.S. policy that has concerned all the Caribbean countries is the U.S. penchant for bilateralism. Caribbean leaders have publicly opposed this and also, as one described it, [U.S.] "attacks, in a kind of crusade, against some multilateral organizations where decision-making is democratic."[18]

Given the deep economic problems of most Caribbean nations, they have not surprisingly joined in the Third World call for a New International Economic Order, support for which has brought them into some disagreement with the developed countries as a whole and the United States in particular. Apart from the issue of aid, including the desirability of more multilateral aid, the Caribbean has joined with the rest of the Third World in promoting commodity stabilization programs, reduction in protectionism in the industrial countries, transfer of technology, and other schemes. The need for more global approaches to development is highlighted by Jamaica, which despite having conformed to conditions demanded by the IMF, the World Bank, and the U.S. Agency for International Development, continued in the 1980s to have a depressed economy because of the decline in commodity prices.[19] Although Jamaica favored a case-by-case approach in line with U.S. policy, it still found common cause with other countries in similar economic straits.

The demands for a New International Economic Order (N.I.E.O.) were strident in the 1970s, and not surprisingly the Caribbean socialist governments of Guyana, Jamaica, and Grenada were then its strongest supporters, heightening the conflict between these governments and the United States. In the 1980s, with global negotiations stalled and bilateralism on the rise, Third World demands have been muted and rephrased by many governments in moderate terms so that U.S.-Caribbean antagonism on this issue is unlikely now to produce major confrontations. It is to be noted that the Caribbean's Third World orientation has been reflected in regional areas as well—in the leading role played by Jamaica in the formation of the International Bauxite Association in 1974; in Trinidad and Tobago's attempt, twice rejected in the 1970s, to join OPEC; and especially in the Caribbean's enthusiasm for the Sistema Economico Latinoamericano (SELA) formed in 1975 on Venezuelan and Mexican initiatives. SELA was designed as an alternative to the OAS, at least in the economic sector, as a Latin American rather than U.S.-dominated organization. SELA assists members in marketing raw materials, seeking equitable arrangements with multinationals and financing national development projects and programs.

Finally, economic conflict for Caribbean nations has perhaps been most problematic in the regional sphere itself. As has been the case with many integration movements, Caricom has suffered from conflicts between the more and less developed members and between the demands of the integration movement and those of economic survival. Regional trade as a percentage of total trade grew about 3 percent between 1967 and 1973, then dropped 4 percent by the mid-1970s to 7 percent of total trade.[20] It has since hovered around the 7 percent range. But between 1983 and 1986, intraregional trade dropped by a precipitous 26 percent.[21] From the earlier country analyses, it is clear that the Caricom market has been much more important to the small Eastern Caribbean islands than to the other countries. Among the larger countries, Guyana has been more dependent on trade with Caricom than Jamaica or Trinidad. Our earlier analysis indicated that Trinidad and Tobago is in an especially peculiar position: Caricom trade has constituted about 10 percent of its exports and an even smaller percentage of imports, yet Trinidad has been the major trading partner for most members of the community. The fact is that Trinidad has had a consistent trade imbalance with the community, aggravated in the 1970s by its oil-based wealth, and that Trinidad, Barbados, Jamaica, and Guyana have had consistent trade imbalances with the Eastern Caribbean. Although both Carifta and its successor Caricom have written corrective provisions into their agreements, the operationalization of these preferences for the less developed countries (LDCs) has been another matter. For example, among these provisions in the Caricom agreement is the harmonization of fiscal incentives intended to increase the attractiveness of the LDCs for foreign and local investment in industry. The Caribbean Development Bank has also created special funds for LDC development. Despite this, however, LDCs find it hard to attract investment and still lag far behind their more developed counterparts in technical and industrial advancement.

The perception of the unequal distribution of gains from regional integration led to grumbling by the LDCs almost from the inception of the integration movement. When the time came to move on to Caricom, LDCs hesitated. Antigua in particular was concerned that the new common external tariff would raise the price of imported Caricom products more than goods from North America or Europe. In the end, only the more developed countries signed the Caricom accord in August 1973. After much debate, all the Eastern Caribbean countries joined in July 1974.[22]

In the 1970s there were other issues for Caricom to handle. Guyana's nationalistic policies led to import restrictions which were intensified when the oil crisis aggravated balance-of-payments deficits. Again, both Guyana and Jamaica searched for broader markets to help alleviate their trade problems. In addition, several countries imposed foreign exchange restrictions and currency changes—for example Jamaica's two-tiered official-floating exchange rates—which gave their manufacturers a competitive edge while reducing Caricom imports. As one analyst explained:

> Although the increase in intraregional trade consists of a large number of manufactured items not previously traded, this indicates neither diversification nor specialization of production as was intended. On the contrary, it represents duplication in production (some of nonessential items) so that when foreign exchange crises arise and the struggle between national and regional goals is manifest, it becomes difficult for any government not to cut back on nonessential imports, even at the risk of breaking the regional agreement.[23]

This situation continued into the 1980s when Trinidad finally introduced import licensing and foreign exchange rationing as a result of declining oil revenues.

In the late 1970s, Trinidad and Tobago's enhanced oil wealth produced not only a great imbalance in the Caricom trade sttructure but led to complaints by other countries that Trinidad was not doing enough to assist them. This dissatisfaction was accompanied by an intensification of interest in Venezuelan initiatives, which, as we have seen, was a source of annoyance for Trinidad's Prime Minister Williams. Trinidad complained that the oil facility that was established by Venezuela and Mexico was less generous than the one established by Trinidad and Tobago, but had attracted more attention. The turn to donors outside the region also led to the failure of a smelter arrangement that Trinidad was hoping to initiate with aluminum supplies from Guyana and Jamaica. The arrangement was effectively torpedoed when Jamaica decided to pursue the idea with Mexico instead. (Mexico later pulled out of the deal.) Trinidad's reaction to these slights was to downgrade its participation in the integration movement, sending low-level officials, if any, to functional meetings.

The additional conflicts caused by the Caribbean's ideological polarization in the 1970s have already been cited. Because of these economic and political differences, between 1975 and 1982 no Caricom heads-of-state summit, normally an annual event, was held. Even functional cooperation was undermined as many territories sought their own services, in particular air and educational services. In this negative climate, Eastern Caribbean governments managed to pursue their own collaborative goals: the existing West Indies Associated States Council and Eastern Caribbean Common Market were transformed into the Organization of Eastern Caribbean States in 1981. Finally, even after Caribbean leaders met in 1982 and revived their commitment to the community, the events in Grenada in 1983 led to further polarization. In 1984, Caribbean leaders decided to salvage the community and return to urgent economic problems and the goals of economic cooperation. Subsequent meetings have been relatively harmonious, focusing on measures to reduce the barriers to intraregional trade and also boost extraregional exports. How effective these measures will be remains a matter of conjecture in the late 1980s.

Notes

1. For the text of the OECS treaty, see Jack Hopkins, ed., *Latin America and Caribbean Contemporary Record*, vol.1, 1981–1982 (New York: Holmes and Meier, 1983): 685–689. At the time of writing, the Eastern Caribbean states were taking measures toward political union.

2. For a brief description of the Lomé association, see Arthur S. Banks, ed., *Political Handbook of the World 1986* (Binghamton, N.Y.: Center for Social Analysis of the State University of New York, 1986): 679-80. For a more detailed treatment, see Ellen Frey-Wouters, *The European Community and the Third World: The Lomé Convention and Its Impact* (New York: Praeger, 1980).

3. William G. Demas, "The Caribbean and the New International Economic Order," *Journal of Interamerican Studies and World Affairs* 20 (3), August 1978: 251.

4. The *Declaration and Action Programme on the Establishment of a New International Economic Order* is contained in two resolutions, 3201 and 3202, passed at the Sixth Special Session of the General Assembly, May 1, 1974. For a comment on the regional/interregional linkage, see Demas, "The Caribbean," 253–254.

5. On the negative aspects of import substitution and the new thrust to export promotion, see Joan Edelman Spero, *The Politics of International Economic Relations* (New York: St. Martin's Press, 1985): 225–259.

6. Vernetta Calvin-Smith, "The Role of the Ministry of External Affairs in the National Export Promotion Thrust of Trinidad and Tobago," in Anthony P. Gonzales, ed., *Trade Diplomacy and Export Development in a Protectionist World:*

Challenges and Strategies for Caribbean States, Occasional Paper 5 (Trinidad: Institute of International Relations, 1985): 52.

7. Alma H. Young, "Belize," in Jack Hopkins, ed., *Latin America and Caribbean Contemporary Record,* vol.1, 1981–1982: . 395–396.

8. Data on trade with Venezuela are for 1966. No data are reported for 1967.

9. See United States Central Intelligence Agency, National Foreign Assessment Center, *Communist Aid Activities in Non-Communist Developing Countries 1975* (Washington, D.C.: CIA, 1976), p. 33; *Communist Aid 1979 and 1954–79* (1980), p. 19; and U.S. Department of State, *Soviet and East European Aid to the Third World 1981* (February 1983).

10. Republic of Trinidad and Tobago, Ministry of Finance, *Review of the Economy 1983* (Port-of-Spain: Government Printery, 1983): 53.

11. On the Venezuelan-Caribbean relationship, see Andres Serbin, ed., *Geopolitica en las Relaciones de Venezuela con el Caribe* (Caracas, Venezuela: Fundacion Fondo Editorial Acta Cientifica, 1983).

12. See the text of the San José accord in *LACCR,* vol.1, 1981–1982: 651–652, and see Rita Giacalone de Romero, "The Venezuelan Financial Crisis: Its Impact on Foreign Policy Toward the Caribbean," *Caribbean Studies Newsletter* 13 (2), Summer 1966: 7-8.

13. Giacalone, ibid., p. 8; and Veronica Casanova P., "Venezuela hacia el Caribe y Cooperacion Sur-Sur," paper presented at the 11th Annual Meeting of the Caribbean Studies Association, Caracas, Venezuela, May 28-31, 1986, pp. 14–26.

14. CBI data from *Business Bulletin 1984* is reproduced in *LACCR,* vol,4, 1984–1985, p. 1007.

15. Jack W. Hopkins, "Antigua and Barbuda," in *LACCR,* vol. 1, 1981–1982: 493.

16. The protest suggestion is gleaned from interviews with Eastern Caribbean diplomats. Dominica and some of the other smaller Caribbean countries later accepted a Commonwealth proposal that would provide funding for their U.N. missions. For more details, see Chapter 8.

17. A U.S. military official is quoted as saying that Mitchell would not receive more economic aid if he did not accept military assistance. See Joseph B. Treaster, "Caribbean War Games: Not Everyone Is Delighted," *New York Times,* September 16, 1985, p. 2.

18. Statement by Guyana's Executive President, Hugh Desmond Hoyte, at the 40th Session of the United Nations General Assembly, October 23, 1985 (U.N. Doc. A/40/PV. 46), p. 8.

19. See, for example, Statement by the Right Honorable Edward P. G. Seaga, M. P., P. C., Prime Minister of Jamaica, to the United Nations General Assembly, 40th Session, October 14, 1985 (original), pp. 11–13.

20. Demas, "The Caribbean," 251.

21. The 7 percent range is calculated from UNCTAD data in the *International Trade Statistics Yearbook 1985* (New York: United Nations, 1987). The 26 percent drop was noted in a Caribbean News Agency report, July 2, 1986 from the Caricom summit meeting in Georgetown. Trade improved in 1987: An increase of 8 percent was recorded.

22. This paragraph and the next few pages draw substantially from my "Changes in the Regional Foreign Policies of the English-speaking Caribbean,"

in Elizabeth G. Ferris and Jennie K. Lincoln, eds., *Latin American Foreign Policies: Global and Regional Dimensions* (Boulder, Colo.: Westview Press, 1981): 227–228.

23. Anthony T. Bryan, "The CARICOM and Latin American Integration Experiences: Observations on Theoretical Origins, and Comparative Performance," in Inter-American Development Bank, *Ten Years of CARICOM* (Washington, D.C.: IDB, 1984): 84.

5. Patterns and Directions in Policy: Diplomacy

The third issue-area of interest to the Caribbean foreign policy specialist must be the diplomatic area. This is somewhat of a residual category of international relations, and we have selected three non-exhaustive indicators to analyze in this study: patterns in the establishment of diplomatic relations, official visits (defined not just as *state* visits, a more used category, but as any government-government visits), and voting and attendance patterns in the United Nations. The U.N. is widely recognized as perhaps the most important area of diplomatic activity for small states that cannot afford the extensive diplomatic network established by larger, richer nations.[1] In addition to these categories of international behavior, which will again be analyzed with a view to determining the direction of Caribbean activity, a section will be reserved for a discussion of Caribbean–Latin American relations, an arena of Caribbean activity that has grown in importance but one plagued by certain difficulties. As was the case in Chapters 3 and 4, discussion here will also center on patterns of cooperation and conflict.

General Patterns of Interaction

Diplomatic Relations and Visits

It is logical to assume that small states, with limited financial resources, have to choose carefully not so much the states with which they want to establish relations as the states with which they want to *formalize* diplomatic relations. Thus an analysis of a small state's diplomatic relations network is most useful in giving us an idea of its external priorities. A hierarchy in diplomatic relationships can be readily established: states in which there are resident missions are at the top, followed by states to which ambassadors are accredited, followed by the numerous states with which a country has non-formalized links. At the other end of the spectrum, international relations specialists also recognize that missions *received* (as opposed to sent) are also significant in showing how the host country is perceived abroad or how important the host is and to whom.

Because the list of countries with which Caribbean states have established diplomatic relations is quite long (100 countries in the case of Jamaica), the discussion here will be quite general. All states have established relations with the United States, Canada, Western European countries, and Japan, along with English-speaking Caribbean colleagues. We should note that the European linkages also include links to the EEC, headquartered in Brussels, and to various U.N. agencies headquartered in Geneva. Also, most states have relations with the Vatican. A second group of relationships has been established with the circum-Caribbean and Latin American nations: All the Caribbean states have representation of some sort to the OAS and diplomatic links to Venezuela, and there are a varied but selective number of Latin American linkages, the most popular being with Argentina, Colombia, Brazil, Mexico, and Costa Rica. Most English-speaking Caribbean states also have relations with their neighbors Suriname, Haiti, and the Dominican Republic. Finally, a third line of relationships is with Africa and Asia: India has been the favorite Asian nation for the states in our study, and links have been established in Africa with Ethiopia, Ghana, Nigeria, Sierra Leone, and other West African states. In the Middle East, relationships have generally been established with Syria and Lebanon, sometimes Cyprus, and more recently, some of the wealthy Arab states, including Saudi Arabia and United Arab Emirates. International linkages have clearly been dictated by economic concerns, consular interests, and ethnic considerations.

Although size and length of independence are determining factors with respect to the extensiveness of the network of diplomatic relations, the most interesting linkages have nothing to do with size but with political preference. Thus no Caribbean state has had diplomatic relations with South Africa. Another internationally ostracized state, Israel, has fared better among Caribbean countries: Jamaica, Trinidad and Tobago, and Barbados established relations with Israel just after independence, relations that were kept inactive but never broken off, and later, relations with Israel were established by Bahamas, Saint Lucia, Antigua and Barbuda, and Belize. As for Caribbean relations with socialist countries, most states have relations with a limited number of Eastern European countries, generally the more "open" socialists (Romania, Yugoslavia, and Hungary). Guyana, Trinidad and Tobago, Barbados, and Jamaica established relations with Cuba in 1972, and Bahamas, Grenada, and Saint Lucia followed. After the change of government in 1980, Jamaica cut off relations with Cuba, but Grenada has retained an inactive linkage after the changes of 1983. Guyana established relations with the Soviet Union in 1970, as did Jamaica and Trinidad in 1975.

Not unexpectedly, Guyana has established relations with a wider range of socialist countries than have its neighbors. Its links include

East Germany, Bulgaria, Czechoslovakia, Yugoslavia, Hungary, Romania, and the Soviet Union. The list of countries with which Jamaica had diplomatic relations in 1987 also reflects the expansion undertaken during the Manley era. Between 1972 and 1980, Jamaica established relations with the following socialist countries: People's Republic of China, Cuba, Democratic People's Republic of Korea, Guinea, Iraq, Algeria, Hungary, the U.S.S.R., Poland, Czechoslovakia, Vietnam, Libya, Bulgaria, German Democratic Republic, Mozambique, People's Republic of Congo, and People's Democratic Republic of Yemen. (Relations with Nicaragua were also established in this period, but in 1975 before the Nicaraguan revolution). With the exception of Cuba, all these links have remained intact. Again, Grenada's diplomatic links reflect a similar expansion to include many of the countries listed for Guyana and Jamaica. Under Prime Minister Gairy, the pattern of linkages was similar to the general pattern given above: links with North America and Western Europe (including the U.K.), Caricom, Venezuela, and some other Latin American and Afro-Asian countries, including South Korea. (The most publicized Latin American link was with Chile. In contrast, Jamaica cut off relations with Chile after Augusto Pinochet came to power. Barbados never normalized its relations with Chile, established within the first year of independence. Trinidad had relations with Pinochet's Chile, but these could best be described as inactive.) The PRG diplomatic list excluded Chile and included the traditional Caribbean and North America, although links with the United States were downgraded because of the U.S. refusal to accept the designated Grenadian Ambassador.[2] The PRG was committed to preserving ties with Mexico, Nigeria, Algeria, Panama, Sweden, Venezuela, India, Tanzania, Greece, and France. Relations with the EEC were established, and socialist links included "all of the countries of Eastern Europe,"[3] the Soviet Union, Yugoslavia, Vietnam, Mongolia, Laos, Kampuchea, Cuba, Nicaragua, North Korea, Algeria, Syria, Libya, Iraq, and socialist African states. Of these links, the only ones eliminated after 1983 were with Libya, the U.S.S.R., and North Korea. The post-intervention government restored full ties with Washington, downgraded those with Cuba, added China to the diplomatic list, and in the late 1980s was considering ties with Uruguay, Colombia, and Costa Rica, among others.[4]

On the "socialist" question, two other linkages can be discussed. First, despite the U.S. and U.N. decision to recognize the People's Republic of China in the early 1970s, some Caribbean countries have still not extended recognition. Of the four larger countries, Guyana was the first to initiate links with the PRC in 1972 before U.S. President Nixon made his historic trip. The other countries fell in line after the U.S. decision: Trinidad and Tobago and Jamaica in the early 1970s and later Barbados, Bahamas, Grenada and Antigua/Barbuda. But Saint Vincent's Prime Minister Cato decided after a trip to Taiwan in 1981 to establish diplomatic relations with that country, and later, Dominica's Eugenia Charles and Saint Lucia's John Compton also decided to link with Taiwan rather than with the PRC. After independence, St. Christopher/Nevis joined the pro-Taiwan group. Since Taiwan maintains relations with only about twenty-four countries, the position of these countries must be viewed as anachronistic from the diplomatic point of view, if not from the practical economic perspective.

The other linkage of interest is that between the Caribbean and the two Koreas. The non-socialist Caribbean countries have been interested in maintaining links with the Republic of Korea (South Korea) because of its status as a newly industrializing pro-West power. But the Democratic Republic in the north has over time gained status as a member of the non-aligned group and a possible trading partner. Interestingly, some Caribbean countries have resolved the dilemma by establishing relations with both Koreas. Among countries doing so are Barbados, Jamaica, Saint Lucia, and St. Vincent and the Grenadines.

As for the important issue of establishment of diplomatic missions, the four countries which gained their independence in the 1960s established their missions quite selectively. As can be seen in Table 5.1, Trinidad and Tobago far outpaced the other countries in the early establishment of missions and consulates. Along with the traditional northern linkages, Trinidad, so close to the South American mainland, early formalized links with Venezuela and Brazil and with India and Ethiopia, the last two primarily for symbolic reasons. It also established missions in both Jamaica and Guyana while Guyana established a mission in Jamaica only and Jamaica in Trinidad only. A commission was also established to deal with the not yet independent Associated States. Consulates were set up in the U.K. and Venezuela as well as the important New York region. Finally, Trinidad was the first country to seek a formal resident relationship with the European Communities.

In all, Trinidad and Tobago's relationships have tended to be more diverse than those of the other Caribbean countries. Still, the priority for all four states of relations with the United States, the U.K. and Canada can be seen in the diplomatic data as well as the economic data already examined. We can note, however, the importance of geopolitics in determining diplomatic links. Thus Guyana, like Trinidad, moved fairly quickly to formalize its links with Venezuela—despite or perhaps because of the dispute—and Brazil; and Jamaica formalized its relationship with the Dominican Republic as well as Mexico, where a resident mission was established in the 1970s. In another area, we can speculate that Jamaica's links with Ethiopia were based not only on the importance of that country as headquarters of the Organization of African Unity but on symbolic ethnic considerations. Finally, Barbados had the least diversification in its overseas missions. As can be seen in the 1987 data, missions in Venezuela and Belgium were added in the 1970s and in Trinidad in the 1980s but Barbados depends heavily on multiple accreditation. Even with multiple accreditation, Barbados' links remain heavily North American and European.

Table 5.2 gives the more comprehensive data on diplomatic links for the entire group of Caribbean countries in the 1980s. Consular data are omitted, although they are discussed briefly later. The list shows an expected expansion from 1970, but holds no great surprises. All the Caribbean countries give priority to maintaining links with the United States, the U.K., Canada, and the EEC, as well as being represented at the U.N. in New York. Beyond these basic ties, links with Venezuela are also ubiquitous. Only Trinidad and Guyana have high commissions in India (clearly a link based on ethnic considerations). Jamaica and Guyana have missions in the Soviet Union, Jamaica's dating from the Manley era. Trinidad, Jamaica and Barbados have accredited missions to the Vatican, and Saint Lucia has an ambassador to the Vatican resident in Castries, indicating the importance these countries place on the religious tie. Jamaica has the only accreditation to Israel. Finally, the selection of African linkages is interesting in its variety: Trinidad and Tobago has the only Caribbean mission in Nigeria, accredited to a large number of West African states. Jamaica has retained its mission in Addis Ababa; and Guyana has selected non-aligned Zambia. Trinidad used to have a mission in Addis Ababa, the seat of the Organization of African Unity, but this mission was closed amid the political turmoil Ethiopia experienced in the early 1970s.

Among other missions that have been closed are Guyana's mission to Jamaica and Jamaica's missions in Paris and in Nassau, all of which were not viewed as cost-effective, as well as Jamaica's mission in Cuba after Jamaica broke off relations with that country. Also for Jamaica, accreditations in the 1970s to Lusaka, Beijing, New Delhi, Accra, and Dar-es-Salaam do not appear on the 1987 list. Finally, as of June 1987, the Venezuela ambassadorship was vacant as well as the accreditation to Egypt. As for Barbados, it is worth mentioning that after the Grenada intervention in 1983, diplomatic relations with Cuba were maintained despite some official sentiment that they should be broken. The then Minister of External Affairs stressed that it would be disadvantageous for Barbados to ignore the importance of Cuba in Latin America.[5]

At the time, the foreign minister also argued that Barbados had "failed in not according the wider Caribbean the type of priority it merits," and he announced that to remedy this a diplomatic mission would be established in Grenada and honorary consuls would be appointed in all the other twelve Caribbean Community states.[6] As can be seen from our data, Barbados later decided not to establish a separate mission in Grenada but to accredit the new Trinidad mission to Grenada. This Trinidad and Tobago mission was only fully established after the Grenada intervention and was catalyzed by the disharmony that that event produced between the two countries. Prior to 1983, Trinidad had a high commission in Barbados, but Barbados had not yet sent a high commissioner to Trinidad. After Trinidad's high commissioner indicated that he had not been informed in advance of the plans for a U.S.–Eastern

TABLE 5.1. Missions of Caribbean States Circa 1970[a]

Barbados

Canada
United Kingdom[b]
United States[c]

United Nations (New York)[c]
OAS (Washington)

Non-resident/accredited: Cuba, France, Netherlands, Belgium, Israel, West Germany, Brazil

Consulate: U.S. (New York)

Guyana

United States
United Kingdom[a]
Jamaica
Brazil
Venezuela

United Nations (New York)

Non-resident/accredited: Trinidad, Barbados, Associated States, Haiti, Dominican Republic, Netherlands, Yugoslavia, West Germany, U.S.S.R., France, Sweden

Consulate: U.S. (New York)

Jamaica

United States
United Kingdom
Canada
Trinidad and Tobago
Mexico

United Nations (New York)
United Nations (Geneva)
OAS (Washington)

Non-resident/accredited: Barbados, Guyana, Associated States, Dominican Republic, Haiti, Venezeula, France, Panama, Argentina, Yugoslavia, Switzerland, EEC-Brussels

Consulates: U.S. (New York, Miami)[e]

Trinidad and Tobago

Belgium[f]
Brazil
Canada
Ethiopia
Guyana
India
Jamaica
United Kingdom
United States[g]
Venezuela

European Communities (Belgium)[f]
United Nations (Geneva)
United Nations (New York)[g]
OAS (Washington)

Non-resident/accredited: Barbados, Colombia, Dominican Republic, Eastern Caribbean, France, West Germany, Haiti, Italy, Luxembourg, Mexico, Senegal, Switzerland, United Arab Republic, Tanzania

Consular offices: Canada (Toronto), U.S. (New York), Suriname and the Netherlands Antilles (non-resident, Georgetown)[h]

a Embassies to U.S. are also permanent missions to Organization of American States. Consular offices exclude those headed by honorary consuls.
b Barbados and Guyana were represented by one High Commissioner until 1970.
c Until the end of 1968, the Permanent Representative to the U.N. was also Ambassador to the U.S.
d Headed by Chargé d'Affaires.
e Jamaica also opened a trade commission in Toronto.
f Ambassador resident in London, chargé d'affaires in Brussels.
g In the early 1960s, the ambassador to Washington also served as ambassador to the United Nations.
h Trinidad also opened a trade commission in Montreal.

Sources: Based on data supplied by Ministries of External Affairs, supplemented by selected data from West Indies and Caribbean Yearbook 1974 (Toronto: Caribook Ltd., 1974).

TABLE 5.2. Missions of Caribbean States 1986-1987

	Resident Missions	Accredited also to
Eastern Caribbean:		
Antigua, Dominica,	United Nations (N.Y.)[a]	Belgium—EEC
St. Lucia, St. Vincent,	United Kingdom[b]	OAS
St. Kitts	Canada[c]	
	United States[a]	Caribbean countries
	Headquarters[d]	
Grenada	United States	
	Canada[e]	
	United Kingdom	
	Belgium—EEC	
	Venezuela	
	United Nations (N.Y.)	
	Headquarters[d]	Caribbean countries
Bahamas	Canada	
	United Nations (N.Y.)	Cuba
	Haiti	
	United Kingdom	EEC
	United States	OAS
Barbados	Belgium—EEC	Austria, France, W. Germany, Italy, Luxembourg, Netherlands, Switzerland, Yugoslavia
	United States	Bermuda, Costa Rica, Panama, Mexico, OAS
	United Kingdom	Denmark, Finland, Vatican, Iceland, Norway, Sweden
	Canada	
	Venezuela	Brazil, Colombia, Peru
	United Nations (N.Y.)	Bermuda, Cuba, Dominican Republic, Haiti
	Trinidad and Tobago	Grenada
	Headquarters[d]	Bahamas, Eastern Caribbean,[f] Guyana, Jamaica, Suriname
Belize	United Kingdom	
	United States	
	United Nations (N.Y.)	
	Canada	
	Headquarters[d]	Honduras, El Salvador, Nicaragua, Costa Rica, Panama
Guyana	India	
	United Kingdom	France, Netherlands, West Germany, Yugoslavia, Switzerland
	Canada	
	China	
	U.S.S.R.	
	Belgium—EEC	Sweden, Norway, Austria
	United States	
	Zambia	
	Cuba	
	Venezuela	Peru
	Brazil	
	Suriname	
	United Nations (N.Y)	
	Headquarters[d]	Colombia, Barbados, Trinidad, Eastern Caribbean,[f] Grenada, Bahamas, Jamaica, Haiti, Dominican Republic

	Resident Missions	Accredited also to
Jamaica	Belgium—EEC	France, Luxembourg, Switzerland
	Canada	
	Ethiopia	
	W. Germany	Israel, Netherlands, Vatican
	Mexico	Costa Rica, Nicaragua, Panama
	Trinidad and Tobago	Eastern Caribbean,[f] Barbados, Guyana, Suriname
	United Kingdom	Denmark, Norway, Sweden, Egypt
	United States	OAS, Bahamas, German Dem. Rep.,
	U.S.S.R.	Hungary, Poland, Romania
	Venezuela	Argentina, Brazil, Colombia, Ecuador, Dominican Republic, Haiti, Peru
	United Nations (N.Y)	
	United Nations (Geneva)	Austria, Italy, Yugoslavia
Trinidad and Tobago	United Kingdom	Denmark, Finland, France, W. Germany, Norway, Sweden
	United States	OAS, Mexico
	Canada	
	Venezuela	Colombia, Peru, Ecuador
	Guyana	Netherlands Antilles, Suriname
	Jamaica	Dominican Republic, Guatemala, Haiti
	Brazil	Argentina, Uruguay
	India	Indonesia, Japan, Singapore, Sri Lanka, Bangladesh
	Belgium—EEC	Vatican, Luxembourg, Netherlands, Switzerland
	Nigeria	Algeria, Cameroon, Ghana, Guinea, Ivory Coast, Liberia, Senegal, Sierra Leone, Zaire
	Barbados	Eastern Caribbean[f]
	United Nations (N.Y.)	Cuba
	United Nations (Geneva)	Yugoslavia, Austria, Italy, Romania

a There was a bilateral arrangement for sharing facilities between St. Lucia and Dominica at the U.N. Dominica closed its U.N. operations in 1986. In 1987-1988, Dominica and the other Eastern Caribbean territories (except Antigua, St. Kitts, and St. Vincent) accepted a Commonwealth proposal to partially fund their U.N. operations.
   Dominica, St. Kitts, St. Lucia, and St. Vincent each have one ambassador for both the U.N. and the U.S./OAS. St. Vincent covers Washington from the U.N. St. Lucia did the same until 1984, but now has staff in both places. St. Kitts covers the U.N. from Washington.
b The London mission is an OECS one with shared facilities.
c OECS mission.
d That is, non-resident.
e Grenada participates in the OECS High Commission. It also has a consulate general in Toronto.
f Although the broad characterization is used, the number of countries actually on the accreditation list is not necessarily all of those in the Eastern Caribbean.

Sources: Ministries of External/Foreign Affairs, Diplomatic and Consular Lists/Yearbooks and information supplied by diplomatic personnel. Guyana's accreditations are from Caribbean Yearbook 1979/80 (Toronto: Caribook, Ltd., 1980)

Caribbean invasion of Grenada, Barbados Prime Minister Adams demanded his recall, and Trinidad in turn asked Barbados not to send its high commissioner to Port-of-Spain. Full relations were eventually restored in 1986. As for the honorary consulates, by 1987 Barbados had these in the Bahamas and Jamaica only, while the ambassadors to Dominica, St. Lucia, St. Vincent, and Guyana were resident in Barbados. Grenada too has undergone some changes. Under the PRG, resident missions were sent to Moscow, Cuba, and the EEC. The last has of course been retained but the others have not.

In numerical terms, the number of resident missions would seem to correlate rather precisely with the size (not necessarily the wealth) of the Caribbean country (see next chapter for details). Trinidad and Tobago and Guyana (13 missions), and Jamaica (12 missions) lead the list, although Trinidad far outnumbers the others in accreditations[7] (42 to 33 for Jamaica and 18 for Guyana). Barbados has 7 resident missions and 32 accreditations, a proportionally large number; Grenada has 5 independent missions and one joint mission in Ottawa, a respectable showing for such a small country. (Grenada may rejoin the joint commission in London soon.) The Bahamas and Belize have 5 and 4 missions respectively, and the other Eastern Caribbean states maintain only very basic resident linkages, collectively so in the case of the U.K. and Canada. All these countries have minimal accreditations.

More than a few words need to be devoted to the diplomatic arrangements of the Eastern Caribbean states. Because of financial constraints, joint representation has been an obvious alternative, either in terms of having a single ambassador—the route taken for the London and Ottawa missions—or, more recently, only the pooling of resources and space, for example, by St. Lucia and Dominica at the U.N. The problems involved in these arrangements are discussed more appropriately in Chapter 8. Here we will simply note that although the London arrangement was intended to be "joint" in the sense of the appointment of a single ambassador, Dominica and Grenada had their own representatives. Under the PRG, Grenada left to form its own mission, and Antigua/Barbuda opted for its own representative in 1985. Thus the London arrangement has become more a matter of sharing facilities than sharing representation; even so, some members, notably Antigua, are not enthusiastic about the financial arrangements. The Canada mission, on the other hand, still has a single ambassador.

Another Eastern Caribbean strategy, one also used by some of the larger countries during the early post-independence period, is the sharing of personnel between Washington and New York. In the case of St. Kitts and St. Vincent, there is one mission: St. Kitts covers the U.N. out of Washington, and St. Vincent does the opposite. Saint Lucia had the same arrangement as St. Vincent until 1980. All the Eastern Caribbean countries, except Grenada and Antigua, have the same ambassador responsible for both the United States and the U.N. Interestingly, the ambassadors of Dominica and St. Kitts are resident (at the date of writing) in Dominica and St. Kitts.

Again, we can summarize the discussion numerically in terms of the direction of diplomatic linkages. If we exclude international organizations from our calculations, the Eastern Caribbean countries and Belize maintain all their missions with developed Western countries (DCs). Grenada maintains 4 of its 5 missions with DCs, with one mission in Latin America. For Barbados, 4 of its 6 resident missions are in developed countries, one mission is in Latin America and another in the Caribbean. Three of the 4 missions of the Bahamas are in developed countries, with one in Latin America (actually Francophone Haiti). Guyana has only 33 percent of its missions (4 out of 12) in DCs, 3 in socialist countries, 3 in Latin America, 1 in the Caribbean (Suriname), 1 in Africa, and 2 in Asia. (Numbers do not add up to 12 because of category overlaps.) In other words, Guyana pays more diplomatic "attention," as it were, to LDCs than to the Western DCs. Jamaica has half of its missions in developed countries, 1 in a socialist country, 1 in Africa, 2 in Latin America and 1 in the Caribbean. And Trinidad has 4/11 (36 percent) of its missions in Western developed countries, 1 in Africa, 1 in Asia, 2 in Latin America, and 3 in the Caribbean. In sum, Trinidad and Guyana have the least concentration on the developed Western world and the only missions in Asia, and Trinidad pays the most attention to the Caribbean.

All the Caribbean countries also maintain a number of consulates, mainly headed by honorary consuls. Among those not headed by honorary representatives, most of the Eastern Caribbean states have U.N. missions that double as consulates;[8] Grenada also has a consulate general in Toronto; Trinidad and Barbados have consulates in Toronto and New York; Guyana in New York (having closed its Toronto consulate for financial reasons); and the Bahamas in New York and Miami. Jamaica has the most varied consular offices: in New York, Miami, Toronto, Panama City, San José, Belize City, and in Colon in Panama. The consular locations of course reflect the residency and travel choices of Caribbean nationals and thus reflect important popular influences on foreign policy.

One final aspect of diplomatic relationships must be discussed and that is missions "received." While missions "sent" are highly important in understanding a country's foreign policy, missions "received" also reflect a country's ties and are an indicator of the level of international importance of the country. Table 5.3 gives the missions hosted by each Caribbean country. The data exclude organizational representation, but it should be mentioned that delegations to the European Community can be found in many countries, including Belize, Barbados, Jamaica, Grenada, and Trinidad and Tobago.

Once again, Jamaica, Guyana, and Trinidad and Tobago stand out in this list in terms of the number of missions hosted. Judging by the numbers, we have to conclude that Jamaica has the most visibility in

TABLE 5.3. Missions Received, 1986-1987

	Number of Missions	Sending Countries
Antigua and Barbuda	2	U.S., U.K.[a]
Bahamas	2	U.K., U.S.
Barbados	9	Brazil, Canada, China, Colombia, Republic of Korea, Trinidad/Tobago, U.K., U.S., Venezuela
Belize	6	Colombia, Mexico, Panama, Honduras,[b] U.K., U.S.
Dominica	2	Taiwan, Venezuela[b]
Grenada	3	U.S., Venezuela, U.K.[a]
Guyana	16	Brazil, Canada, China, Colombia, Cuba, German Dem. Rep., India, D.P.R. (North) Korea, Libya,[b] Suriname, Trinidad/Tobago, U.S., U.K., U.S.S.R., Venezuela, Yugoslavia
Jamaica	28	U.S.S.R., Colombia, Spain, U.K., D.P.R. Korea, Rep. of Korea, Trinidad/Tobago, Australia, Israel, Belgium, Canada, Mexico, U.S., Panama, Peru, France, China, West Germany, Brazil, India, Nigeria, Haiti, Netherlands, Argentina, Venezuela, Costa Rica, Japan, Bolivia[b]

St. Christopher/Nevis	1	Taiwan
Saint Lucia	2	France, Venezuela
St. Vincent	2	Taiwan, U.K. [a]
Trinidad and Tobago	19	U.S., Barbados, Canada, China, Colombia, France, India, Mexico, Jamaica, Rep. of Korea, Japan, U.K., Venezuela, Brazil, Argentina, West Germany, Vatican, Netherlands, Nigeria

[a] Resident representative (First Secretary); High Commissioner resides in Barbados.
[b] Chargé d'affaires.

Sources: Ministries of External Affairs, Diplomatic and Consular Lists/Yearbooks; information from diplomatic personnel; Caribbean telephone directories; The Europa Yearbook 1986: A World Survey (London: Europa Publications, 1987).

the international community. In terms of regional representation, the missions received are quite diverse for the major Caribbean states: Developed countries, including Japan, are again important, but Latin American representation rivals Western developed representation, with Venezuela again clearly predominant. The pattern of representation confirms the position of Guyana as socialist host in the Caribbean; half of its missions received are from socialist countries. Representation from Africa is particularly weak, with only Jamaica and Trinidad hosting missions (from Nigeria). Also noteworthy is the fact that Trinidad is the Caribbean base of the Vatican. Note that Taiwan has sent missions to the few countries with which it has diplomatic relations.

An important point is that despite the diversity, in many countries the U.S. mission overwhelms the others through sheer force of numbers. Thus in the Bahamas the U.S. mission houses 17 people, in contrast, for example, to the U.K. mission which has a staff of 4. (The U.S. staff is boosted by an Internal Revenue Service attaché and two narcotics attachés.) In Barbados, a traditional seat of British influence in the Caribbean, the British mission is quite large, 20 persons, but does not at all compare to the U.S. mission, which had a staff of 44 in 1987. As with missions sent, there are larger numbers of accredited missions received, as well as consulates and honorary consulates, but an analysis of resident missions is sufficient for our purposes.

Another way to gauge the hierarchy of diplomatic linkages as well as the importance of a country in world affairs is to analyze the pattern and number of official visits the country sends and receives. An official, particularly a high-level official, who goes abroad not only goes in search of economic and other practical benefits but also makes a political statement about what linkages are of interest to the sending country and the receiving country. Tables 5.4 and 5.5 therefore give numerical information on the pattern of these visits across the years to 1984, an arbitrary cutoff date. As a cautionary note, it should be stated that the data are derived from the Foreign Broadcast Information Service (FBIS), a Central Intelligence Agency source. FBIS culls data from a variety of news services, including the Caribbean News Agency. We assumed that there was a tendency to overreport news from socialist countries, even though the news bank is now a declassified public source of information. But we also discovered a bias in concentration on the Bahamas and Belize, along with a deemphasis on the more southerly countries, especially Trinidad and Tobago. It turned out that despite the overreporting of Bahamian news, the number of Bahamian visits reported were low, which led us to believe that the bias was not fatal for our particular focus of research. FBIS is the most convenient and easily manipulated source of information on visits, which are underreported in major U.S. newspapers and scantily or selectively dealt with in regional newspapers such as *Caribbean Contact* or newsletters such as *Latin American Regional Reports*. A visit is defined in bilateral terms in order to differentiate it from a meeting. Special care was taken to eliminate redundancy, that is, to ensure that visits were not counted twice. A final caveat to the reader: these visits are not intended to represent the total visits actually made and received but simply those reported in the media.

We expected the pattern of visits to conform to the patterns uncovered for diplomatic links so far and indeed they do. The data were so weak in the 1960s in both the FBIS and a collection of other regional and international sources tested that the analysis of the immediate post-independence period for the Big Four was eliminated. However, data were collected for 1974, just after the independence of Grenada and Bahamas, and for 1978–1984, when the rest of the Caribbean emerged to independence. Because of the different chronologies involved, we cannot compare all the twelve countries for the total period, at least not in terms of total number of visits sent and received. But of the six countries independent throughout the period, Jamaica sent and received by far the most visits, which confirms its status as the most internationally visible Caribbean nation. Jamaica maintained a relatively high visit visibility through 1980, with a decline after the Manley years.

During the Manley years, Jamaica's diplomatic reputation clearly hinged on a high level of international socialist interest. All of the 13 visits to and 17 visits from socialist countries noted in Table 5.5 took place in 1974, 1978–1980. A further 12 visits sent at this time and 12 visits received were to and from Third World countries that could be classified as militantly nationalist (Iraq, Libya, Algeria, Guinea, and Grenada for visits sent; Tanzania, Angola, Zimbabwe, Guinea, Nicaragua, Grenada, Guyana, North Korea, and Vietnam for visits received. Two visits sent and one received from Mexico could also be included.) Especially salient during the Manley years is the number of visits sent to strongly nationalist countries in the Middle East and North Africa, specifically Algeria, Iraq, and Libya. Jamaica sent 9 visits to these countries, contributing to the ranking of the Middle East/North African region as the second highest target of Jamaican activity after Latin America. But again Latin America emerges as the favored target of Caribbean activity. Note that about the same amount of activity with developed countries is noted for both the Manley and Seaga periods. The difference lies in the targets themselves: Manley's DC activity included links with countries such as Portugal, Norway, the Netherlands, and Canada, whereas the Seaga administration's attention was more heavily focused on the United States.

Table 5.4 also shows that Jamaica not only received the highest absolute number of visits, even compared with Guyana (which may also be overreported) but also the highest proportion of high-level visits. In absolute numbers, Guyana comes next, supporting general Caribbean analyses that have noted Guyana's thrust for more international visibility dating from the late 1960s. Again, as shown by the diplomatic data, Guyana's importance stems from its association with socialist countries: of the 37.5 visits sent, 16 were to socialist countries, excluding Grenada,

TABLE 5.4. Visits Sent and Received, Independence to 1984[a]

		1974	1978	1979	1980	1981	1982	1983	1984
Antigua/Barbuda	S	--	--	--	--	1 (1)	0	3 (3)	0
	R	--	--	--	--	0	1 (1)	0	1[b]
Bahamas	S	4 (2)	0	0	0	0	2 (2)	2 (2)	0
	R	3	0	0	½[c]	0	0	0	½[d]
Barbados	S	1 (1)	1 (1)	1	3 (2)	3 (2)	2 (2)	1	3[b] (2)
	R	3 (1)	2	1	3 (2)	4 (2)	4 (3)	2 (1)	3
Belize[e]	S	2 (2)	8 (5)	0	9 (6)	11 (10)	6 (6)	5 (5)	9 (6)
	R	1	0	1	0	2 (2)	0	2[f]	3
Dominica	S	--	0	5 (1)	1 (1)	6 (6)	3 (3)	2 (2)	3[b] (3)
	R	--	0	0	0	1	0	0	3
Grenada	S	1	0	3 (2)	13 (9)	5 (4)	9 (8)	10 (8)	0
	R	0	0	2	2 (1)	4	4 (2)	1	5 (2)[g]
Guyana	S	6 (4)	4 (4)[h]	4 (1)	7 (4)	3½ (1½)[d]	5 (5)	2 (1)	6 (4)[b]
	R	3	12 (5)[h]	2 (1)	0	6 (1)	5	10 (2)	10 (5)[b]
Jamaica	S	7 (3)	14½ (11½)[i]	11 (7)	18 (11)	7 (7)	1 (1)	3½ (3½)[d]	7 (6)
	R	5 (3)	23 (9)[j]	11 (4)	8 (3)	4 (3)	4 (4)	4 (3)[k]	4 (1)

St. Kitts	S	--	--	--	--	--	--	--	0	0
	R	--	--	--	--	--	--	--	0	1[g]
St. Lucia	S	--	--	1	1	1 (1)	1 (1)	0	1 (1)	2 (2)
	R	--	--	0	0	0	0	0	1 (1)	3 (1)[b]
St. Vincent	S	--	--	0	0	2 (1)	4 (4)	1 (1)	0	2 (2)
	R	--	--	0	0	1	0	0	0	0
Trinidad/Tobago	S	6 (4)	2 (1)	1	0	1	0	0	1 (1)	2½ (1)[d]
	R	8 (3)	3 (3)	2	2	0	1	2 (2)	1	6 (2)

a   Data are only those reported in the source. No significant visits were reported for the 1960s, so there are no sample data representative of the period just after the independence of the "Big Four." High-level visits (heads of state, deputy heads, and their foreign ministers) are indicated in parenthesis.

b   EEC delegation or mission.

c   Visit was not "voluntary" but made in connection with a fisheries dispute.

d   Visit(s) were received as a by-product of an international or regional meeting.

e   Although Belize was not independent in 1974-1980, data are given to highlight the "internationalization" phase of the border dispute in the 1970s.

f   Includes one visit from the pope as head of the Vatican.

g   Includes one visit from the Commonwealth secretary-general.

h   Includes one visit from a CMEA delegation and one from a delegation representing Cuba's Council of Ministers.

i   Talks with Norway's prime minister were held during a visit to West Germany.

j   Includes one visit from a CMEA delegation and one from the Commonwealth secretary-general.

k   Includes one visit from the queen of England.

Source: Foreign Broadcast Information Service, Latin America Daily Report, relevant years.

TABLE 5.5. Total Visits Sent And Received Since Independence, By Region

		Western Developed Countries[a]	Socialists[b]	Developing Countries				Total[c]
				L.A.	Carib.	Africa	Asia	
Antigua/Barbuda	S	2 (2)	1	0	0	0	1	4
	R	1	0	0	1	0	0	2
Bahamas	S	4 (1)	0[d]	1[d]	3	0	0	8
	R	6	½[d]	½[d]	1½[d]	1	0	4
Barbados	S	4 (3)	4	5	3	0[f]	4	15
	R	6	4	2	6[e]	2[f]	3[g]	22
Belize	S	9 (5)	0	12	7	0	3	31
	R	2	0	3	2	0	0	7[h]
Dominica	S	6 (3)	1	8	5	0	1[i]	20
	R	2	1	0	1	0	1	4
Grenada	S	6 (4)	18[j]	18	9[k]	2[l]	2	41
	R	3 (1)	6	4	5	1	2	18[m]
Guyana	S	1½[d]	16	3	9	3	3[g]	37½[d]
	R	2	26	7	8	2	7	48
Jamaica	S	17 (9)[n]	13	24	2	9[o]	6½[d,p]	69
	R	9 (3)[n]	17	18	13	6	5[g]	63

St. Lucia	S	0	1	5	0	1	6
	R	4	0	0	0	0	4
St. Vincent	S	4 (2)	0	0	1	2	7
	R	1	0	0	0	0	2
Trinidad/Tobago	S	5 (1)	1	5	3½^d	1	13½^d
	R	4 (1)	7	5	7	5	23

a Includes Japan. Visits to and from the U.S. are noted in parenthesis.

b Includes U.S.S.R., Eastern Europe, Cuba, North Korea, People's Republic of China, Vietnam, and Cambodia.

c Overall totals do not necessarily add up to regional distribution totals because of category overlap. Totals are not comparable across all countries because dates of independence differ. St. Christopher/Nevis is excluded from the table because it sent no visits in 1983 and 1984 and received only one in 1984, from the Commonwealth secretary-general. Note that visits counted are only those recorded in the source.

d See Table 5.4 for explanation.

e Includes Martinique and Bermuda.

f Includes Southern Africa delegation.

g Includes one visit to/from the Middle East.

h Includes one visit from the pope.

i Countries not specified.

j Does not include left-wing countries such as Mozambique, Algeria, Libya, Nicaragua, and Guyana to which Grenada sent visits.

k Includes Suriname.

l North Africa only.

m Includes a visit from the Commonwealth secretary-general.

n Four visits were sent under the Manley administration, two in 1980. All three visits received were after 1980.

o Includes seven from North Africa.

p All but one half were from the Middle East.

Source: Foreign Broadcast Information Service, Latin America Daily Report, relevant years.

and of the 48 received, 26 were from socialist countries. Of the non-socialist allies, the data for Guyana show a strong orientation towards the Caribbean, followed by Latin America and Asia (Table 5.5).

Grenada follows next in importance as far as state visits are concerned. Although it received fewer visits than Guyana did, it actually sent more than that country. Again, most of the activity took place in the PRG era, during which Grenada sent 25 visits to countries of similar ideological orientation (socialist *and* left-wing) and received 10 such visits. Grenada's next most favored region has been Latin America, followed by the Caribbean.

Barbados and Trinidad occupy the middle positions in terms of visit activity. They both show orientations toward Latin America, the Caribbean, and the developed Western world. China is their only regular socialist contact in the data collected. The data for Barbados contain two points of interest: The change from Taiwan (visited in 1974) to the PRC is highlighted; and in October 1983 Barbadian officials hosted a delegation from the fledging Southern African integration organization, the Southern African Development Coordination Conference. (The delegation was noted in the news source as being on a Caribbean tour, but the only actual mention of a visit was for Barbados.) Trinidad and Tobago also stands out as having the lowest percentage of high-level visits sent. On visits received, it is noteworthy that the Caribbean as a whole receives relatively low-level officials while sending out a high percentage of prime ministers and foreign ministers. This is not an unexpected finding, but it confirms the subordinate role of small states in the international system.

The Bahamas sent and received a smaller number of visits than its colleagues. Of the 8 sent, 4 were to Western developed countries, 3 to the Caribbean. St. Lucia sent most of its visits to Latin America, primarily Venezuela, and received all the noted visits from Canada and the EEC. St. Vincent sent most of its visits to the traditional Western countries, but they also included Taiwan and the Republic of Korea. Antigua's interests are similar, although its links are with the PRC, not Taiwan.

The number of official visits reported for Dominica and Belize is rather surprising given the small size of these countries. As noted earlier, there is a consistent pattern in FBIS data towards overreporting of Belize, but no similar pattern for Dominica was found. The data indicate that prior to 1980, Dominica was leaning toward such countries as Cuba and Guyana, but that in the 1980s the prime focus of interest has been Latin America, with a diverse group of countries having been visited. Dominica's visits to and from France and to Martinique should also be mentioned in order to point to the importance of geography in foreign affairs. As for Belize, it is clearly very active in sending visits to Latin America, specifically its Central American neighbors, to the United States, the U.K., and the Caribbean, especially Jamaica.

Overall, the importance of Latin America in Caribbean affairs is perhaps the most interesting finding of this research, interesting enough to warrant a relatively detailed look at the Caribbean–Latin American relationship in a later section of this chapter. For the moment, we can turn now to the third area of importance to an assessment of diplomatic performance—the analysis of voting patterns at the United Nations.

The Caribbean at the United Nations

The importance of the United Nations for the Commonwealth Caribbean states was highlighted in the diplomatic data above by the fact that all states, even the smallest, have maintained a presence in New York and many states accredit their U.N. mission to relatively distant countries. The U.N. is not only the place where countries with limited resources can meet with geographically distant colleagues; it is also the place where a voice is given to small states that would not otherwise be heard in a world dominated by larger, wealthier countries. In addition, as described in Chapter 4, Caribbean countries depend on economic assistance from the various United Nations agencies and therefore their participation in the organization is seen as producing desired benefits.

Our interest in this diplomatic section is to ascertain the level of activity of the Caribbean states at the U.N. and the patterns and direction of Caribbean cooperation at the organization. How active are the Caribbean states at the U.N.? Clearly the level of activity, which can be judged by the number of offices held, the number of resolutions sponsored, speeches made, and a host of other indicators, depends partly on the country's financial resources. A large country has the financial means to staff a large mission with sufficient personnel to ensure it a high level of visibility in U.N. activities. A large, wealthy country can also influence others by the very fact that it has economic resources to distribute. Nevertheless, the small country does have influence by virtue of its vote, and although it may not have the staff to service all the committees of the U.N.,[9] it should be able to participate in most votes on the floor of the plenary. Table 5.6 gives the number of absences of each country during the plenary session of 1985, the date we closed our voting analysis and the year after St. Kitts was admitted to the U.N. Since a one-year analysis of data can lead to inaccurate conclusions based on environmental peculiarities, data for two other years are also given.

A caveat is in order: A country's representatives may deliberately absent themselves from voting, either in protest, disinterest, or to avoid having to cast a vote on a controversial issue. Nevertheless, the level of absences for some Caribbean states is too high for it to be seen only in this light, and we feel therefore that these absences are a legitimate indicator of interest. The four larger countries have across the years been able to participate quite fully at the U.N., reflecting the financial argument raised earlier. However, we can note that Guyana's participation continued at a high level even during difficult financial years. The same applies to a lesser degree to Jamaica. This suggests that the difficulties

TABLE 5.6. Participation in the U.N., Number of Absences

	1985	1982	1975
Antigua/Barbuda	9	88	--
Bahamas	4	15	33
Barbados	16	0	0
Belize	102	90	--
Dominica	106	130	--
Grenada	23	19	6
Guyana	4	3	9
Jamaica	10	0	1
Saint Lucia	19	76	--
St. Vincent	23	139	--
St. Christopher/Nevis	103	--	--
Trinidad and Tobago	2	1	5
Total Recorded Votes	171	180	85

Sources: United Nations, Index to the Proceedings of the General Assembly, (30th, 37th, and 40th sessions), "Voting Chart of Resolutions Adopted by Recorded or Roll-Call Vote." (N.Y., United Nations, 1975, 1982, 1985).

lie less in finances than in personnel (see Chapter 8). For the rest, Grenada and Bahamas have reasonably good records of attendance considering problems of size, and Antigua, Saint Lucia, and St. Vincent have improved tremendously. The countries that are clearly only minimally active at the U.N. are Dominica and Belize and, at least for the moment, St. Kitts. An analyst has to assume that these countries have compensated for this lack by focusing their foreign policy on bilateral channels.

In analyzing the Caribbean's voting record for clues as to the direction of foreign policy, we can ask the extent to which the Caribbean sides with the United States or the U.S.S.R. in the East-West competition, the extent to which they side with one another, with Latin America, and with the Third World. Full U.N. records are used for the years 1975, 1979, 1982, and 1985. The choice of these years conforms to our use throughout this work of certain representative and important years. However, instead of 1974, which was used earlier, 1975 is used simply because that was the first year that the U.N. produced comprehensive voting charts.[10] For the 1960s, full U.N. data are not readily available. Therefore, to assess the direction of Caribbean voting in those years, we have used some representative but by no means comprehensive data.

In 1967, based on an analysis of all the recorded-vote resolutions (19) listed in the U.N. Yearbook for that year, Barbados voted 3 times (15.8 percent) with the United States and 6 times (31.6 percent) with the U.S.S.R., Guyana 3 times with the United States and 9 times (47.4 percent) with the U.S.S.R., Jamaica 6 times with the United States and 10 (52.6 percent) with the Soviet Union and Trinidad 5 (26.3 percent) and 11 times (57.9 percent) respectively. (Abstentions are included as similar votes, and all resolutions in which the United States and the U.S.S.R. voted similarly are excluded.) Thus the pattern of voting more closely with the U.S.S.R. than with the United States was already established. Barbados was the least likely to vote with either side, and Trinidad and Jamaica had the highest percentage of voting coincidence with the Soviet Union. As most analysts will readily concur, the pro-Soviet votes of the Caribbean have been in actuality mainly pro–Third World votes—that is, the Soviet Union has sided with the Third World in many matters, especially colonial and economic issues, brought before the U.N.

To determine how closely the Caribbean votes conformed to Third World votes—absent the ability to analyze all the votes of all the Third World countries—we can consider some of the crucial issues of importance to the Third World and see whether the Caribbean votes the "right" way on these. Thus in 1967, on disarmament matters, Barbados and Guyana supported 1 out of 3 resolutions while Jamaica and Trinidad supported all 3. On colonial issues, Barbados voted yes 3 out of 8 times, Trinidad 4, Guyana 5 and Jamaica 6. (All four countries abstained on the issue of the granting of independence to the Eastern Caribbean territories). On South Africa, all four had perfect records.

Another political subject that may be said to be a Third World issue is the Arab-Israeli conflict, in the sense that voting against Israel and for the Arab states has become the non-aligned norm. No resolutions on that subject were noted in the limited data given in the U.N. Yearbook. However, there was an emergency session on the Middle East in the same year, 1967, in which four resolutions were passed. Three resolutions were specifically targeted toward Israel, the fourth forwarded the records of the emergency session to the U.N. secretary-general. Trinidad voted yes on all the resolutions, Guyana on 3—the 3 that referred to Israel— and Jamaica and Barbados abstained on 3. Without more systematic data then, we can conclude that Jamaica and Trinidad had the best Third World records and Barbados the least.

We can also calculate the cohesiveness of Caribbean states in terms of the well-known Modified Rice formula:[11]

$$IC = \frac{\# \text{ yes votes } - \# \text{ no votes } - 1/2 \text{ absences}}{\text{total votes excluding absences}} \times 100$$

For 1967, based on the data available, the index is 49.6 percent. Including the Middle East emergency session votes, the index is 56.1 percent. The relatively low figures indicate that the four Caribbean countries did not coordinate their voting.

The data for the other years (Table 5.7) are more reliable since they are comprehensive. In terms of the U.S.–Soviet Union dichotomy, it is somewhat surprising that Trinidad and Tobago (not Guyana) has the highest percentage voting coincidence with the Soviet Union in 1985 (82.7 percent) and the second highest, after Guyana, in 1982. This means that Trinidad outranked Grenada in that year and again suggests that pro–Third World votes are more significant than pro-Soviet voting. Guyana topped the list in voting similarity with the Soviet Union in the three years considered prior to 1985. Overall, all of the larger Caribbean countries had relatively high percentages of votes with the Soviet Union. For Trinidad, there is a definite pattern of increase over the years, whereas for Jamaica, Barbados, and Guyana, the peak year was 1982. Highly noteworthy is the jump in pro-Soviet coincidence for Barbados between 1975 and 1979 (from 49.1 percent to 62.6 percent). Regional specialists may note that this jump occurred after the more conservative Barbados Labor Party came to power in 1976. Again, this highlights the difference/coincidence between Third World stances and cooperation with the Soviet Union. (Political and other influences on foreign policy are discussed in more detail in the Chapter 6.)

The Bahamas and Grenada follow the pattern of the four larger countries in voting similarity with the Soviet Union. As with Barbados, the Bahamas exhibits a big jump in voting similarity between 1975 (30.2 percent) and 1979 (62.4 percent). As we compare this with the early performance of the Big Four, we are led to conclude that for most

Caribbean states, a few years elapse before their voting record stabilizes into a Third World pattern. The conclusion is supported also by the data for Antigua and St. Vincent. The Bahamas shows an increase in pro-Soviet coincidence continuing through 1985, whereas Grenada shows a decline that is extremely steep (from 78.7 percent to 23.3 percent) even given the impact of the events of 1983.

The data for the smaller countries are more difficult to interpret because of the large number of absences in these countries' voting records. Saint Lucia seems to be in the process of stabilizing its voting pattern, with its voting coincidence with the Soviet Union increasing gradually. St. Vincent seems to be doing the same, although for both, the level of voting coincidence with the Soviet Union remains relatively low compared with that of their Caribbean colleagues. Of the Eastern Caribbean states, Antigua has the highest level of pro-Soviet voting (72.2 percent in 1985). It is too early to tell in what direction St. Kitts will travel on this dimension of Caribbean diplomacy, but Dominica and Belize have extremely low percentages of pro-Soviet votes.

It is interesting to note that increases in Third World voting have generally coincided with Caribbean involvement in another diplomatic thrust—namely, participation in the Non-Aligned Movement. Guyana, Jamaica, and Trinidad and Tobago joined the movement in 1970, Grenada in 1979, Saint Lucia and Belize in 1981, and Bahamas and Barbados in 1983. Dominica and Antigua have observer status, but the former rarely attends meetings and its voting record reflects its disinterest in official non-alignment. Of those that have joined the movement, only Belize's voting behavior can be described as inconsistent with the voting behavior of most non-aligned nations at the U.N.

The other side of the coin—voting similarity with the United States on issues in which U.S.-Soviet agreement is lacking—reveals low percentages of Caribbean-U.S. similarity that are somewhat surprising. The highest percentage of pro-U.S. voting in the 1970s and 1980s is for Grenada in 1985 and that is only 27.8 percent. For most countries, the current range in voting similarity is between 10 percent and 15 percent. Barbados and the Bahamas declined from 26.4 percent in 1975 to 10.5 percent and 8.3 percent respectively for 1985. Jamaica and Antigua have the same 1985 percentages as Barbados. The percentages for Trinidad, St. Lucia, and St. Vincent are slightly higher, that for Guyana slightly lower. Even when we exclude from our calculations the large number of absences for Belize, Dominica, and St. Kitts, the voting similarity with the Soviet Union is at least twice as much as that with the United States. In 1985, Dominica cast only 3 out of 46 votes with the United States. St. Kitts and Belize did much better, respectively casting 25 percent and 20 percent of their votes with the United States. It can probably be concluded that absences are more damaging to U.S. influence than to Soviet efforts.

A few additional points on U.S.-Caribbean voting patterns must be made. The data show that for some reason 1979 was a relatively good

TABLE 5.7. U.N. Voting Coincidence Between Caribbean States and the U.S. and U.S.S.R. (percentages)[a]

		1975	1979	1982	1985
Antigua/Barbuda	U.S.S.R	--	--	36.8	72.2
	U.S.	--	--	5.1	10.5
Bahamas	U.S.S.R.	30.2	62.4	61.8	72.2
	U.S.	26.4	23.8	11.0	8.3
Barbados	U.S.S.R.	49.1	62.6	77.9	69.2
	U.S.	26.4	23.8	10.3	10.5
Belize	U.S.S.R.	--	--	16.2	19.5
	U.S.	--	--	1.5	7.5
Dominica	U.S.S.R.	--	--	8.8	18.8
	U.S.	--	--	3.7	2.3
Grenada	U.S.S.R.	62.3	62.6	78.7	23.3
	U.S.	17.0	18.8	2.9	27.8
Guyana	U.S.S.R.	73.6	70.3	82.4	78.2
	U.S.	13.2	20.8	8.8	9.8
Jamaica	U.S.S.R.	69.8	69.3	75.7	69.9
	U.S.	15.1	19.8	11.0	10.5

		Col 1	Col 2	Col 3	Col 4
St. Kitts/Nevis	U.S.S.R.	--	--	--	15.0
	U.S.	--	--	--	9.0
Saint Lucia	U.S.S.R.	--	100.0	38.2	57.1
	U.S.	--	0.0	8.8	11.3
St. Vincent	U.S.S.R.	--	--	8.1	57.1
	U.S.	--	--	0.7	11.3
Trinidad/Tobago	U.S.S.R.	66.0	67.3	79.4	82.7
	U.S.	15.1	19.8	11.0	11.3
Total Recorded Votes		69	125	158	152
of which					
Votes excluded[a]		16	24	22	19

[a] Votes on which the U.S. and the U.S.S.R. voted alike (including abstentions) are excluded. Some percentages are affected by the high level of absences. See Table 5.6.

Sources: United Nations, Index to the Proceedings of the General Assembly, (30th, 37th, and 40th sessions), "Voting Chart of Resolutions Adopted by Recorded or Roll-Call Vote." (N.Y., United Nations, 1975, 1982, 1985).

year for the United States in terms of Caribbean cooperation. Many Caribbean countries increased their voting agreement with the United States in that year so that voting agreement averaged about 20 percent, quite high considering the percentages for 1985. A closer examination reveals that in 1979 there were 9 resolutions on financing of forces and 19 resolutions on the U.N. budget, issues on which the U.S.S.R. voted no in opposition to most U.N. members, including the Caribbean states. This quite traditional Soviet aversion to increased financing reduced the pro-Soviet votes for that year and increased the pro-U.S. votes.

The voting data show that Grenada had the lowest percentage of pro-U.S. votes of all the Caribbean states, a 2.9 percent voting similarity in 1982. One might conclude that the data reflect a high level of absences, but in fact there were only 19 absences in that year. Rather, the data reflect the abysmal state of U.S-Grenada relations under the PRG and the PRG's high level of pro-Soviet voting. As we have seen, in the period after 1983, Grenada's voting coincidence with the Soviet Union has declined dramatically, whereas that with the United States has increased, though by no means proportionally. Finally, the fact that Bahamas had the lowest percentage of pro-U.S. votes in 1985—that is, of all the countries for which there are few absences—is indicative of the deterioration in U.S. relations with that country, a decline that began around 1983 and is still continuing. However, the voting record is rather deceiving because the Bahamas had a high level of abstentions that can be interpreted as favorable to the United States.

The abstention question is a rather important one, for an examination of the U.N. records will quickly show that "no" votes are quite rare in general and extremely rare among Third World states. Aside from the votes on which the United States and U.S.S.R. themselves abstain, abstentions on the part of small states are generally not so much an indicator of indecisiveness or disinterest as a deliberate attempt not to antagonize a superpower "patron" while not taking an anti–Third World stand. With the possible exception of Guyana, the superpower that Caribbean states do not want to displease is the United States. Hence, the records point to a correlation between high levels of abstention and high levels of pro-U.S. clientalism. As shown in Table 5.8, the highest number of abstentions was 72, cast by Grenada in 1985 (compared with 4 in 1975, 0 in 1979, and 13 in 1982; interestingly, in 1982 the abstentions were on issues such as disarmament and financing, which the Soviet Union usually opposes.) The Bahamas has the most abstentions in three of the four years and the second highest number in 1985: 15 in 1975, 7 in 1979, 20 in 1982, and 27 in 1985.

Since the pro-Soviet votes of the Caribbean are presumably very largely pro-Third World votes, it is important to consider the performance of the Caribbean on the issues in more detail. Judging from the agenda of the non-aligned nations, the Third World can be said to feel strongly about such issues as decolonization, anti-racialism and apartheid, eco-

TABLE 5.8. Abstentions of Caribbean Countries at the U.N. [a]

	1975	1979	1982	1985
Antigua/Barbuda	--	--	1	14
Bahamas	15	7	20	27
Barbados	13	2	9	10
Belize	--	--	4	7
Dominica	--	--	5	9
Grenada	4	0	13	72
Guyana	0	2	9	3
Jamaica	3	2	13	15
St. Kitts/Nevis	--	--	--	15
Saint Lucia	--	1	5	25
St. Vincent	--	--	4	24
Trinidad and Tobago	3	4	7	8

[a] See Table 5.7 for vote totals and exclusions.

Sources: United Nations, Index to the Proceedings of the General Assembly, (30th, 37th, and 40th sessions), "Voting Chart of Resolutions Adopted by Recorded or Roll-Call Vote." (N.Y., United Nations, 1975, 1982, 1985).

nomic and social development, and disarmament. More specific Third World causes include siding with the Arab states against Israel and condemning South Africa, not only on apartheid but also on Namibia. All these issues except disarmament attract Soviet cooperation, hence the coincidence in voting.

An analysis of the voting records for 1975 reveals few controversial votes, at least for the countries involved in this study. With the exception of Bahamas and Barbados, the Caribbean countries supported resolutions on decolonization. The Bahamas abstained on general issues relating to the implementation of the Declaration on the Granting of Independence to Colonial Countries and Peoples and the dissemination of information, as well as on the specific questions of French Somaliland, Western Sahara, and Timor. Barbados and Grenada abstained on the questions of Samoa, Guam, and the U.S. Virgin Islands, and Barbados on the implementation of the Declaration on the Granting of Independence. On the question of Rhodesia, crucial at that time, the Caribbean states voted the Third World way, as also on the issue of South Africa. On disarmament matters, the Caribbean countries were all supportive (but the Bahamas was absent), and all fully supported the Charter on the Economic Rights and Duties of States. The Caribbean also agreed with various financing and budgetary measures proposed by the U.N. On the other hand, the Bahamas also abstained on two resolutions calling for a program of action and a world conference to deal with racism and racial discrimination, and the Bahamas and Barbados abstained, objecting to the wording of a resolution dealing with the elimination of discrimination against women.

The most problematic resolutions for the Caribbean in 1975, a pattern set for the other years as well, dealt with the problems in the Middle East and with human rights issues. Again, the Bahamas and Barbados were most likely to vote against or abstain on resolutions condemning Israel, and they were occasionally joined by Grenada. The most controversial resolution of that year was one equating Zionism with racism. On that issue, the Bahamas and Barbados voted against, Jamaica and Trinidad abstained, and Guyana and Grenada voted yes. Finally, on human rights issues, although the Caribbean nations have supported general declarations, they have differed on specific cases. In 1975, Chile was the specific case: Bahamas, Barbados, and Grenada abstained on the question of the human rights situation in Chile. In sum, we can say that Guyana, Jamaica, and Trinidad and Tobago were most inclined to side with the Third World in their voting in 1975, Grenada somewhat less so, and Barbados and Bahamas least but still supportive of crucial issues.

The pattern for 1979 is not terribly different. Again the Caribbean supported the many resolutions passed on disarmament and decolonization, including Namibia, though Bahamas abstained on the issue of a nuclear-free zone in South Asia and on East Timor. Bahamas also abstained on two South Africa resolutions, one dealing with the Israel–South Africa link. Voting on the Middle East was also more harmonious, with only one resolution dealing with the Camp David Accords resulting in a divided Caribbean: On this, the Bahamas, Barbados, Jamaica, Saint Lucia, St. Vincent, and Trinidad all abstained; as Dominica did not participate in the 1979 session, this means that only Grenada and Guyana voted yes against the United States. The only other controversial resolutions centered on the situation in Kampuchea. On the credentials aspect, Grenada, Guyana, and Jamaica voted no and Trinidad and Tobago abstained (Bahamas and Barbados voted yes), and on the substantive issue, Grenada and Guyana objected, Jamaica and Trinidad abstained. On human rights, the only abstention was that of the Bahamas on Chile. Thus again, the Caribbean, with some exception for Bahamas, voted with most of the Third World in 1979.

The picture for 1982 and 1985 is somewhat more complicated, not least because of the rise in the number of resolutions tabled. Voting in 1982 on most economic issues was by consensus. Voting on colonial issues and on South Africa and general declarations on racism showed full Caribbean support for the Third World position. The only problematic colonial issues were East Timor and—going beyond just colonialism—the Malvinas or Falklands. On East Timor, a resolution criticizing Indonesia received negative votes from Antigua and Saint Lucia, abstentions from Dominica and Jamaica, and approvals from Trinidad, Guyana, Grenada, Belize, and Barbados. (This resolution barely passed 50-46 with 50 abstentions, so the Caribbean countries' dilemma was a generalized one.)

With the exception of Grenada, the Caribbean had supported Britain in the Falklands war, or rather had supported the islanders, who did not want independence from Britain. Resolution 37/9, sponsored by the Latin Americans, called for a settlement of the dispute and the nonuse of force and was supported by both the United States and the Soviet Union; Britain rejected it on the grounds that it did not mention Argentina's refusal to declare a formal cessation of hostilities. Antigua, Dominica, and Belize joined Britain against, Grenada supported the resolution, and the other countries abstained. On related issues, Grenada voted no on a resolution dealing with the situation in Kampuchea, and Guyana and Trinidad abstained; on the situation in Afghanistan, Grenada was the only dissenter, one of twenty-one countries supporting the Soviet Union.

The Caribbean record on disarmament at this session is somewhat checkered. Trinidad's and Barbados' records were the best on these issues, while Bahamas, Guyana, Saint Lucia, Jamaica, Belize, and Grenada all abstained at various times. In addition, Grenada voted no on a resolution dealing with cooperation in reducing military expenditures and on three resolutions on chemical and bacteriological weapons. Altogether, Grenada abstained four times and voted no four more times, Guyana abstained six times, Jamaica four, Saint Lucia twice, and Belize once. Two of these votes were tied into other controversial issues: On the establishment of a nuclear weapons free zone in South Africa, Bahamas, Belize, and Grenada abstained, and on "Israeli nuclear armament," Saint Lucia and Jamaica abstained.

As usual, the situation in the Middle East caused some division in the Caribbean votes. Barbados and Bahamas abstained on a number of issues, and they were joined twice by Jamaica and once each by Antigua and Trinidad. Again, human rights issues were controversial: On Chile, the Bahamas, which had been a consistent abstainer, was joined by Belize, Dominica, Saint Lucia, St. Vincent, and Trinidad. The same countries abstained on Guatemala and on El Salvador, except that on the latter, Saint Lucia voted no. Guyana also abstained on a general resolution on further promotion and protection of human rights. Finally, Grenada abstained on some financial measures, including peacekeeping financing, and Bahamas on some internal budgetary and personnel matters.

A record number of resolutions were tabled at the historic fortieth session in 1985. Again, most economic resolutions were adopted without a vote, and the Caribbean concurred on those that were not. An important exception was Grenada's abstention on affirming the Charter on Economic Rights and Duties of States. Grenada also abstained on such Third World resolutions as one dealing with the progressive development of international law related to the New International Economic Order, on the indivisibility of economic, social, cultural, and political rights, "long-term trends in economic development," and "economic measures as a means of economic and political coercion against developing countries."

Almost all decolonization votes were adopted unanimously at this session. There was a Caribbean consensus on Namibia as usual, except for St. Kitts, which was absent on these resolutions. Only on Mayotte, for which the U.N. favors independence even though the islanders voted for association in 1976, was there a "problem" vote with Grenada and Saint Lucia abstaining, as did the United States. On specific related issues, none of the Caribbean countries voted against condemning the Soviet Union on Afghanistan this year, Guyana remained the only abstainer on the Kampuchea issue, and only Belize voted against a resolution on the Falklands, with Bahamas, Grenada, St. Kitts, Saint Lucia, and St. Vincent abstaining. (Thus five countries that abstained in 1982 did not continue to do so.) A new issue, condemnation of the trade embargo against Nicaragua, drew abstentions from Antigua, Barbados, Dominica, Jamaica, Saint Lucia, and St. Vincent, approval from Trinidad and Guyana, and rejection from Grenada and St. Kitts.

On apartheid, Grenada voted with the United States against sanctions, the only Third World country to do so, and abstained on most other resolutions, although it agreed on an international convention against apartheid in sports. Belize also abstained on a resolution dealing with "programme of work of the Special Committee against Apartheid" as well as on "relations between South Africa and Israel," on which Barbados, Jamaica, Saint Lucia, St. Vincent, and Grenada also abstained. Thus more countries had reservations about this aspect than before. On related issues, Grenada also abstained on the general "Report of the Committee on the Elimination of Racial Discrimination," which the United States opposed.

The pattern of voting on disarmament was even more complex than in 1982. Grenada abstained or voted no on most of the large number of resolutions in this area, including the prohibition against chemical and bacteriological warfare—ironically, this time siding with the United States rather than the Soviet Union. It was the only Third World country and one of only four countries to vote against a resolution citing the urgent need for a comprehensive test-ban treaty. (The other dissenting countries were the United States, the U.K., and France.) St. Kitts also registered a relatively large number of abstentions and a negative vote on the chemical issue. However, almost all the Caribbean countries abstained on some disarmament issues: Bahamas abstained frequently, as it had in the past; Antigua, St. Lucia, St. Vincent, Jamaica, and Barbados abstained more than twice. Trinidad abstained on curbing the naval arms race and prohibition of the nuclear neutron weapon, and Guyana registered one abstention on the neutron issue. Overall, the record on disarmament is mixed, but it is not at all clear that the record of many other Third World countries is much better.

On the Middle East, Grenada again either voted no or abstained generously, even when it was the only abstainer or only joined by the United States, as was the case with resolutions on the status of the Palestinian refugees. Other countries were ambivalent: Antigua, Saint Lucia, St. Vincent, Jamaica, Barbados, Dominica, and Bahamas abstained on a number of issues, including (not all countries) Israeli aggression against Iraqi nuclear installations, convening an international peace conference on the Middle East, Israeli human rights practices, conditions of peace in the Middle East, and the status of Jerusalem. Only Guyana and Trinidad had excellent records on the Middle East.

The record on human rights in 1985 was as mixed as before. Bahamas, Belize, Grenada, Saint Lucia, St. Vincent, and Trinidad abstained on El Salvador, on Guatemala, and on the persistent issue of Chile. St. Kitts was absent on the first but joined the abstainers on the second and third resolutions. On the non-regional questions, human rights in Afghanistan and Iran, Bahamas and Trinidad were the only abstainers. On a general resolution on measures against Nazi and fascist activities, Antigua, Bahamas, Belize, Grenada, and St. Kitts abstained. Finally, on financing and budgetary issues, the Caribbean countries were supportive, except that there were a large number of absences on peacekeeping questions and Grenada and St. Kitts absented themselves on budgetary matters.

To summarize this rather extensive survey of Caribbean voting patterns across the years, in terms of both content and direction, our qualitative analysis would suggest that the Caribbean countries have adopted Third World stances on such issues as Namibia, South Africa, economic and social development, decolonization, disarmament, and even U.N. financing issues. However, in the 1980s, this Third World orientation seems to be on the decline for some countries, in that consensus on South Africa and on disarmament is waning. Of the group of countries being surveyed, Guyana and Trinidad have maintained the most consistent Third World stances across the years. In other areas of voting activity, the Middle East and human rights, the Caribbean has always been somewhat divided. Although certainly human rights has never been a Third World issue per se, the Third World was strongly identified in the 1970s by its backing of the Arab cause in the Middle East. Here again, pro–Third World stances made in the 1970s seem to be eroding in the 1980s. Most of this erosion comes from the conservatism of Grenada and some of the smaller islands in the 1980s.

This conclusion is supported by calculations of the cohesion of the Caribbean states in U.N. voting. Since Third World issues have provided commonalities for many diverse nations, changes in this area must affect the cohesiveness of regional groups, unless all the members happen to change their orientation at the same time. The Modified Rice Index of Cohesion, which measures how closely the Caribbean voted together in the various years, was 76.9 percent in 1975, 96.8 percent in 1979, 86.3 percent in 1982 and 75.8 percent in 1985. For the sake of comparison, it may be noted that indexes calculated for another study for 1976 show cohesion percentages of 94.2, 91.4 and 94.3 for the Middle East/North Africa, Sub-Saharan Africa, and Asia/Pacific respectively, and 74.3 percent for Latin America and the Caribbean (combined).[12] This reflects the fact that the Latin American and Caribbean regions were rather slow in assimilating Third World goals and aspirations. By 1979, the Caribbean was a highly cohesive unit. The decline in 1982 may be attributed to the intensification of ideological differences between Grenada and the others, and the decline in 1985 is also most clearly associated with deviation on the part of Grenada but is also much more general, as we have seen.

A final point may be made in this section with respect to Latin American–Caribbean cooperation. At the United Nations, the Caribbean has no caucusing group of its own but is a sub-group within the Latin American bloc and therefore we can expect some closeness in voting. Analysis indicates that Latin America, like the Caribbean, became more Third World–oriented in its voting in the 1970s, although some of the smaller countries, for example in Central America, have retained a relatively strong pro-U.S. record. Although we did not try to analyze all the votes of all the Latin American nations across the years, we did look at the voting pattern for Venezuela, the English-speaking Caribbean's main focus in Latin America. In 1975, Venezuela agreed with the Soviet Union 58.5 percent of the time, a slightly lower percentage than for most of the Caribbean, and with the U.S. 18.9 percent of the time, slightly more than the Caribbean average. In 1985, the percentages were 83.5 percent and 11.3 percent respectively, very close to the profile for Trinidad and Tobago. Venezuela voted with the U.S.S.R. on the bulk of resolutions but, like Trinidad and most of the Caribbean, agreed with the United States on the situation in Kampuchea, on Afghanistan, on peacekeeping financing, and on some disarmament matters. It voted against only one resolution, dealing with the scale of assessments, a resolution with which the United States also disagreed and Trinidad abstained. Overall, Venezuelan voting patterns were similar to those of the more "progressive" Caribbean nations, and we can probably conclude that the voting patterns of Latin America and the Caribbean are similar in their reflection of the differences between Third World–oriented countries like Venezuela and other pro-U.S. countries, such as Honduras and Guatemala.

A Note on Non-Alignment and Patterns in Caribbean Diplomacy

In the consideration of the Caribbean's Third World stances, a note on the significance of non-alignment for Caribbean diplomacy should be included. As we observed in the section on U.N. voting, most of the English-speaking Caribbean states have joined the Non-Aligned Movement—Jamaica, Guyana and Trinidad in 1970, Grenada after the takeover in 1979, Saint Lucia and Belize in 1981, and Barbados and Bahamas in 1983. Dominica and Antigua/Barbuda have observer status. As for St. Vincent, on independence, prime minister Cato said that he would not seek admission to the Non-Aligned Movement because such participation "is to be aligned."[13] Prime Minister Mitchell has made no attempt to change this policy. St. Kitts/Nevis is also not a member of the movement.

Membership in the movement does not imply homogeneity of views about the meaning of non-alignment. For Guyana, the most committed member, having hosted two foreign ministers conferences, non-alignment has conformed to the self-reliant, usually anti-U.S., Third World mainstream. Membership in the movement has been not just a practical policy but a means for Guyana to acquire prestige and respect through taking "principled" stances on major international issues. As one diplomat put it: "Membership in the movement does not get a country love but respect."[14] Through non-alignment, Guyana also hopes to win friends in support of its foreign policy goals, although the strategy can also be critiqued as one that distances Guyana from any close alliances. In the past, Grenada and Jamaica have been of similar mind as Guyana on the virtues of non-alignment. Maurice Bishop noted early in his administration that "non-alignment for us is a positive concept characterising a vigorous and principled approach to international issues. It is an affirmation of that fundamental attribute of all peoples and states to sovereignty, independence and the right to freely determine their own domestic and foreign policies."[15] Similarly, Michael Manley has written that Jamaica, having decided to disengage from "slavish" obedience to the West, found the Non-Aligned Movement to be "our natural and proper home . . . Jamaica had joined the movement under our predecessors, but had never been active. It is the degree of activity which was to separate the present from the past."[16]

The other Caribbean countries have been less active in the movement, primarily because they view it in a more practical or instrumental way— as a means to achieve international (mainly economic) changes that cannot be gained through individual action. There is no doubt that the political goals of the movement—decolonization, anti-racism, disarmament—are goals which the Caribbean nations inherently espouse, but the anti-American bent of the organization has conflicted with the perspectives of most Caribbean countries. As a result, many Caribbean diplomats insist that their countries are "truly" non-aligned, but not necessarily as viewed by the Non-Aligned Movement. In other words, they maintain that their countries follow an independent path, criticizing both the United States and the Soviet Union, and voting for the "right" position without regard to economic or other consequences.

The data we have collected and analyzed in this chapter showed that the Caribbean as a whole has a relatively good record on the kinds of Third World issues espoused by the Non-Aligned Movement and that many of their votes are clearly a matter of principle rather than reward or intimidation. Votes on Namibia and apartheid and on the Falklands/ Malvinas issue fall in this category. On the other hand, geopolitical and economic considerations also appear to influence Caribbean voting, resulting in a relatively large number of abstentions on crucial issues. Guyana and Trinidad and Tobago, by virtue of their consistency in Third World voting, have the best record in votes with members of the Non-Aligned Movement. Because Guyana's votes are in some instances (for example, Kampuchea) influenced by friendship with the Eastern bloc, it is Trinidad that probably has the best record on *independence* in voting. Of the smaller countries, we saw that Antigua votes the most strongly with the Third World, and an analysis of its abstentions suggests that it is also the most independent voter in the Eastern Caribbean.

Overall, the Caribbean position is atypical of many countries which, although favoring one superpower or the other, have found in the Non-Aligned Movement a useful forum for cooperation with the Third World both for pragmatic reasons and on philosophical grounds. Our analysis of patterns in Caribbean diplomatic activity has shown that although the Caribbean is on the whole Third World-oriented in its principles, in practice its linkages (as shown by diplomatic missions and official visits) remain much more selective, targeted mainly at its traditional developed-country allies.

Diplomatic Issues: Conflict

Because the category of diplomatic conflict covers such a wide range of controversies, we will only highlight the most significant disputes that have arisen between the Caribbean countries and the states they have chosen as their major diplomatic partners. We will therefore confine the discussion to problems experienced with the United States, with Latin America, and internally within the Caricom region. Diplomatic disputes are clearly inseparable from the economic and security problems that we have discussed. The distinction maintained here is therefore quite arbitrary but necessary for organizational purposes.

The United States

The Caribbean's diplomatic problems with the United States have arisen primarily out of the desire of these small states to assert their independence, if not economically then at least in the political arena. The data on U.N. voting that we have considered show a generally low voting coincidence between the Caribbean states and the United States. As the Caribbean countries became more nationalist and Third World–oriented in the 1970s, their voting stances became more annoying to the United States. Not only did the Caribbean join the rest of the Third World on economic issues but also their political stances were more antagonistic to the United States. Among these stances have been votes against Israel, including Caribbean votes on the resolution equating Zionism with racism in 1975; revolutionary Grenada's insistence on supporting the Soviet Union in Afghanistan; abstentions (and Grenada's and Guyana's vote against) on resolutions dealing with the Camp David Accords; abstentions and votes against the trade embargo of Nicaragua; and votes on the South African question, especially when collaboration between Israel, the West, and South Africa is cited. As a member of the Security Council in 1986, Trinidad and Tobago also sided with the majority against the U.S. bombing of Libya and in the General Assembly reaffirmed this position in its vote, along with Guyana. (Barbados and Jamaica abstained; Belize and Dominica were absent.)[17]

Outside of the U.N., there have also been some problem areas. The worst has been the result of the ideological differences that pitted Jamaica, Guyana, and Grenada against the United States. The pro-Soviet, pro-Cuba foreign policies of these countries did, as we saw in earlier chapters, lead to charges of U.S. interference in domestic politics through diplomatic pressures as well as destabilization attempts and U.S. support for electoral opponents. Thus after Michael Manley came out publicly in favor of Cuban actions in Angola, despite a request from then U.S. Secretary of State Henry Kissinger that Jamaica at least be neutral, an aid package never materialized.[18] Again, Guyana's assistance to Cuba in ferrying Cubans and military equipment to Angola in 1975, coupled with other "unfriendly" measures taken by Guyana, led to reductions in U.S. aid.

(Barbados also lent logistical support to the Cubans in this venture but not on the scale of the Guyanese.) As for Grenada, one aspect of the hostility between it and the United States was the U.S. refusal to accept Grenada's choice of ambassador to the United States on the grounds of age and unsuitability. The proposed ambassador, Dessima Williams, was only 28 at the time. Diplomatic relations between the two countries remained downgraded throughout the PRG years. As a result, Grenada communicated less and less with the State Department and more through the U.S. representative to the OAS.[19]

Charges of U.S. diplomatic and political intervention and pressures have not always been limited to socialist countries. As noted in Chapter 3, Caribbean countries are increasingly coming under U.S. pressure to control drug trafficking, with cutoffs of aid hinted. Among the more salient bilateral conflicts in this regard has been that between the United States and the Bahamas. In 1983, U.S. officials discovered that Robert Vesco, the fugitive American financier, and a Colombian drug baron had turned one of the Bahamas' many islands into a transit station for drugs.[20] Charges of corruption and involvement of Bahamian government officials in the drug trade, revealed by the U.S. news media, led to investigations and governmental shake-ups over the next few years. In the process, Bahamian problems with the U.S. Drug Enforcement Agency have been publicized. One issue has been the infringement by the agency of the sovereignty of the Bahamas by conducting drug searches and other operations, including helping drug smugglers so that they could then be caught in Florida, without the consent of the government. Another revelation, made by the American media, was that the U.S. ambassador, in an effort to improve relations with the Bahamas, personally intervened to stop a DEA plan to entrap a Bahamian minister in a drug-payoff scheme.[21] Alleged U.S. violations of Bahamian sovereignty spilled over into the elections of June 1987. During the campaign, Prime Minister Pindling accused the Central Intelligence Agency and the DEA of "running drugs through the Bahamas in pursuit of their own nefarious objectives" and stated that "[the U.S.] ought to stop trying to run our country for us."[22] The Progressive Liberal Party's appeal to Bahamian nationalism helped it win reelection handily. However, after the election victory, Foreign Minister Clement Maynard charged that the United States had "interfered" in the election, and the party chairman clarified this to mean that "there were right-wing Republican interests in the United States who did, in fact, give aid and comfort," presumably to the PLP's opponents. As the New York Times reported, in the weeks before the election, U.S. officials in the Bahamas and in Washington had stepped up their criticisms of the government's efforts against drug smuggling,[23] actions that could be construed as attempts to influence the outcome of the elections. These events served to sour U.S.-Bahamian relations, and prospects were for more diplomatic conflict into the late 1980s.

Latin America

While Caribbean diplomatic conflicts with the United States have centered on issues of sovereignty, disputes with neighboring Latin countries have had more specific causes. Again, most diplomatic disputes are tied to security or economic issues: For example, at various times in the history of Guyana's border dispute with Venezuela, diplomats have been expelled or rebuked by Guyana and harshly worded exchanges have taken place. There have been occasional incidents of Guyanese destroying the Venezuelan flag and other demonstrations, none as serious as the machine gunning of the Trinidad embassy in Caracas in 1963 by terrorists incensed at Trinidad's extradition of six young hijackers. More generally, Trinidad's relations with Venezuela have ebbed and flowed, beginning with the push just after independence to end a 33⅓ percent surtax Venezuela had long imposed on Antillean products, and moving through diplomatic problems caused by persistent fishing disputes, concerns about Venezuelan economic and diplomatic initiatives in the Caribbean, and uncertainties over appropriate delimitations of marine territory vis-à-vis Venezuela under the new law of the sea treaty.[24] The only other Latin country which has been involved in direct diplomatic disputes with Caribbean countries has been Cuba. After almost a decade of involvement in Jamaica, Cuban embassy personnel were expelled from Jamaica in 1980 and relations were broken off. Similarly, the close diplomatic relationship between Cuba and Grenada ended in 1983. Neighboring Suriname also expelled its Cuban diplomats around the same time. (Jamaica's relations with the Soviet Union also deteriorated at the end of 1983 when it expelled four Soviet diplomats, in response to which a Jamaican diplomat was expelled by Moscow.)

Caribbean conflict with the wider Latin American region has mainly taken place in the organizational context, given the fact that interactions outside these organizations are limited. Relevant organizations include the OAS, the Latin American and Caribbean Group at the U.N. (GRULAC), and the U.N. Economic Commission for Latin America and the Caribbean.

Within the Organization of American States, the first Caribbean members were not welcomed with open arms. The Latin Americans were clearly concerned about the impact of these small states, which would not contribute much financially to the organization, as well as about the cultural/linguistic and historical differences. They were also bothered by Caribbean membership in the Commonwealth and by the possibility that these countries would be satellites of the United States. Nevertheless, in 1964, a year after Jamaica had applied to the organization, the OAS passed the Act of Washington allowing for the admission of the new states, except those whose territory was the subject of dispute involving an existing OAS member. (The exclusion affected Guyana, Belize, and the Falklands.) The Act of Washington was incorporated into the amended charter of the organization in 1967. Among the issues raised by the proposed membership of the Caribbean states, and accepted by the Latin Americans, were the separation of OAS membership from membership in the Inter-American Development Bank and the separation of OAS membership from membership in the Rio Treaty. Today, the smaller Caribbean islands are not members of the IDB, but Guyana and Belize are, even though they are not members of the OAS. Only Trinidad and Tobago and the Bahamas have ratified the Rio Treaty.

The entry of Trinidad and Tobago into the OAS in 1967 facilitated the entry of the rest of the Caribbean states, including the smaller Eastern Caribbean islands. The relationship between the two groups within the organization has been less antagonistic than might have been expected, primarily because the Caribbeaners early on won admiration through their principled debating stances.[25] Yet there have been many differences between the groups. The Caribbean countries have focused first on amending the charter to gain entry for its excluded members, Guyana and Belize. Throughout the years, they have argued that the admission of states has absolutely no bearing on the bilateral issue of the settlement of border disputes. At last, in 1985 at a time when Venezuela was seeking admission to the Non-Aligned Movement and Argentina needed support in the Falklands issue, they succeeded in having Article 8, the article that provides the basis for the exclusions, made a "transitory deposition" valid only until September 10, 1990. At that time, it will be replaced by a new article establishing rules of admission, and Guyana and Belize will be eligible to apply for membership.

Two recent events have also brought to the fore the differences in orientation between the Caribbean and Latin American members of the OAS. In the Grenada crisis of 1983, most Latin American nations joined with Trinidad and Bahamas in the organization to oppose the U.S.-Caribbean intervention, even though the issue was not put to the vote. The Latin Americans were acting out of a historical attachment to the principle of non-intervention. But in a speech to the OAS in 1985, the Barbados Minister of Foreign Affairs, in trying to account for the ineffectiveness of the organization, noted that the concept of non-intervention as enshrined in the charter is "anachronistic," a response to a specific historical situation when the Charter was first drafted in 1948. Similarly, the OAS concept of collective security, the minister noted, is rooted in the past:

> [We] must recognise that the superpower in our midst is not an enemy or even a stranger of whom we are to be suspicious, but a friend with whom we share fundamental values and with whom we have deep and enduring relations . . . The threats or perceived threats to the security of the hemisphere are more varied, affect some states more than others, and call for a variety of flexible responses.[26]

Although clearly not all of the Caribbean shared Barbados' sentiments, Grenada did serve to highlight the differences in perception, based on differences in historical experiences, between the Caribbean and Latin American nations.

Another event that served to emphasize these differences was the Falklands conflict of 1982. Here the Caribbean, with the exception of Grenada which was apparently concerned about colonial implications, supported Britain against Argentina, causing much resentment on the part of the Latin Americans. But it should be noted that not all Latin American countries supported Argentina: Chile and Colombia, with their own historical disputes, did not, and Mexico and Costa Rica expressed reservations about the use of force to claim territories. Again, as one Barbadian diplomat noted, there were differences in perception at work:

> Both the English-speaking Caribbean states and the Latin American states are profoundly anti-colonial, but there are differences in emphasis which reflect different sensitivities. Latin Americans, subject to many attacks, invasions, interventions and other forms of external aggression, tend to place greatest emphasis in their anti-colonial views on the question of territorial integrity. The Caribbean, on the other hand, remembering that time on the cross when they were literally in chains and their subsequent struggles to gain political and economic freedoms, tend to focus in their anti-colonial outlook on the question of self-determination.[27]

In general, Latin American and Caribbean members of the OAS have cooperated on issues such as the restructuring of the organization and economic development issues. The early decision of the Commonwealth Caribbean states to establish relations with Cuba did place them at odds with most OAS members but the impetus for change was already developing so that no major diplomatic conflict occurred. Again, the coincidence of the development of Third World views in Latin America and in the Caribbean produced a reasonably high consensus within the organization. Even revolutionary Grenada found the organization far from unfriendly. The former Grenadian ambassador to the OAS noted that Latin Americans supported Grenada in its charges of U.S. aggression because of their own historical and economic problems with the United States.[28]

In the area of economic development, Caribbean–Latin American relations have perhaps been more crucial. In ECLA, the U.N.'s Economic Commission for Latin America, now renamed ECLAC, the Economic Commission for Latin America and the Caribbean, the Caribbean has fought first for consideration as a unique unit, a fight led by Trinidad and Tobago's former prime minister Williams. In 1975, he succeeded in getting the commission to create a Caribbean Development and Cooperation Committee, with membership from the Hispanic Caribbean, Haiti, and Suriname, as well as the English-speaking Caribbean, to focus specifically on Caribbean problems. Increased Caribbean visibility eventually led to the addition of the "C" in ECLAC in 1984 but did not diminish the struggles within the organization between the two groups on questions of funding for various functional programs.

Caribbean *working* relations with Latin America within the group at the U.N. are generally described as good by diplomats. Although the membership of the Caribbean countries may have contributed in the earlier days to decreasing the cohesion of the bloc, we have seen that this diminished as Latin America itself became more Third World-oriented, and today the Caribbean reflects divisions similar to those found in Latin America.

In all three organizations mentioned, some of the strongest conflicts have arisen in the area of elective officeholding. The Latin American countries have tended to see themselves as more influential internationally—with a longer independent history, larger, and generally wealthier—and have assumed that they are the best qualified for major positions. The most progress in the area of elective officeholding has probably been made in the U.N. group, where Guyana has represented the Latin American group on the Security Council twice (1975–1976 and 1983–1984), Jamaica once in 1977 and 1978, and Trinidad and Tobago in the 1985 and 1986 sessions. The Big Four Caribbean countries have also spoken for Latin America in a variety of subsidiary organs. Yet Caribbean candidates have been opposed by the Latin Americans in group elections for the highly visible and sought-after post of president of the General Assembly, which has never been held by a representative of the English-speaking Caribbean. In fact, Caribbean diplomats at the U.N. describe the relationship with Latin America as less than happy. One highly placed diplomat explained that although the separate identity of the Caribbean is now sufficiently recognized, there is no feeling of "brotherliness," that the Caribbean is part of the family. Rivalries for officeholding are, overall, relatively muted only because the Big Four in particular have been producing good candidates. According to this diplomat, and the conclusion is supported by others, the Caribbean is partly to blame for this predicament because the "doctrine of responsibility" favors the Latin Americans—that is, many Caribbean states just do not participate actively enough to be taken seriously.[29] Similar sentiments have been voiced by persons associated with ECLAC, where the Caribbean has had great difficulty in being recognized, particularly insofar as elective offices are concerned. Diplomats at the U.N. and elsewhere also note that the Latin Americans themselves are more contentious than other groups in elective as well as substantive matters.

In the Organization of American States, the pattern of conflicts on officeholding has been sharper than in the U.N. because the Caribbean presence in this dominant Spanish group has been accepted more slowly. Valerie McComie, the Barbadian assistant secretary-general points out that despite his elevation to the position in 1980, the Caribbean position within the organization has not improved substantially.[30] For one thing, McComie had been involved in the OAS since 1967 and also was that fairly rare (English) Caribbean species, a fluent Spanish speaker. In the 1960s, when the first Caribbean nations joined, there was an existing gentleman's agreement that the secretary-general would be from the United States and his assistant would be Latin American, generally from the larger countries. In 1969 a deal struck with the United States and supported by the small states led to the election of a small-state candidate (from Panama) to the number two position, while the United States supported Ecuadorian Galo Plaza for the number one post. This election paved the way for the election of someone from the even smaller Caribbean ten years later. Even so, the vote for McComie was close (14 to 13) and required much lobbying on the part of the Caribbean. In 1984, however, McComie was unanimously reelected.

In committee posts, Caribbeaners have made some inroads but much remains to be done. One other change that has benefited the Caribbean is the rule change to allow the chairmanship of the Permanent Council to be rotated. This revision has permitted the Caribbean some say in issues of government. In the Inter-American Development Bank, Caribbean members also helped change the rules so that Guyana and the Bahamas could be admitted in the 1970s. Note that the United States was a strong supporter of Bahamian admission, but the Bahamas was not then a member of the OAS. Caribbean members were also instrumental in getting a change in the composition of the board of directors that permitted them to have their own elected director.

Overall, the problems between Latin America and the Caribbean tend to be of a very general nature, grounded in deep differences in history, culture, and outlook. Most Caribbean analysts and diplomats interviewed include a racial element among these differences: that Latin Americans have had some difficulty accepting the fact that the black nations of the Caribbean must be placed on an equal international footing with societies in which blacks are either too few to matter or have traditionally occupied lower social positions. Whatever the reasons for the differences, however, our analysis here and in previous chapters shows a clear rapprochement between the two regions, and an improvement in relations and perceptions seems to be taking place across time.

Caribbean

Our final area of analysis here concerns diplomatic conflicts within the core English-speaking region itself. The tensions among Caribbean nations are grounded in generalities such as those that affect the Caribbean–Latin American relationship. Despite cultural and historical similarities, the region has traditionally been fragmented and the leaders highly competitive, as readers familiar with the breakup of the West Indies Federation of 1958–1962 will readily admit. This tendency towards fragmentation and individualism has made the harmonizing of foreign policy, a goal of Caricom, difficult. As we saw in earlier sections, the Caribbean states have formed a variety of diplomatic linkages: Although all have links with the West, some have added to that socialist linkages, others have been more strongly oriented to the United States, some have chosen Taiwan over China, South Korea over the North, and so on. Again, as reflected in the U.N. votes studied, Caribbean countries can agree only in a very general way on such issues as apartheid, the situation in Central America, and decolonization matters. A recent addition to this common agenda has been a general concern over the problems of Haiti. On the other hand, the differences were highlighted by Dominica's Prime Minister Eugenia Charles when she noted after the Grenada events that she had "never been keen on saying that there would be any foreign relations involvement as far as Caricom is concerned . . . I have refused to attend a meeting of ministers of foreign affairs of Caricom . . . I think it is unnecessary."[31] Although Dominica's relationship with Caricom has improved since then, the comment reflects the lack of consensus that still pervades the organization. This lack of agreement came to the fore again in 1988 when Caribbean leaders spent more time bickering over who should take the initiative in Haiti than formulating clear positions and policies.

Despite some general communiqués made both at Caricom meetings and in the U.N., the Caribbean states do not work hard toward coordinating their foreign policies. At the U.N., they might meet at the beginning of the General Assembly and compare notes, but they are not in any way bound as a group to a common position. Coordinated stances are not the norm even for the OECS states, which are incorrectly perceived, after Grenada, as having common foreign policy positions.

Events in Grenada did, of course, produce the greatest diplomatic disharmony in the Caribbean to date. Already in the 1970s, the discontent of Trinidad and Tobago over the Caribbean's turn to Venezuela, over Jamaica's rejection of the proposed trilateral smelter project, and over various violations of Caricom rules led to its refusal to attend many Caricom meetings and the downgrading of its representation at those few that it did attend. After the coup in Grenada, Prime Minister Williams tried his best to ignore the new Grenadian government, even refusing to open letters sent by the PRG. Caribbean countries other than Jamaica (in 1979), Guyana, and for a time Saint Lucia (under a short-lived left-leaning government) were no more cooperative, with most refusing to accord the regime full recognition. Relations between Dominica and Grenada and between Barbados and Grenada were especially poor. Harsh verbal exchanges occurred between the Dominican and Grenadian prime ministers, and Grenadian officials complained about being harassed when in transit at the Barbados airport.

As a result of the economic and ideological problems plaguing the Caribbean, no Caricom summit had been held since 1975. In 1982 the heads of government finally met, and despite a move by Jamaica and Barbados to amend the Caricom treaty to exclude members not committed to parliamentary democracy, they agreed to accept ideological pluralism as well as to address some of the economic problems that were destroying Caricom. However, the murders of Prime Minister Maurice Bishop and some of his cabinet members in Grenada in 1983 halted the move toward reconciliation and led to new diplomatic problems. Among these problems must be included the lack of agreement by Caricom members on what action to take in the crisis, the separate action taken by the OECS in inviting U.S. intervention, and the repurcussions of this action. As mentioned earlier, the most salient of the intra-Caricom repercussions was the breakdown of good relations between Barbados and Trinidad. The Trinidadian ambassador to Barbados was recalled and Trinidad requested that Barbados not send a high commissioner to Trinidad. Relations between Barbados and Trinidad remained poor until 1986. Relations between Guyana and Barbados and the Eastern Caribbean also remained strained into 1985. There was a general improvement in the Caricom climate after several relatively successful economically oriented summits were held beginning in 1984.[32] By the late 1980s, with several new faces at the helm of Caricom states, harmony and cooperation were being stressed, and Eastern Caribbean states were moving to cement their diplomatic and economic relationship with a possible political union.

Notes

1. See, for example, Maurice A. East and Charles F. Hermann, "Do Nation-Types Account for Foreign Policy Behavior?" in James N. Rosenau, ed., *Comparing Foreign Policies: Theories, Findings, and Methods* (New York: Wiley, 1974): 297; Robert Keohane, "Who Cares About the General Assembly?" *International Organization* 23 (1), Winter 1969: 141–149; and George L. Reid, *The Impact of Very Small Size on the International Behavior of Microstates* (Beverly Hills, Calif.: Sage, 1974): 277.

2. The decline of U.S.-Grenada relations is detailed in the last section of this chapter.

3. U.S. Department of State and Department of Defense, *Grenada Documents: An Overview and Selection* (Washington, D.C., September 1984): 106–107.

4. Personal interview with Ben Jones, Minister of External Affairs of Grenada, January 23, 1986.

5. Foreign Broadcast Information Service, Latin America Daily Report, October 30, 1984, S1.

6. Ibid., May 17, 1984, S1.

7. The Eastern Caribbean has been counted as one unit for all calculations of number of accreditations.

8. Honorary consulates are not discussed primarily because they are so numerous for the larger territories and, of course, involve less financial and personnel investment on the parts of governments than do other forms of diplomatic and consular representation. Nevertheless, it must be added that the honorary consulates of the smaller territories play very important roles in external representation. Most of these countries have honorary consulates in Toronto.

Interestingly, Saint Vincent has one in Geneva at which a Deputy Marine Commissioner is stationed, with responsibility for important shipping matters.

9. These limitations are discussed in Chapter 8.

10. U.N. voting charts accompany the *Index to Proceedings of the General Assembly* for the various years. In some of the charts, changes in a country's vote are recorded along with the original vote. In that case, the changed vote has been used. If vote changes are not recorded, as is the case with most of the 1980s records, obviously they have not been used here. Users of these charts should also be very careful to compare vote descriptions with the vote noted. This is because vote descriptions are sometimes noted where no vote has been recorded; in other instances, resolutions described as having been adopted without a vote, are then accorded a vote. Fortunately, these errors are few, and efforts have been made to eliminate them in this analysis.

11. The modified index is adopted from Joseph Harbert, "The Behavior of Ministates in the United Nations," *International Organization* 30 (1), Winter 1976: 117.

12. Not all issues were included in the study, only what were referred to as "Third World" issues. See J. Braveboy-Wagner, *In Search of Self-Reliance: An Analysis of Trends in, and Factors Affecting, Cooperation Among Developing Nations* (Ph.D dissertation. Ann Arbor, Michigan: University Microfilms, 1979): 71–73, 132–135.

13. Quoted in Arthur S. Banks, ed., *Political Handbook of the World 1986* (Binghamton, N.Y.: Center for Social Analysis of the State University of New York and the Council on Foreign Relations, 1986): 468.

14. Interviews with Noel Sinclair, Permanent Representative of Guyana to the United Nations, December 15 and 22, 1986.

15. Address by His Excellency Mr. Maurice Rupert Bishop, Prime Minister and Minister of Foreign Affairs of Grenada, to the 24th Session of the General Assembly (U.N. Doc. A/34/PV. 27, October 11, 1979): 6.

16. Michael Manley, *Jamaica: Struggle in the Periphery* (London: Third World Media Limited in association with Writers and Readers Publishing Cooperative Society Limited, 1982): 68.

17. Resolution 38, 41st General Assembly (1986).

18. On the Angola issue, see Manley, *Jamaica: Struggle in the Periphery*, 110–117.

19. Interview with Dessima Williams, former Grenada ambassador to the OAS, March 21, 1986.

20. *New York Times*, June 14, 1987, p. 20.

21. For a succinct summary of events in the Bahamas, see Dean Collinwood, "Bahamas," in Jack Hopkins, ed., *Latin America and Caribbean Contemporary Record*, vol. 4, 1984–1985 (New York: Holmes and Meier, 1986): 624–625.

22. *New York Times*, June 14, 1987, p. 20.

23. Ibid., June 21, 1987, p. 16.

24. The new treaty, opened for signature in 1982 and closed December 9, 1984, establishes a 12-mile territorial limit, with a 200-mile economic zone. Disputes over delimitation are to be handled by diplomatic means. Venezuela joined the United States, Turkey, and Israel in opposing it, but 155 nations have signed the convention so far. Venezuela's objections are based on its territorial problems with Colombia and Guyana.

25. Interview with Valerie McComie, Assistant Secretary-General of the OAS, March 21, 1986.

26. Statement of the Minister of Foreign Affairs, Barbados, to the 15th Extraordinary Session of the General Assembly of the Organization of American States, Cartagena, Colombia, December 1985 (original), pp. 12–13.

27. Speech to the Inter-American Bar Association by Ambassador Peter D. Laurie of Barbados, *Relations Between the English-Speaking Caribbean and Latin America*, Washington, D.C., October 19, 1984 (original), p. 4.

28. Interview with Dessima Williams, March 21, 1986.

29. Interviews with Noel Sinclair, December 15 and 22, 1986.

30. Interview with Valerie McComie, March 21, 1986.

31. Foreign Broadcast Information Service, Latin America Daily Report, January 16, 1984, S1.

32. Some details of the Grenada situation are discussed in Chapter 8. For detailed descriptive accounts see, among others, Hugh O'Shaughnessy, *Grenada: An Eyewitness Account of the U.S. Invasion and the Caribbean History That Provoked It* (New York: Dodd, Mead, 1984); and Anthony Payne, Paul Sutton, and Tony Thorndike, *Grenada: Revolution and Invasion* (New York: St. Martin's Press, 1984).

6. Influences on Caribbean Foreign Policy

The last few chapters described the outcome of Caribbean foreign policy—that is, the behavior and activities or interactions of the English-speaking states. In this regard, we have concentrated on providing the reader with as much data as possible from which to draw appropriate conclusions. The question to be answered in this chapter is this: What accounts for the policy, behavior, and decisions made by Caribbean states in the external arena? Figure 1.1 proposed a framework for analysis of the influences on Caribbean foreign policy, focusing on the effect of national and external factors and the characteristics of the decision-making system. This framework will be filled out in the next few pages.

Constraining Influences

In the analysis of the foreign policy of more powerful states, national capability factors and interests are stressed as paramount in foreign policy decision-making. However, because of the small size and limited resources of states like those in this study, we must make a departure from mainstream analysis to first consider the constraints on policy. Clearly size is the primary constraint or the basis of most other constraints. Small-sized states have limited resources, both financial and human, and limited national capability, including military capability, compared with their larger counterparts. They are therefore less active in international affairs, pursue more limited national interests, and are inclined to react rather than initiate major foreign policy activities. In interviews conducted for this book, several diplomats also attributed the preference of their countries for bilateral over multilateral interaction to the recognition of the limited influence small states have on global issues. Small states are also highly vulnerable to global political and economic changes. Although small size is a limitation for all Caribbean states, it is also clear that among Caribbean states themselves there are variations, with limitations particularly acute for the ministates of the Eastern Caribbean.

"Level of development" (measured in terms of per capita GNP) is usually also cited as an important national attribute in discussing influences on foreign policy. Underdevelopment can be viewed as a constraining factor for most Caribbean countries, reducing national capability and also limiting these states' ability to diversify and vary their international economic linkages. The experience of the OPEC members in the 1970s shows that wealth can increase international influence, regardless of size. Except for Trinidad and Tobago, Caribbean countries have not had the resources and opportunity to exercise influence based on wealth. Again, the severity of the constraints imposed by underdevelopment will vary among Caribbean countries.

A look at the twelve Caribbean countries under study suggests that size and wealth/development are not intimately linked in the Caribbean context and therefore must be listed as two separate constraints. For example, Trinidad, Barbados and Bahamas are richer than their larger counterpart Jamaica, and Guyana is poorer than many of its smaller colleagues. Some simple quantitative tests (Pearson's r correlation) confirm the lack of a significant relationship between size and wealth in the Caribbean context. Further tests also confirm the separate influences of size and wealth, in terms of issue-areas: The pattern of correlations revealed that size is relevant mainly to the level of diplomatic activity (state visits, diplomatic missions), whereas GNP per capita correlates primarily with economic interaction (trade, aid).[1] (See Table 6.1.)

Another constraint on Caribbean foreign policy behavior stems from geographic location. The Caribbean nations' geographic location has given them throughout history a particular strategic value to the larger (great) powers. Although the countries are no longer militarily strategic, they are today politically and economically strategic to the United States, which since the establishment of a tutelage over the hemisphere under the Monroe Doctrine, has perceived its own interests as best served by the preservation of democracy, stability, and, after World War II, anti-communism in the countries of the Western Hemisphere. Moreover, from an economic standpoint, as President Reagan noted at the height of ideological conflict in the region, the Caribbean is a major source of bauxite and petroleum, and half of the U.S. trade and two-thirds of its imports pass through the region.[2] Geopolitical considerations have therefore limited the ability of Caribbean states to act in ways that might displease the hemisphere's superpower.

Finally, Caribbean actions in foreign policy are also constrained by these countries' economic dependence on a few Western countries, particularly, as we have seen, on the United States. Their dependence is a product of their history, insofar as colonialism brought them into the global capitalist economy as suppliers of raw materials to the industrial countries. The resulting monocultural/monoproduct economies and trade dependence have locked Caribbean states into external relationships that are difficult to change. Moreover, economic dependence is usually assumed

154

TABLE 6.1. Influences on Caribbean Foreign Policy Behavior: Significant Correlations, Size and GNP by Activity

Dependent Variables	Population 1970	Population 1984	GNP 1970	GNP 1984
Pop. 1984	.99[b]	1.0	--	--
GNP 1984	--	--	--	1.0
Exports	--	--	--	.81 (1974) N=11 / .85 (1980) N=12 / .89 (1985) N=12
Imports	--	--	.81 (1974)[c] N=11	.77 (1974) N=11 / .81 (1980)[b] N=12 / .75 (1985)[c] N=12
Regional exports (Caribbean)	--	--	--	.76 (1974) N=11 / .74 (1980) N=12 / .80 (1985)[c] N=12
Regional exports (Latin America)	--	--	.82 (1974)[c] N=11 / .85 (1980)[b] N=12 / .90 (1985)[c] N=12	--
Regional imports (Caribbean)	--	.79 (1980)[c]	--	--
Regional imports (Latin America)	.72 (1974) N=11 / .87 (1985)[b] N=12	.72 (1974) N=11 / .77 (1980)[c] N=12 / .88 (1985)[b] N=12	.66 (1974) N=11	--
Visits sent	.82 (1974) N=6 / .79 (1979) N=9	.73 (1979) N=9	--	--
Visits received	--	.90 (1979)[b] N=9	--	--
Regional visits sent (Caribbean/Latin America)	.85 (1974) N=6	.84 N=6	--	--
Missions sent[d]	.85[b] N=12	.82[b] N=12	--	--
Missions received[d]	.97[c] N=12	.96[b] N=12	--	--

TABLE 6.1. Influences on Caribbean Foreign Policy Behavior: Significant Correlations, Size and GNP by Activity

Dependent Variables	Independent Variables			
	Population		GNP	
	1970	1984	1970	1984
Regional missions sent (Caribbean/Latin America)[d]	.77[c] N=12	.75[c] N=12	--	.61 N=12
DAC aid	.73 (1982) N=11	.75 (1982) N=11	.92 (1975) N=5 .98 (1979) N=4	--
Bilateral aid	--	--	.94 (1975) N=5 .99 (1979) N=4	--

[a] Correlations are Pearson's r. All are significant at or above .05. The year in parenthesis relates to the dependent variable.

[b] $p \leq .001$.

[c] $p \leq .005$.

[d] 1980s only.

Sources: Population and GNP: United Nations Conference on Trade and Development, Handbook of International Trade Statistics 1973 (New York: United Nations, 1975) and World Bank, World Bank Atlas 1986 (Washington, D.C.: World Bank, 1986); trade data: International Monetary Fund, Direction of Trade Statistics Annual/Yearbook, 1970, 1980, 1981, 1979-1985 (Washington, D.C., 1971, 1981, 1982, 1986), and United Nations, International Trade Statistics Yearbook, 1977, 1980, 1985 (New York: U.N., 1979, 1983, 1987); visits: Foreign Broadcast Information Service, Latin America Daily Report, 1974, 1978-1984; diplomatic missions: Ministries of External/Foreign Affairs, Diplomatic and Consular Lists/Yearbooks, Caribbean Yearbook 1979/80 (Toronto: Caribook, Ltd., 1980), and information supplied by diplomatic personnel; aid: Organization for Economic Cooperation and Development, Geographic Distribution of Financial Flows to Developing Countries 1969-1976 (Paris, 1977), and 1982-1985 (Paris, 1987), and United Nations Conference on Trade and Development, Handbook of International Trade and Development Statistics, Supplement 1985 (New York: United Nations, 1987).

to be reflected in political and diplomatic behavior. Thus international relations researchers have held that voting behavior of smaller countries in international organizations is often linked to the level of aid they receive. A more recent variation of this thesis holds that international compliance results from more generalized dependency factors.[3] Again, simple correlation tests on data collected for our descriptive chapters can help in illuminating the relationship between economic dependence and compliance for the Caribbean countries (Table 6.2). We found that economic closeness to the United States, measured by level of aid from and level of trade with that country is indeed strongly related to diplomatic and security closeness measured as voting agreement, visits sent, and commercial purchases of arms. Moreover, diplomatic closeness measured as visits sent has been linked in the 1980s to official military aid received. In sum, the Caribbean relationship with the United States, and by inference with the West in general, is multidimensional. Although simple correlations cannot tell us which variable is the cause and which the effect, it seems logical to assume that the economic relationship has engendered diplomatic and security closeness.

TABLE 6.2. The Caribbean and the United States: Issue-Area Intercorrelations[a]

	1	2	3	4	5	6	7	8
1. Military aid from U.S., 1950-1986	1.0							
2. Commercial arms purchases from U.S., 1950-1986	.61 (82) .65 (85)	1.0						
3. Visits to U.S.		.85 (74)[b]	1.0					
4. Visits with U.S.	--	--	.63 (82/84)	1.0				
5. Voting agreement with U.S.	--	--	--	--	1.0			
6. Exports to U.S.	.88 (74)[c] .76 (80)[c] .68 (85)[c]	--	.99 (69/74)[b,c] .99 (74/74)[b,c] .94 (80/74)[b] .88 (85/74)[b]	.57 (85/84)	--	1.0 (.92--.99)[d]		
7. Imports from U.S.	.95 (69)[b] .75 (74) .67 (80) .68 (85)	--	.96 (74/74)[b,c] .90 (80/74)[b] .94 (85/74)[b]	--	--	.99 (74/69)[b,c] .73 (74/74) .67 (74/80) .63 (74/85) .98 (80/69)[b] .84 (80/74)[c] .89 (80/80)[c] .90 (80/85)[c] .68 (85/74) .61 (85/80) .58 (85/85)	1.0 (74/80)[c] .68 (74/80)[c] .95 (74/85)[c] .83 (80/85)[c]	
8. Financial aid from U.S.	.83 (82)[b]	--	--	-.91 (84/85)[b]	.95 (79/75)[b] .98 (79/79)[b] -.95 (69/82)[b] -.95 (79/85)[b]	-.98 (85/67)[b]	--	1.0 (75/82)[b,c] .98 (75/82)[b,c]

[a] Correlations are Pearson's r, significant at or above .05. Ns are 11 or 12 except where indicated. Year in parenthesis refers to the dependent variable first, followed by the independent variable. For example, a correlation between visits and exports followed by (69/74) indicates that the relationship is between exports in 1969 and visits sent in 1974. The perfect correlation of 1.0 refers to unlagged relationships of a variable with itself.

[b] N=6 or less.

[c] $p \leq .005$.

[d] Exports for all years are highly intercorrelated, with Ns of only 4 for 1967 data and 11 or 12 for 1970s and 1980s.

Sources: Arms assistance: U.S. Department of Defense. Foreign Military Sales, Foreign Military Construction Sales and Military Assistance Facts as of September 30, 1986 (Washington, D.C.: Data Management Division, Comptroller, DSAA, 1986); Visits: Foreign Broadcast Information Service, Latin America Daily Report 1974, 1978-1984; Voting agreement: United Nations, Index to the Proceedings of the General Assembly, 36th, 37th and 40th sessions (New York: U.N., 1975, 1982, 1985); Trade: International Monetary Fund, Direction of Trade Statistics Annual/Yearbook, 1970, 1980, 1981, 1979-1985 (Washington, D.C.; 1971, 1981, 1982, 1986); and United Nations, International Trade Statistics Yearbook, 1977, 1980, 1985; (New York: United Nations: 1979, 1982, 1987); Aid: Organization for Economic Cooperation and Development, Geographical Distribution of Financial Flows to Developing Countries 1969-1976 (Paris, 1977), and 1982-1985 (Paris 1987); United Nations Conference on Trade and Development, Handbook of International Trade and Development Statistics, Supplement, 1985 (N.Y.: U.N., 1987).

Determinants of Caribbean Foreign Policy

The factors that determine or influence the pattern and direction of Caribbean foreign policy include those domestic sources or attributes commonly mentioned by Caribbean diplomats—history, geography, economic need, culture, and society—as well as other factors, such as the dynamics of the political and decision-making processes, that are rarely mentioned by officials. From the Caribbean's historical background of colonialism and slavery has come an external orientation that opposes colonialism and, theoretically at least, economic and political neo-colonialism. A certain amount of selectivity is at work in this area, however, because perspectives on intervention are naturally colored by ideology and political preference. British colonialism also left a legacy of parliamentary democracy, translated externally into a preference for ties with democratic nations, and a special relationship with Britain and Canada, embodied in participation in the Commonwealth. Colonialism has also left Caribbean countries with an economic structure that continues to engender close economic linkages with Britain and the West.

Geography, which has already been discussed as a constraining factor, can also be viewed as a determining factor in Caribbean foreign policy. The proximity of these states to the United States has led to a close relationship with that superpower, while relationships are growing on all dimensions with the geographically proximate states of Latin America. Similarly, while Caribbean underdevelopment and dependence are constraining influences on policy, economic need, defined within these constraints, has determined Caribbean economic relationships with the West as well as linkages with the Third World and other attempts to diversify economic relations. Geopolitics, which constrains Caribbean policy, also determines it in promoting close ties with the United States and wariness in dealing with socialist nations.

As to the effects of culture and society, Caribbean societies are multiethnic, a factor in determining links with Afro-Asia and also the major motivation behind firm diplomatic stances against racism and racial discrimination in international forums. The Caribbean value system is included here as a determinant of foreign policy. Caribbean foreign policy reflects a strong popular conservatism and inculcation of Western values. The attachment to the Western value system can be attributed to colonialism and modernization (Westernization), to the presence of U.S. bases in some countries during and after World War II, to the major role played by multinational enterprises and the general external orientations of these economies, and to the societal structure that emerged out of these influences. That structure has been characterized by an economic elite of landowners and merchant traders, a black middle-class political elite that has sought to emulate the values and financial success of the upper class, and a primary focus on land ownership and small-business ownership among the lower strata of the middle classes. In these circumstances, pro-Western materialist values have held sway, becoming entrenched under the pressures of modernization, and fostered by tourist economies and by a high level of migration and travel to the United States, Canada, and the U.K. Caribbean value systems reflect strong anti-communism, and belief in the virtues of democracy and capitalism. Foreign policy has both reacted to these values and helped engender them, making socialist experimentation (other than democratic socialism) highly suspect in the eyes of the general Caribbean populace.

Caribbean foreign policy is also determined by systemic factors in that, the Caribbean nations, as small states, continue to be strongly influenced by changes taking place in the international environment. As we have seen, in the early post-independence period, Caribbean states reacted to the tight bipolar international system by declaring themselves to be solidly on the side of the West. Choice was severely circumscribed in a world in which there were few fence-straddlers and in which the effects of choosing "the other side" were subversion and intervention on the part of the offended superpower. As the late 1960s brought detente or cooperation between the superpowers, the third bloc was able to achieve significance. Increased flexibility on the part of the United States allowed the Caribbean states to move closer to this third bloc. The stratification of the international system, that is, the relative powerlessness of the developing states, engendered the bloc's focus on economic development issues and Caribbean identification with these issues. But the tightening up of the international system, beginning in the last years of the administration of President Carter and becoming consolidated under President Reagan, had an imitative effect on the small Caribbean states in that it not only reduced their freedom of maneuver but also strengthened the forces of conservatism in the region.

In the systemic area, it is clear that the Caribbean's relationship with the United States is most crucial. But it must be emphasized that systemic factors are global, going beyond the geopolitics described earlier as both a constraint and a determinant of Caribbean foreign policy. Changes in U.S. and Soviet policy have a rippling effect around the globe. Soviet-U.S. hostility still reduces the freedom of maneuver of third-bloc countries, albeit less aggressively than in the 1950s. In particular, because of the global influence of the United States, policy changes in that country have a wide systemic effect. Thus President Reagan's preference for bilateralism, free trade and private enterprise has had a dampening effect on Third World demands for international economic changes and in fact appears even to have encouraged individual governments to open up their economies in order to receive U.S. aid. Global and Third World trends in turn have affected regional attitudes and behavior.

Caribbean states can no longer be considered as merely reactive to changes in the international system—having demonstrated in the 1970s the range of choices open to small states—but systemic factors still have to be considered in Caribbean foreign policy decision-making. Thus it was a misreading of global changes that led Grenada's PRG to pursue an aggressively anti-U.S. foreign policy. The PRG subscribed to a thesis of "hegemonic decline" that underestimated the will and influence of the United States. The government's assessment of the external environment that colored internal decision-making was reflected in policy statements such as the following:

> One of the main characteristics of the present international juncture is the changing balance of forces. Previously imperialism led by the U.S.A. held unchallenged sway over mankind. Now the socialist community is strong and growing still. The U.S.S.R. is the equal, at least, of the U.S.A. Other poles of power have developed through the ability of the OPEC countries to exact from the rapacious West adequate compensation for their natural resource: petroleum. . . . Though it remains powerful U.S. imperialism is on the decline.[4]

Similar assessments were made even during the last days of the regime. As one former government and party official noted: "[The Central Committee's] analysis was that imperialism was too weak to attack them. There was Lebanon, which had reached a flash point. There were a number of other things, and imperialism could not attack them at that time. They felt that after a while the socialist countries could understand and come to their defense."[5] Indeed, this assessment seemed logical based on a number of factors, including the U.S. retreat from a "world policeman" role after Vietnam; the effects of OPEC actions and subsequent U.S. acquiescence to talks with the Third World; the perception of President Carter as weak and ineffectual; the fall of the Shah in Iran and Somoza in Nicaragua; negative political reaction to President's Carter's attempt to make much of the stationing of a Soviet "brigade" in Cuba; U.S. powerlessness in the face of the Soviet invasion of Afghanistan; and Fidel Castro's coup in permitting thousands of Cubans, including social undesirables, to leave for the United States in the Mariel boatlift.

On the other hand, the PRG erred in downgrading the importance of the increasingly hard-line policies of the Carter and Reagan administrations, the U.S. use of economic pressures against recalcitrant regimes, including Jamaica and Grenada itself, the increasing militarization of the Caribbean, and in the sub-system, the Caribbean's antipathy (which improved to the level of tolerance after 1982) and capacity for action. The PRG also misread its socialist allies in expecting more economic assistance than was given and in expecting military assistance in a crisis. In other words, Grenada's foreign policy stance of militancy, anti–U.S. imperialism, and friendship with socialist nations was impelled not only by domestic preferences but also by particular misperceptions of the global and regional systems.

Finally, up to this point we have not mentioned the influence of *political system*, one of the basic attributes of comparative foreign policy theory. Comparative foreign policy theorists have generally classified political systems into "open" and "closed," positing that the former are more active in the international system than the latter. Our analysis to this point suggests that this dichotomy makes little sense in the Caribbean context, where personalism/authoritarianism has been rampant even in the midst of the maintenance of democratic norms. Among the states in our study, only Guyana can be identified in some sense as a closed society, and Guyana has, in fact, been especially active on the international scene. Rather, an examination of the Caribbean position indicates that the significant political differences have been those of ideology. The socialist Caribbean states have attempted to pursue a "different" foreign policy based on diplomatic visibility and diversification of linkages on all dimensions, although this is not necessarily reflected in reality.[6]

The nature of the political system (meaning therefore the political and development ideology) not only directly influences Caribbean choices and behavior but also appears to be a screen or mediating factor between all the other constraints and determinants and foreign policy behavior. In other words, socialist states have perceived themselves as capable of overcoming the constraints and modifying some of the effects of history, geography, society, economic need, and the influence of the international system in non-traditional directions. Thus there is a centrality to the role of ideology in foreign policy.

We can also consider the influence of political system from the point of view of changes in regime. Except for the socialist departures, in particular in Guyana and Grenada, there have been few major changes initiated by the various governments that have come to power in the Caribbean. The differences are rather ones of degree. Thus some governments have been more favorable to the United States than others, and some have been more Third World-oriented than others. However, many changes are rhetorical or attitudinal or on paper only, in political manifestos or policy documents for public consumption. St. Vincent provides a good example: Prime Minister Mitchell is more liberal than his predecessor Cato, but although he has downplayed St. Vincent's role in the Regional Security System, he has not made major changes in the country's economic and diplomatic policies. In other countries, notably Guyana and Trinidad and Tobago, changes have been made by governments in power rather than through changes in regime. (Both became more nationalistic in the 1970s.) Indeed, then, it is not surprising that an analysis of variance conducted on the available data (for the non-socialist countries) revealed significant changes in external activity only for Barbados and Dominica and only in the area of trade. Trade with Latin America, and imports in general, increased more than might have been expected under the Adams government compared with the earlier Barrow government, and for Dominica exports grew significantly during the Eugenia Charles era.[7] Overall, shifts in government are at best only a mild influence on the Caribbean's external behavior.

All the determinants listed above affect Caribbean foreign policy behavior as a whole, that is, in all issue-areas. Nevertheless, it can be said that geopolitical and systemic influences have been particularly important in the security issue-area, that economic need and societal modernization are particularly relevant to the obvious economic development issue-area, and that the effects of history, geography, society and ideology are particularly felt in the diplomatic issue-area.

Decision-Making

In the Caribbean, as elsewhere, foreign policy actions implement decisions made within the context of the operational environment described above. Therefore it is important to know who are the major decision-makers on foreign policy issues, by whom they are influenced, and how in general decisions are made. In this process, factors at the individual, societal, and governmental-bureaucratic levels are all involved.

The players in the game of foreign policy are usually given as the head of state (performing ceremonial functions), the head of government, the foreign affairs minister, the foreign policy bureaucracies, various technical ministries that provide experts on functional issues, and legislatures that hold the purse strings. Many others in the informed elite and the public have some influence on foreign policy but are not directly involved in the policymaking process. Rather, their involvement may be informal, consultative, or at the parliamentary level during the second reading of legislation before parliament.

Government

Caribbean countries (with the exception of Guyana) have a dual system of leadership, with a governor-general or president and prime minister. Central decision-making power rests with the prime minister who is the leader of the majority party in parliament, and his or her cabinet, composed of members of parliament chosen by the prime minister. The cabinet is described constitutionally as being the principal executive instrument of policy with general direction and control of the government, and it is responsible to parliament. Cabinet operates on the principle of collective responsibility, which means that cabinet discussions are, theoretically, confidential and once a decision has been taken, members who publicly disapprove must resign.

In the Guyanese variant, the cabinet is still the central decision-making body in which the prime minister plays an important role, but power is centralized in the hands of an executive president. In all cases, the parliament's responsibility is to question proposed changes in policy, to vote them down if necessary, or to delay them through various procedural tactics.

Parliaments also have particular control over budgetary matters. But in the Caribbean the majority parties have usually had solid majorities in parliament, and this, coupled with the generally low popular priority given foreign affairs, has meant that cabinet decisions are usually simply rubber-stamped in parliament. Cross-over voting is rare in the Caribbean. For this reason, intraparty dissension, particularly at cabinet level, is therefore more important in understanding policymaking than is parliamentary dissension. For example, consensual decision-making and effective policymaking has been adversely affected in the 1980s in Trinidad and Tobago because of infighting within the ruling National Alliance for Reconstruction. At the extreme, the 1983 crisis in Grenada was attributable to major differences in both organization and policy among the high-level members of the ruling party. Still, except for Grenada where the Westminster (British-style) system had been discarded, intraparty dissension has not reduced in any significant way the prime minister's control over policy.

As in domestic policy, so too in foreign policy the most influential figure is the prime minister. The history of Caribbean politics has been to a large extent the history of various personalities: Grantley Adams, Alexander Bustamante, Eric Williams, Norman Manley, Michael Manley, Eric Gairy, Maurice Bishop, L.F.S. Burnham, Tom Adams, Lynden Pindling, Vere Bird, John Compton, Milton Cato, Eugenia Charles, and many others. In the past, prime ministers tended to assume the portfolio of foreign minister because they felt that they were in the best position to deal with the complexities of foreign affairs. If they did not assume the role themselves, they entrusted it to good friends and party loyalists who were unlikely to question prime ministerial judgments. Since foreign policy issues were not on the whole high-priority issues for the public or for politicians, prime ministers exercised inordinate influence on the policy process. During Eric Williams' tenure, for example, the foreign policy bureaucracy heistated to make any decisions without the nod of Whitehall, even when the prime minister was no longer foreign minister. Foreign policy was weakened by this and by the fact that the prime minister made many decisions without consulting the bureaucracy. Again, in Barbados, a commission of inquiry set up by the Adams government to look into the previous administration's policies concluded that under Barrow, "all government business revolved around [the prime minister],"[8] including, presumably, foreign affairs. In pre-1979 Grenada, given Eric Gairy's dominance and the weakness of the civil service bureaucracy, foreign policy decisions were individual prime ministerial decisions.

Today, although prime ministerial dominance in foreign policy persists in the smaller Caribbean countries, the situation is changing in the larger countries. As societies become more technologically advanced and more bureaucratically complex and as post-independence personalities die, the decision-making process is also becoming more complex and the role of personality declining. In such circumstances, experienced foreign ministers are assuming more and more of an advisory rather than merely supportive role. Prime ministers in the more developed

Caribbean countries are entrusting the foreign ministry to persons they consider highly qualified by reason of their backgrounds and/or experience, although these persons are usually also party loyalists, often deputy party leaders. Whereas upon independence, the prime ministers of the Big Four—Williams, Bustamante, Barrow, and Burnham—all assumed the job of foreign minister, twenty-five years later, we find that that situation pertains only to some of the smaller Eastern Caribbean countries, specifically Dominica, Saint Lucia, St. Kitts, and St. Vincent. (Former Prime Minister George Price of Belize also held the foreign ministry position until his electoral defeat in 1984.) Instead, in Trinidad and Tobago, the ministry at various times has been entrusted to academics with specialties in international relations or a related area (Trinidad has been the only country to appoint foreign ministers rather than draw them from the elected representatives, and several Trinidadian foreign ministers have lacked political experience); seasoned politicians (including Errol Mahabir, a deputy prime minister); and a former opposition leader who joined the ruling alliance (Basdeo Panday). In Barbados, the Minister of Foreign Affairs at the time of writing, J. Cameron Tudor, is a seasoned politician who headed the ministry in 1971–1972. Another holder of the position in the past, Henry Forde, had international legal training. In Seaga's Jamaica, a former prime minister and deputy party leader, Hugh Shearer, was entrusted with external affairs, a position he held before. These and many other individuals have qualified for the position of Minister of External Affairs by their experience and backgrounds, as well as their party standing.

Nevertheless, as in any political system, the influence of foreign ministers, and of cabinet ministers as a whole, still depends to a large extent on their relationship with the prime minister. Policy and personality conflicts between prime minister and foreign minister inevitably result in the shifting of the latter to another ministry, or in the extreme, as in Trinidad in 1988, in the complete exclusion of the former from policymaking positions. Foreign ministers who are personally close to the prime minister will exercise a great deal of influence. Such is the case for example in Grenada, where Prime Minister Herbert Blaize has given the external affairs portfolio to Ben Jones, who is not only an experienced politician (a deputy party leader) but also a close friend. Jones' personal relationship has allowed the prime minister to grant him a great deal of autonomy in running his ministry and others (Legal Affairs, Tourism) entrusted to him. Antigua is also an interesting case. The foreign minister and deputy prime minister is, at the time of writing, the prime minister's son. This relationship appears to have allowed Lester Bird more flexibility than accorded most Caribbean foreign ministers; his tendency has been to make anti-U.S. and other pronouncements that clearly go against the tone set by his father. Although Vere Bird clearly remains the chief influence on policy, as seen in the Grenada crisis when the father's policy superseded the son's lack of enthusiasm for invasion, Lester Bird appears to exercise a great deal of independence and influence in foreign policy decision-making.

Overall, the importance of foreign ministers in the policymaking process seems to be increasing. Indeed, some foreign ministers appear to be exercising relatively free rein on foreign affairs because their prime ministers are more preoccupied and more knowledgeable about domestic matters. Another reason why foreign ministers can be assumed to have more influence than in the past is the increasing vulnerability of the leadership. Post-independence leaders lasted long because of their reputations as anti-colonialists, populists, and political initiators. The new leaders are less durable and less dominant in an era of widespread economic and political malaise. Max Weber's characterization of the move from charismatic authority to rational-legal authority fits here, even though the two cannot be so sharply differentiated.[9] As the Caribbean moves away from the era of dominant leaders, though not necessarily away from personality politics, and as these societies become more technologically complex, the need for more open decision-making has increased.

The decisions of the foreign minister and prime minister must secure cabinet and legislative approval before being implemented. As noted earlier, parliaments tend to have only token influence on decisions, since the tradition in the Caribbean has been for the ruling party to exercise wide majorities in parliament. Opposition members have usually paid more attention to domestic than foreign affairs, unless particular salient issues are being discussed, and in many of those cases (for example, the Grenada crisis or, in Guyana, aggression by Venezuela), unity rather than dissension has been promoted.

In the past, cabinet decisions were assumed to be prime ministerial decisions. However, today, especially in the larger countries, more open decision-making is taking place. Prime ministers obviously will always set the tone for the conduct of cabinet business: For example, Trinidad's former Prime Minister George Chambers was reported to have treated cabinet discussions in somewhat cavalier fashion; Prime Minister Robinson in his first months of office was noted as being intent on having more meaningful discussion,[10] but later disclosures suggested that his style was quite authoritarian. The capacity for influence of the members of the cabinet will therefore depend on the particular style of the prime minister, whether the latter encourages constructive criticism or expects conformity. Whether the cabinet merely operates on "groupthink" or not also depends on the experience and personality of the members: Some members of Caribbean cabinets are more experienced than their prime ministers and are known to have strong personalities and viewpoints themselves. Therefore, while the cabinet system demands an overall consensus among members on policy matters, there is undoubtedly lively debate in cabinet on some issues in some countries. In fact, in recent years lively debate has been superseded by detrimental conflict in Grenada and Trinidad and Tobago, where coalition-type arrangements have broken down under the weight of policy differences among government factions.

Decision-making analysts focus to a great degree on the personality, motivations, and perceptions of the crucial members of decision-making units. We attempt to discuss this to some extent in a particular situation described in Chapter 7. Nevertheless, it can be noted here that the perceptions of Caribbean decision-makers are influenced by social background characteristics: policymakers' educational level, age, sex, social class, and career experiences are among factors that influence the way decision-makers think and therefore the actions they take. Although a thorough statistical survey of these factors is not undertaken in this book, we can generalize that Caribbean leaders and other central elites have on the whole been quite well educated (many, if not most, university-educated), some with educational and life experiences in Britain and others in the United States. Younger elites have been trained at the University of the West Indies. Most major policymakers have been male, over 45, and from the middle class.

The effects of these characteristics on the actual decision-making process will vary according to issue and personality. However, some examples can be given here. It has often been noted that Jamaica's Prime Minister Edward Seaga was born in Boston and educated at Harvard University. His sympathetic views of the United States must in some degree be related to this past, although in earlier days he was said to be on the left rather than on the right. On the other hand, Eric Williams' nationalism was spawned by experiences at Howard University and with the Anglo-American Commission formed after World War II. Again, the New Jewel Movement (NJM) leaders were influenced by educational experiences in the United States and the U.K. Younger policymakers are generally more radical than their older colleagues, as reflected in the leaders of the NJM. There are also obvious generational differences between Vere Bird and his son Lester Bird in Antigua. In general, it can also be said that elites trained at the University of the West Indies are more sensitized to Caribbean and Third World problems than those trained abroad. Social background also affects style as well as policy content: The fact that Trinidad's former Prime Minister Chambers was considerably less educated than his predecessor and cohorts may have led him to defer to others in policymaking; in addition less-educated leaders have tended to have more populist styles than their highly educated cohorts. As to the effect of sex, the paucity of female decision-makers makes it impossible to tell what the influence of this factor might be, but the general propositions of the literature that women might be more "doveish" in foreign policy are not borne out by the one example the Caribbean has had of a female in the position of chief decision-maker.

One other interesting aspect of the effect of social background on decision-making concerns the influence of social closeness among decision-makers both in a particular country and across countries. For example, the older Caribbean leaders undoubtedly developed a familiarity with and respect (if not always affection) for one another that influenced not only internal Caricom relationships but also efforts to harmonize foreign policies. The fact that Guyana's late Prime Minister Burnham, Barbados' late Prime Minister Barrow, and Jamaica's Michael Manley knew one another in England before they entered politics must have played some role in determining the close relationship between their countries. Again, persons interviewed for this study from St. Vincent and Saint Lucia made much of the fact that their leaders, Mitchell and Compton, were apt to coordinate their policies more than usual because they are cousins. On the other hand, generational differences appear to have aggravated policy differences between Maurice Bishop and Eastern Caribbean leaders.

Bureaucrats

As foreign policy concerns have broadened, ministries other than the foreign ministry have become involved in the foreign policy process. In particular, the rise of legal and security issues has meant that attorneys general and ministers of national security and their staffs have come to play vital roles in certain matters. Their importance is reflected in the distribution of portfolios of many Caribbean governments. For example, in some countries, the foreign minister is also attorney general, and in Barbados (post-Adams) and Belize, the prime minister is also minister of defense. However, it is the Finance and Planning and Economic Development ministries that have seen the greatest rise in importance in foreign affairs. In fact, they have dominated the External Affairs ministry in the smaller Caribbean islands.

The importance of the economic ministry lies in the fact that it handles external aid projects, a role that dates from pre-independence times when external donor agencies urged the designation of a specific agency to handle aid.[11] The thesis is that technicians are better equipped to handle these matters than are foreign affairs generalists. The importance of the finance portfolio is shown in the fact that in Trinidad and Tobago, Barbados, Jamaica, Bahamas, St. Kitts, Saint Lucia, and St. Vincent, the prime minister is also, at the time of writing, minister of finance. In Dominica, the prime minister is not only finance minister but is also in charge of trade and industry, which are other important aspects of foreign as well as domestic economic relations. In Antigua, the foreign minister is also minister of economic development, and in Belize, he is also in charge of economic development and finance. In Guyana, there is a Department of International Economic Cooperation within the office of the prime minister. The rise of the economic ministries has created some difficulties in coordination between these and the foreign ministries. Other technocrats who have become involved in varying degrees in foreign policy are those in agriculture, tourism, and energy departments, as well as in functional areas such as health and education.

Despite the acknowledged need for technocratic input into foreign policy, the contribution of experts to the policy formulation process is much more limited than their contribution to the implementation process. The implementation stage calls for managerial expertise, and here the major role is played by permanent secretaries who head the administrative staff of the various ministries, including the foreign ministry. Permanent secretaries should be active advisers and intermediaries between their staffs and the ministers in charge, but on the whole the advisory function is subordinated to the mediation and coordination role. In some Caribbean countries, their chance to advise on foreign policy comes through the Foreign Affairs Committee (FAC) of cabinet, interministerial committees composed of senior civil servants as well as senior cabinet ministers who discuss the issues sent to them by the Ministry of External Affairs and then send their decisions on to cabinet. The level of formality of the committee and its ministerial composition vary according to the country. In Trinidad and Tobago, for example, it is a permanent committee and it has included representatives from External Affairs, Customs, Agriculture, Finance, and Legal departments.[12] In the smaller islands, the arrangement tends to be informal and the composition narrower. The problem is that the committees appear to seldom meet, although they might be influential on some major decisions. (For example, in the Grenada crisis, Foreign Affairs Committees were activated in several countries.)

The permanent secretary of the foreign ministry in particular has a stronger influence at the preliminary stage, before the minister takes his proposals to the cabinet or to the FAC. The extent of this influence on foreign policy depends on the relationship between the foreign minister and the permanent secretary. Generally speaking, the contacts between the permament secretary and the foreign minister are ad hoc rather than regularized, often with the secretary himself approaching the minister. Thus decision-making from the top down is reinforced. As for the rest of the foreign ministry staff, other than the permanent secretary, their input is through the permanent secretary (and before that, through division heads where these exist). Generalizing across our twelve states, regular institutionalized meetings between minister and staff, other than the permanent secretary, seem to be rare, these being conducted instead on an ad hoc basis. Permanent secretaries too seem to prefer one-to-one contacts with staff rather than formal meetings. On the whole, it is only in the smaller countries that the higher-level staff are likely to approach the ministers directly with a foreign policy initiative. Thus on the input side of the decision-making ladder, the foreign policy staff exercises only minimal influence, through reports and suggestions made to the permanent secretary.

Similarly, while the decision-making structure in foreign policy also includes the staff abroad, the extent of an ambassador's influence on

168   INFLUENCES ON CARIBBEAN FOREIGN POLICY

policy (as opposed to policy implementation) depends on the person's relationship with the foreign minister and, even, the prime minister. Although the influence of career ambassadors is screened through the permanent secretaries, political appointees, including all the ambassadors of the smaller countries, usually enjoy direct access to high party officials and politicians and may bypass permanent secretaries in communicating their views to the top. As to the rest of the staff abroad, their influence on policy is even more indirect than that of their counterparts at home, being screened through both the ambassador and the permanent secretary at headquarters.

To sum up, although small size and prime ministerial dominance under the Westminster model of government have combined to make the prime minister the most important figure in Caribbean decision-making in general, and foreign policy decision-making in particular, the importance of foreign ministers and other heads of technocratic ministries is rising as foreign affairs becomes increasingly complex. The smaller the country, the more likely it is that the prime minister will also assume the portfolio of foreign minister, but in the larger countries, the trend is toward experience rather than just party loyalty. The fact that foreign ministers tend to be seasoned politicians, many with particular experience in foreign affairs, leads us to assume that the relationship between foreign minister and prime minister is today becoming truly an advisory one. In fact, there is evidence to indicate that the prime ministers of newer breed are less knowledgeable about foreign affairs and therefore more dependent on their foreign ministers.

Next in line of influence in foreign policy is of course the cabinet as a whole, which has to approve all decisions and usually does, but not necessarily without dissension. The legislature tends to rubber-stamp these decisions, given the tradition of dominance of the majority party, although parliamentary oppositions have spoken out on salient issues. At the bureaucratic level, the chief influencer is the permanent secretary, who has an input on foreign affairs committees, advises the minister, and coordinates the implementation of policy. However, in cases where decision-making is personalized by the prime minister, ambassadors may be more influential than the permanent secretaries. Finally, senior civil servants from other ministries may have some influence on FACs or directly with the ministers. Other members of the foreign policy and civil service staffs do better at implementing policy than at influencing it.

Society

It remains the case for the Caribbean, as for most countries, that people are more interested in domestic issues than in foreign policy. In the early 1970s, one scholar wrote of Trinidad and Tobago:

> The news media have made a valiant attempt to report on regional and international matters but by and large suffer from what the rest of the

society suffers: lack of proper research facilities which are vital and necessary to write insightful and penetrative articles. . . . Public opinion on foreign affairs has been singularly lacking since the public operates under the very constraints of the local news media, and is not well-informed. . . . Important events affecting and concerning Trinidad and Tobago come and go with little informed comment. The extension of diplomatic relations with Cuba by the Commonwealth Caribbean States, for example, evoked virtually no public response in the local press. When comments appear they are . . . likely to be the responses of ethnic groups. Fine illustrations were a spate of letters in the local press criticizing the Government's extension of diplomatic relations with Uganda or the virulent reaction to local Syrians coming out on behalf of financial support for Arab States during their struggle with Israel.[13]

In another work, the same writer notes that when the government was contemplating whether to join the OAS in the 1960s, a public opinion poll was conducted that not only received "poor" response (the "poor" is not further elaborated in the article) but showed that only 53.6 percent of respondents knew what the OAS was.[14]

As Johan Galtung and others have pointed out, the bulk of the population in most societies is uninformed and not very influential on foreign affairs, so the Caribbean is not exceptional.[15] There is a "center" comprising people with above-average incomes and education, mainly professional and managerial occupations, and usually urban and sub-urban, who are relatively well informed and pragmatic, but the periphery of public opinion consists of people at the lower rung of the social ladder who tend to hold "absolutist" opinions.[16] The Caribbean equivalent of the "absolutist" group can be assumed to be those who respond virulently along the lines the writer mentioned.

Actually, public awareness of foreign affairs differs from Caribbean country to country depending on government priorities. In Guyana, the government has first been forced to give priority, especially at certain times, to the issue of relations with Venezuela and then has consciously promoted itself internationally, hoping to acquire both external and domestic prestige. Given these circumstances, the Guyanese people have not been uninformed, although their influence has been limited by the authoritarian (and up to 1985 highly personalist) nature of the government. Similarly, Jamaican awareness of foreign affairs was increased in the 1970s by the government's international activeness, and the people, having been drawn into the important issue of whether Jamaica should reject the International Monetary Fund, were actually able to *influence* foreign affairs through the electoral process. Finally, the strong Caribbean reaction to events in Grenada in 1983—manifested through polls and letters to the editor from all strata of society—shows that as in most countries, foreign issues can generate much popular concern when they hit close to home. None of this, of course, means that the people as a whole have had much influence on foreign policy. It does mean, however, that they are not as apathetic or uninformed on major, highly relevant, issues as the earlier assessment might imply.

Another development has served to sharpen awareness of foreign affairs in the 1970s and 1980s. The news media in the Caribbean have changed quite a bit since the early 1970s, benefiting particularly through the establishment of the Caribbean News Agency, which distributes information on a wide variety of international topics. Regional reports also appear regularly in most newspapers as the Caribbean has become more socially and culturally, if not economically and politically, integrated. Regional newspapers have been founded and regional distribution of local newspapers improved. As skills and training opportunities have opened up, journalists and commentators have addressed international issues in both the print and electronic media. Moreover, interviews with diplomats suggest that governments do care what is written about them and that diplomats, especially the younger ones, read relatively widely, although reactions depend on who the particular author is. Again, none of this means that the "periphery" has become any more influential or even that elite opinions are crucial to foreign policy decision-making and behavior. The influence of the elite will vary according to the decision-making structure previously discussed, with outside influences minimal in cases where personalistic decision-making is the norm. But we can probably hypothesize that the more developed the Caribbean society, the larger and better informed the elite is on foreign policy matters and the more the government will take elite opinion into account. Clearly, in all of this we are implying that the elites do have some influence and therefore must be taken into account. But what is the extent of this influence?

Elites may exercise direct influence by becoming involved in formal politics, but elites often have important indirect influence by their informal social links with politicians. The smaller the state, the easier it is to exercise this type of influence. Academic elites are sometimes invited to brief politicians or would-be politicians on issues, or politicians may attend lectures and participate in academic conferences in which various points of view are aired. A visit to some libraries within Ministries of External Affairs turns up some locally produced academic reports. At the broadest level, Caribbean intellectual elites have often founded political parties and groups that discuss foreign as well as domestic policy and put some pressure on ruling elites for change. And the relatively new fetish for polling, initiated by those in the academic sector, has provided governments with better knowledge of changes in the popular mood. In addition, there is some, albeit small, "circulation" of elites, that phenomenon well known in the more developed societies by which business and academic elites circulate into government and back.

The study of the effect of elite opinion on foreign policy is limited by the fact that except in the case of in-depth analyses of how particular decisions were made, the actual process by which general elite opinion is translated into policy cannot be ascertained. Analyses of Jamaican elites have shown that right after independence, the elite—business and political, opposition and ruling—were highly pro-West in cultural and political orientation and that this orientation declined remarkably, to be replaced by a Third World orientation in the 1970s. In the early 1980s, the attitude of the elites changed radically again to a pro-West one.[17] The assumption is made that Jamaica's changes in foreign policy have been the product of changes in elite attitudes in general and not just in the attitudes of the ruling political elite. However, this assumption does not ring true.

First, our knowledge of events in Jamaica also highlights the importance of the "mass" dimension in engendering changes, in that the rise of Michael Manley was facilitated by societal disaffection reflected in growing unrest in the late 1960s and early 1970s. Similarly, mass action in Trinidad and Tobago in 1970 led to changes in both domestic and foreign policy, as previously discussed. Even where unrest has not occurred, the general populace influences foreign policy through electoral changes generated by public dissatisfactions, even though those public dissatisfactions are usually based on domestic rather than foreign policies. In other words, elite influence has often merely reflected or responded to mass demands.

Second, the data on elite attitudes in Jamaica indicate that except for 1962, when there was an elite consensus on the virtues of a pro-West policy, changes have been a reflection of changes in attitudes on the part of the *ruling* elite only. The breakdown of changes for the political elite show an expected increase in the polarization of attitudes. In 1962, 71 percent of Jamaica Labor Party (JLP) elites and 82 percent of People's National Party (PNP) elites preferred a pro-West policy; in 1974, the percentages were 62 percent and 16 percent respectively; and in 1982, 83 percent and 0 percent. No JLP elites chose a Third World or non-aligned orientation in 1982, but 59 percent of PNP elites did, and another 18 percent chose these as their second choice.[18] Since foreign policy orientations are not shared across political groups, except for the 9 percent of JLP people and 18 percent of PNP elites who chose the category "self-interest" as their first choice of foreign policy preference, Jamaican ruling elites have no choice but to ignore their competitors in determining their foreign policy. The figures are even more interesting for the business elite, which has displayed a high degree of consistency in its pro-West orientation—from 100 percent pro-West in 1962, to 71 percent in 1974, to 85 percent in 1982. Thus the changes in Jamaican foreign policy of the 1970s were initiated against the preferences of the business elites. We therefore have to conclude that in Jamaica, at least, the elite is only influential insofar as its views conform to the political orientations of the ruling elite.

Although other Caribbean societies are less polarized than Jamaica, in the sense that the opposition tends to share some general perspectives on foreign policy with those in power, opposition groups in parliament and outside have not had much say in foreign policy. Partly this is attributable to the nature of the Westminster party system in which the opposition's role is to keep the government "on its toes" rather than to share in decision-making as in the U.S. system. Partly, too, the weakness of the opposition in the Caribbean and the personalist bent of most governments have prevented the opposition's effective participation in politics. There have been weak or fragmented oppositions in Guyana, Trinidad and Tobago, Jamaica, Antigua, Saint Lucia, Dominica, and the Bahamas. Finally, the traditional priority given to domestic policy in electoral politics has meant that the opposition in and outside of parliament has concentrated its attention on issues of greater popular concern. There are exceptions: occasional opposition disapproval of government spending on foreign missions and conferences; opposition vocalness on foreign events of great visibility and importance, such as Venezuela's assaults on Guyanese territorial integrity (the Guyanese opposition has vigorously defended Guyana's integrity while accusing the government of using the dispute to militarize the country); Jamaica's troubles with the IMF in the 1970s and its relationship with Cuba (the opposition was highly critical); and the takeover in Grenada in 1979 and subsequent events, which provoked continuing criticism from opposition parties throughout the Caribbean. However, these opposition comments were intended to boost the outgroup's image and chances of election rather than to modify government policies.

The elite studies referred to earlier also highlighted the fact that in Jamaica it has been possible to initiate foreign policies that have not been approved by the business sectors. This is significant in that it goes against the tenets of dependency theory that posit the existence of such close linkages between the ruling and business elites in peripheral countries that foreign policy choices are inevitably favorable to the West.[19] It also suggests that the importance of business elites in Caribbean foreign policy varies by country and government priority and that they can perhaps best be viewed simply as one of a number of interest groups that lobby governments on certain issues. It should be noted that the influence of interest groups also varies according to the level of development of the country: The smaller the state, the more pervasive is the influence of particularly favored groups, usually business, or even a particular business leader. In sum, we should not overestimate the importance of elites in Caribbean foreign policy. It would seem that real influence lies only with ruling political elites and their advisers, along with other elites who share (but perhaps occasionally disagree with) the governing elite's perspectives.

Within these parameters, the three groups that can possibly influence foreign policy decision-making in the Caribbean are labor, business, and the military. In countries everywhere, the military generally gets involved in policymaking on security issues. However, although the military and paramilitary have increased in importance over the years in the Caribbean, they are the implementers rather than the influencers of foreign policy. There appears to be some occasional and ad hoc policy consultation with chiefs of police or military heads on matters involving the Regional Security System, drug interdiction, and other issues depending on the country, but communication is usually through the minister of national security rather than directly. This leaves business and the unions. Given the close relationship in much of the Caribbean between unions and political parties, the unions might be expected to exert some influence on foreign policy. In fact, although they have some control in domestic economic matters, they have relatively little to do with foreign policy issues. Occasionally, they voice opposition or approval of foreign policy measures. At rare times, it may lead to some action: For example, dock workers in Trinidad have at various times refused to handle cargoes from South Africa and Venezuela, the latter in solidarity with Guyana. Again, throughout the Caribbean, union leaders have often been elected or appointed to government positions, thereby exercising indirect influence, and some countries have posted labor attachés at their foreign missions. But beyond these indirect links, union influence on foreign policy remains limited.

On the other hand, despite the findings for Jamaica earlier discussed, business influence has been much stronger than that of other groups, given the importance of the business sector in the implementation of governments' economic policies, especially in the areas of trade and tourism. The various chambers of commerce and manufacturing associations often speak out on international economic matters and in some countries are actually consulted for expert advice when relevant decisions are being made. Regional industry groups also influence their local counterparts.

Much has also been said of the power of multinationals to influence governments, and in the past, companies such as Tate and Lyle, Bookers, Texaco, and the bauxite companies did have an inordinate influence over their hosts, simply because their contribution to domestic revenues was so crucial. Over the years, buyouts, takeovers, and localization policies have reduced the power of multinationals in the Caribbean, as elsewhere. Today influence is more indirect, through government-to-government relations, especially for U.S. multinationals. Close bilateral ties between the United States and various Caribbean countries have generated arrangements favorable to U.S. investment and policy in these states, and U.S. investors and bankers tend to exercise influence more through relationships with the U.S. government than privately. In view of this, it is also important to consider the way in which government officials from the United States and other developed countries and other individuals operating with the approval of their governments work with government officials in Caribbean countries. For example, Jamaican officials in the Seaga administration consulted frequently with U.S. congressmen, trade representatives and other officials. A private group of businesspersons, led by David Rockefeller, worked through the Reagan administration to promote investment in Jamaica. Moreover, the bauxite companies in Jamaica, the Reagan administration, and the Jamaican government all cooperated in seeking to expand production in Jamaica. In other words, there has been more consultation than was the case under the traditional high-handed modus operandi of the multinationals.

We should add that the consideration of the relationship between officials from developed and Caribbean countries is also necessary in understanding the general decision-making process of Caribbean societies—foreign policy outcomes depend on the closeness and the nature of the interaction between these groups of officials. In the 1960s, James Rosenau used the term "penetrated" system to define societies in which non-members participate "directly and authoritatively" in the decision-making process.[20] While Rosenau is very specific about the "direct" nature of this participation, we would extend the concept to include indirect but highly influential participation. To give an example, during recent Bahamian elections, Prime Minister Pindling suggested that he might reappoint a former government official forced to resign amid charges of money laundering for a U.S. organized-crime figure. Reacting to this, the U.S. deputy assistant secretary of state for the Caribbean said: "You can't expect the United States to ignore that. I don't want to anticipate what action we would take, but we are giving it a great deal of thought."[21] The official's reponse was, given the nature of the U.S.-Bahamian relationship, obviously intended to strongly influence the outcome of (in this case) a domestic issue. Again, in the case of Jamaica, Prime Minister Seaga's close cooperation with U.S. officials gave them great influence over Jamaica's policy. On the other side of the ideological coin, extremely close links developed between Maurice Bishop and Cuban President Fidel Castro and between the two countries. Some have even suggested that Cuban government officials participated actively in Grenada's decision-making.[22] Still, for the Caribbean, external influence has usually come from the West: In interviews with bureaucrats in the small Eastern Caribbean islands, the close relationships between the U.S., Canadian, and U.K. ambassadors and the prime ministers and other major government personnel were consistently highlighted. Ambassadors are often treated by local politicians as if they are government ministers, and their views are given primary consideration.

Finally, we should mention a few social associational groups that speak out and try to lobby on foreign affairs matters. The best known is the Caribbean Council of Churches and its local counterparts, which are uniquely active in preparing and distributing reports and papers on international issues and speaking out in public forums. Also very active are press associations (where they exist), which not unlike similar associations in developed countries, tend to discuss foreign issues without actually lobbying for particular policies, although individual journalists and commentators write within their own ideological contexts. As we discussed earlier, the media are playing an increasingly important role in bringing foreign affairs to the people and may even influence policy itself. Last, the role of Caribbean nationals living abroad should be mentioned. Where they are present in large numbers (Canada, the U.K., the United States), they influence their native country's foreign policy by the very fact of their presence; hence the ubiquitous presence of Caribbean consulates and honorary consulates in these countries. They also have tended to form community groups and political organizations that speak out on domestic and foreign policy and engage in political fund-raising and other activities. Officials and politicians from the home country give importance to these groups by frequently addressing them in lectures and social events. In fact, this effort to impress groups abroad has become a foreign policy activity in itself.

Because many if not most Caribbean countries allow dual citizenship, Caribbeaners abroad can often still vote in elections at home, and some may actually be recruited or recruit themselves for political office. They also have the potential to influence officials in their adopted countries on matters affecting the Caribbean. The extent to which groups of nationals abroad work to affect policy both in the Caribbean and abroad varies. For example, a New National Party support group in New York raises funds for the Grenada ruling party but does not try to advise the government, although individual members may. On the other hand, the Jamaican Progressive League (JPL), a pro-Manley group formed in New York in 1938, not only raises funds but actively tries to influence policy. While Michael Manley was in power, the JPL sought through U.N. ambassador Andrew Young to strengthen the bond between the Jamaican government and President Carter. In doing so, it claims to have opened up new bauxite markets in the United States. It also claims to have helped improve tourism through various publicity efforts. Interestingly, the JPL apparently tried unsuccessfully to sensitize Manley to the U.S. view, but in this area its impact was minimal. After Manley lost power, the JPL continued to work for U.S. immigration law reforms. This and a Trinidadian dual citizenship law have also been the main concerns of the Trinidad and Tobago Alliance, another New York–based group. This group has non-profit status, which limits its political activity, and it confines itself to discussions and suggestions. Overall, it seems that Caribbean politicians give relatively high priority to interacting with nationals abroad, and increasingly are depending on the fund-raising abilities of these groups.[23]

*   *   *

To summarize, Caribbean decision-making, at least on day-to-day issues, is influenced by a number of political/bureaucratic and societal actors. At the governmental level, the views of the prime minister, foreign minister, and cabinet are key, and in ideal circumstances, there is consultation with foreign policy personnel headed by the permanent secretary. At the societal level, the ruling elite tends to take its cue primarily from its own clique of advisers and friends, but business groups, academic elites, the media, and nationals abroad wield varying degrees of influence even when not directly supportive of the ruling elite. In terms of the patterns of public influence on decisions, we can draw on the international relations literature to see how these work. Specifically, Donald Puchala's three models depicting the influence of public opinion on policy are of interest here. In Model A, the masses influence the elite, which in turn influences the government, resulting in a change of policy. The changes in the 1970s in Trinidad and Tobago clearly fall into this category. (In Jamaica and Grenada, a different version was played out: The masses influenced the oppositional elite, which in turn implemented changes when it came to power.) In Model B, the government produces a change of public opinion. This is probably the normal Caribbean model, where the government controls foreign policy to the extent that the public acquiesces in whatever has been decided. (In one major exception, Trinidad's government was unsuccessful in persuading its people that its non-intervention in the Grenada crisis was the proper course.) And finally, in Model C, the elite moves to shift government policy *and* mass opinion. This has been done, with varying success, by opposition elites or by dissenters in the ruling elite.[24]

The decision-making structure and influence relationships just described and the operational environment previously discussed, together suggest a model of how foreign policy is made in the Caribbean. However, the complexity of influences described is idealized. The strength of different influences and indeed the *influencers* of policy vary according to the issue and situation. In particular, the overall picture given applies to day-to-day decision-making. However, decision-making analysts have found it important to analyze how decisions are made in crisis when time is of the essence and decision-makers are under a great deal of pressure. Our analysis above indicates that decision-making in the Caribbean is quite concentrated even under normal circumstances. This enhances the probability that decisions and therefore policy will be personalized, narrowly conceived with many options unexplored, and not necessarily supported by the informed public. In Chapter 7, we see how this trend in decision-making is aggravated by crisis conditions.

Notes

1. Given the small size of the sample (12), statistical results must be viewed as suggestive rather than definitive. To compensate for size, we have raised the acceptable strength of the correlation, normally accepted as .30 in the social sciences, to .50. The level of probability is that normally accepted in the social sciences, 95 percent or .05. The statistical tests were done on data collected for the descriptive chapters and therefore cover only a sample of years.

2. Cited in "Caribbean Basin Initiative Speech, President Reagan's Address to the Organization of American States, Washington, February 25, 1982,"

reproduced in Jack Hopkins, ed., *Latin America and Caribbean Contemporary Record*, vol. 1, 1981–1982 (New York: Holmes and Meier, 1983): 716–722.

3. Among those who have looked at the relationship between foreign aid and international behavior are Kul B. Rai, "Foreign Aid and Voting in the U.N. General Assembly, 1967–1976," *Journal of Peace Research* 17 (3), 1980: 269–277; and N. Richardson, "Political Compliance and U.S. Trade Dominance," *American Political Science Review* 70 (4), December 1976: 1098–1109. Bruce Moon has been the main proponent of the broader dependency perspective. See Bruce Moon, "The Foreign Policy of the Dependent State" *International Studies Quarterly* 27 (3), September 1983: 315–340. Moon's dependency measures include treaties, arms sales, IGO membership concentration, export concentration, and military assistance.

4. U.S. Departments of State and Defense, *Grenada Documents: An Overview and Selection* (Washington, D.C., September 1984): Section 106, 17–18.

5. George Louison in *Internal Events Leading to the U.S. Invasion of Grenada* (New York: Grenada Foundation Inc., 1984): 33–34.

6. In fact, t-tests were performed, using the data collected for the descriptive chapters, to analyze the differences between Guyana/Jamaica and the rest of the Caribbean in the mid-1970s, Guyana/Grenada/Jamaica and the rest of the Caribbean in 1979, Guyana/Grenada and the rest of the Caribbean in 1982, and Grenada/Jamaica under socialism and in the non-socialist eras. The only significant differences uncovered were between Grenada/Guyana and the rest of the Caribbean for state visits in 1982, meaning that these countries sent and received more official visits than their counterparts. The mean scores for groups for visits semt were: 7.0 and 1.67, t-value was −3.32, and p = .01. For visits received, means were 4.5 and 1.22, t-value −2.57, p = .03.

7. The results of the ANOVA or t-tests for regime changes were:

Barbados pre- and post-1976:
Imports

Group means	142.00	560.15	t = −5.36	p=.03

Exports to Latin America
Group means	5.85	24.50	t = −5.12	p=.03

Imports from Latin America
Group means	19.50	141.20	t = −7.86	p=.01

Dominica pre- and post-1980:
Exports
Group means:	10.10	25.60	t = −22.37	p=.03

8. Quoted in Gerald Samuel, *Barbados Foreign Policy From 1966–1978*, M.S. thesis, Institute of International Relations, University of the West Indies, Trinidad and Tobago, 1979, p. 222.

9. Max Weber, *The Theory of Social and Economic Organization* (New York: Free Press, 1947). Charismatic authority was considered applicable to "transitional" societies. Weber's type of categorizing, based essentially on a dichotomy of traditional versus modern society, has been criticized since the 1960s as too unidirectional and ethnocentric. Indeed, charismatic authority does not preclude the establishment of rational-legal norms of conduct.

10. Anthony Milne, "Role and Origin of Cabinet," *Trinidad Express*, January 4, 1987, p. 19.

11. Personal interview with Nicholas Braithwaite, adviser to Grenada's prime minister, January 23, 1986.

12. Basil Ince, "The Administration of Foreign Affairs in a Very Small Developing Country: The Case of Trinidad and Tobago," in Vaughan A. Lewis, ed., *Size, Self-Determination and International Relations: The Caribbean* (Mona, Jamaica: Institute for Social and Economic Research, 1976): 329.

13. Ibid., p. 314.

14. Ince, "Leadership and Foreign Policy Decision-Making in a Small State: Trinidad and Tobago's Decision to Enter the OAS," in Basil Ince, Anthony T. Bryan, Herb Addo, and Ramesh Ramsaran, *Issues in Caribbean International Relations* (Lanham, Md.: University Press of America, 1983): 279.

15. See, for example, Johan Galtung, "Foreign Policy Opinion as a Function of Social Position," in J. N. Rosenau, ed., *International Politics and Foreign Policy* (New York: Free Press, 1969): 551–572.

16. Ibid.

17. See Wendell Bell, "Foreign Policy and Attitudes of Elites in Jamaica: The First Twelve Years of Nationhood," in R. Millett and W. Marvin Will, eds., *The Restless Caribbean: Changing Patterns of International Relations* (New York: Praeger, 1979): 149–165; and Wendell Bell and J. William Gibson, Jr., "Independent Jamaica Faces the Outside World: Attitudes of Elites After Twelve Years of Nationhood," *International Studies Quarterly* 22 (1), March 1978: 5–48; and William Jesse Biddle and John D. Stephens, "Dependency and Foreign Policy: Theory and Practice in Jamaica," paper presented at the Latin American Studies Association Annual Meeting, Boston, October 23–25, 1986.

18. Biddle and Stephens, "Dependency," Appendix Tables 2 and 3.

19. Biddle and Stephens explain this deviation by suggesting that the role of "organized action of subordinate classes" be considered, which fits in with our own ideas. They also note that some businessmen supported Manley's moves against the bauxite companies (a) because of the shortage of foreign exchange and (b) because the bauxite companies "had not developed sufficient linkages to the local economy to tie a substantial sector of the bourgeoisie to their own [the bauxite companies'] immediate interests." See p. 20.

20. James Rosenau, "Pre-Theories and Theories of Foreign Policy" in R. Barry Farrell, ed., *Approaches to Comparative and International Politics* (Evanston, Ill.: Northwestern University Press, 1976): 65.

21. *New York Times*, June 14, 1987, p. 20.

22. Former PRG Attorney General Lloyd Noel said that the Cuban ambassador invited himself to cabinet meetings until Bishop withdrew this privilege. Released committee minutes also show that Major Leon Cornwall, Grenada's ambassador to Cuba, complained that the Cubans had greater access to the NJM hierarchy than he did and were directly informed on many matters.

23. All research on New York groups was done by Rebecca Rhodin, graduate student at the City University of New York.

24. Donald Puchala, *International Politics Today* (New York: Dodd, Mead, 1971): 67.

7. Decision-Making in Crisis: The Grenada Case

As we saw in Chapter 6, the process of making foreign policy decisions is a complex one, involving, as most decision-making models elaborate, a central decision-making unit whose structure (organization, cohesion, formality, size, openness to change) is as important as the perceptions, attitudes, beliefs, and motivations of its members. These decision-makers must take into account the environment in which they operate, that is the national and international influences described in Chapter 6, and also elaborated in the scholarly literature on decision-making.[1] Decision-making analysts also consider as important the analysis of communication patterns: These are described by Richard Snyder as who communicates with whom and how, how much information comes in from outside the decision-making unit, and how flexible the decision-making unit is in accepting the information; and they are described by Michael Brecher as "the transmission of data about the operational environment by mass media, internal bureaucratic reports, face-to-face contact, etc."[2] The final outcome of the process, the *decision*, of course feeds back into the operational environment.

Bahgat Korany has criticized those scholars of the Third World who focus on the "psychological-perceptual" school of decision-making. This school concentrates on the perceptions and behavior of the leadership and the elite.[3] Despite this, our own research up to this point has confirmed that in the Caribbean the tradition of elite dominance of foreign policy remains strong. The dynamics of bureaucratic politics described by Graham Allison[4] is relatively muted in an environment in which bureaucrats implement rather than influence. Nevertheless, we saw in Chapter 6 that many factors in the operational environment also play important roles in influencing foreign policy outcomes.

Although we may assume that personalized decision-making will be strengthened in times of crisis, we should not expect operational considerations to be downgraded even at those times. Crisis decision-making obviously differs quite a bit from day-to-day decision-making: Decisions must be taken in an atmosphere of urgency, sometimes secrecy, often with limited information available. Because of the salience of these decisions, scholars of the field have concentrated on crises rather than on everyday decision-making. One of the most thorough researchers in this area has been Glenn Paige, who generated a large number of hypotheses gleaned from an analysis of the U.S. decision to go to war in Korea. Among his findings were the following: that crisis decisions tend to be reached by ad hoc decisional units that vary within narrow limits of size and composition; that the greater the crisis, the more harmonious the relationships among decision-makers, the more the leader's solicitation of subordinate advice, and the greater the interdepartmental collaboration; that the greater the crisis, the greater the felt need for information and the more the directed scanning of the international environment for information; that the greater the crisis, the greater the propensity for decision-makers to supplement information about the objective state of affairs with information drawn from their own past experience; and that the greater the confidence in existing information, the greater the amount of contrary evidence and the greater the authority of the sources required to bring about a change in interpretation.[5] We expect in our analysis of the Grenada crisis to also consider the influence of the nature of the decision unit and aspects of the information question. The analysis is undertaken not so much to shed light on what happened during this particular crisis but to better understand how the decision-making machinery worked in this crucial situation.[6]

In October 1983, the Caribbean was confronted by the breakdown of order in Grenada occasioned by the infighting between two factions of the revolutionary government. From the point of view of the average Grenadian and those outside the country, the crisis had begun on October 13 when Prime Minister Maurice Bishop was placed under house arrest for resisting the demands of the party's central committee that he share leadership with his deputy Bernard Coard. In the course of the infighting, Bishop, three cabinet members, and several supporters had been executed, and an unknown number of the public had been killed and wounded when soldiers in armored tanks stormed the fort where Bishop and supporters, who had earlier released him from house arrest, had gathered. After the killings, which took place on October 19, the army announced that it had taken over, and imposed a 24-hour curfew, with instructions that violators be shot on sight. (On October 25, curfew hours were reduced to 8:00 p.m. to 5:00 a.m.)

The situation was clearly one of crisis, both in an objective sense and in the perception of Caribbean decision-makers and the general populace. The Caribbean had not been immune to social unrest: large-scale demonstrations bordering on riots had taken place in Jamaica in 1968, in Trinidad and Tobago in 1970, and in Grenada prior to independence. Furthermore, partisan electoral violence had become the norm in Jamaica. Nevertheless, the scale of violence in Grenada was unprecedented in the Caribbean and obviously called for urgent responses from the various governments.

Certain factors in the operational environment must be emphasized. First, the social history of the Caribbean islands must be understood. They share a historical and cultural closeness that was once formalized in political federation. Despite political fragmentation and economic disagreements, the social and cultural bonds of the Caribbean community remain deep. However, the links are not uniformly distributed across countries. Historically, the Eastern Caribbean countries, including Barbados, have been the most tightly interlinked through migration. A strong secondary linkage developed with Trinidad, which by virtue of being more developed than the other islands, became a mecca of migrants during the federation and after. More remote from these linkages is Jamaica, which has historically looked northward to the United States, and on the fringes of the social community are Bahamas and Belize. Guyana, on the southern mainland, though not a participant in the federation, formed a tertiary area of linkage, not through migration but through its strong interest in Caribbean unity that at one point (1971) led it to propose a union with the Eastern Caribbean states.[7] For these reasons, the disappointment felt by the other islands of the Caribbean when Jamaica decided to leave the federation in 1962 was nothing compared with the vexation felt when Trinidad opted for independence. As a result, one seasoned Trinidadian minister dated the dispute that arose between Trinidad and the Eastern Caribbean over the action taken in Grenada back to Eastern Caribbean disappointment over the breakup of the federation.[8]

Another operational influence that must be understood is the Caribbean reaction to Grenada prior to the events of 1983. Since the Grenada coup of 1979—the Commonwealth Caribbean's first unconstitutional takeover—the community, accustomed to harmony in political orientation, had been unsettled and polarized. With the exception of socialist Guyana and socialistic Jamaica (until 1980), Caribbean governments opposed the regime. As we have seen, this opposition was reflected in a range of actions, from Trinidad's attempt to ignore the PRG altogether, to the open verbal hostility of Barbados and Dominica, and the complaints by Grenadian officials of harassment at the Bridgetown airport. The opposition to Grenada was grounded in differences in ideology, in the PRG's refusal to legitimize its status through elections, and perhaps also in a certain intergenerational hostility as the Grenada group of young ideologues with different socialization experiences confronted a tight group of older leaders, most of whom were accustomed to one another and to a certain harmony of interest.

In 1981, the Eastern Caribbean countries formed the OECS. No attempt was made to exclude Grenada, partly because leaders felt they could work with Bishop, himself quite personable and middle class, and partly because Grenada's input was useful and needed for unanimity in a number of policy areas, such as decisions on the joint missions and matters to do with the Caribbean Development Bank. The OECS incorporated a rule of unanimity and since consensus was desirable, it made no sense to create too many problems over Grenada.[9] On the other hand, Eastern Caribbean discomfort with Grenada over security matters was evident in the decision of 1982 to join with Barbados in a regional security grouping that excluded Grenada. The Eastern Caribbean troops that participated in the Grenada action did so within the context of this security community.

The relationship between the OECS and the larger Caricom grouping is also relevant to this discussion. The sub-unit makes its own independent decisions and is equal to, though separate from, the larger body. Eastern Caribbean states have been both politically and economically disappointed by their larger colleagues, and at least one Eastern Caribbean prime minister, Eugenia Charles, has, as we mentioned earlier, refused to view the larger organization as anything more than a trading association. Finally, in the operational area, the relationship between the Caribbean (Grenada in particular) and the United States must be considered. In previous chapters, we have made note of the heavy economic emphasis of most of the Caribbean countries on the United States and of U.S. concerns over instability and socialist gains in the Caribbean in the 1970s. With the defeat of Manley by Seaga in 1980, the victory of conservative parties in Dominica and St. Kitts, the consolidation in power of the Antiguan leadership in the same year, the continuing presence of the Cato regime in St. Vincent, the renewal of the Adams' mandate in Barbados in 1981 and the return to power of Compton in Saint Lucia in 1982, the Caribbean countries found themselves even more than usual aligned with the United States in its concern to keep socialism in check. For all these countries, the chief problem was Cuba, and Grenada's closeness to Cuba heightened their concern.

We turn now to the actual conduct of decision-making during the crisis. As is the case in all decision-making studies, we are limited by the fact that because all participants in the process cannot be interviewed and probably will have selective memories in any event, we must reconstruct events as best as possible from public sources supplemented by limited interviews. Fortunately, enough information exists in primary and secondary sources.

Of the decision-makers involved, the late Tom Adams has supplied the public with the most information about the characteristics of the decision process. According to him, the first formal meeting for Barbados, a cabinet meeting, was held on October 19, the day Bishop was killed. The Barbados cabinet met and agreed to proceed with a "rescue" plan in collaboration with the Eastern Caribbean countries and other "larger non-Caribbean countries."[10] It can be assumed that informal communications had already taken place between Barbados and the Eastern Caribbean countries. In fact, Adams claimed that the idea of intervention originated with John Compton of Saint Lucia.[11] It was natural for the OECS states to turn to Barbados: Adams had given relations with the Eastern Caribbean high priority during his tenure, and the political links were supplemented by security links under the Memorandum of Understanding establishing a defense and security community in 1982. The more controversial issue was therefore the decision to proceed in collaboration with "larger non-Caribbean countries."

Contact with the United States had certainly been made prior to the cabinet meeting. According to Adams in a televised address later, he was told on October 15 by an official in the Barbados Ministry of Defense and Security that he had been approached by a U.S. official about the prospect of rescuing Bishop from house arrest and that a specific offer of transport had been made. The United States denied this and claimed that it had been approached by Caribbean governments that same weekend.[12] Whoever actually initiated the contact, the fact remains that both the U.S. and the Caribbean governments were actively engaged in discussions separately and with each other from that time on. (However, U.S. documents indicate that the actual preparations for the U.S. invasion were not begun until five days before the event.)[13] As for other non-Caribbean countries, the U.K. was invited to participate, but not Canada, whose ambassador had to initiate contact with Adams.[14] However, the invitation to the U.K. does not appear to have been made before the cabinet meeting, as Adams indicated that he first met with the British High Commissioner two days after the cabinet meeting.

As in Barbados, the situation in Grenada was discussed at cabinet meetings in other Caribbean countries. A fair amount of discussion seems to have been generated within the various cabinets, but disharmony appears to have been minimal. Some countries (such as Trinidad) were already firm on the non-use of force, and even the Eastern Caribbean governments focused on immediate actions rather than on intervention. Thus, many countries issued condemnations of the killings and denunciation of the military council. St. Vincent's cabinet rejected a statement prepared by the permanent secretary for foreign affairs condemning the brutality and instead opted for sending a telex to the military government expressing concern for the safety of Vincentian nationals in Grenada and seeking a meeting and dialogue. Trinidad and Tobago announced specific sanctions against Grenada: Trinidad and Tobago would not participate in any Caricom meetings if Grenada were present; no Grenada citizens would be allowed entry into Trinidad and Tobago without a visa; no exports from Grenada into Trinidad and Tobago would be afforded Caricom treatment; and no vessels registered in Grenada would be allowed the facilities of the Caricom jetty in Trinidad and Tobago.[15] And Eastern Caribbean governments generally agreed to refer the matter to the Organization of Eastern Caribbean States.

While the OECS was preparing to meet on Friday, Saint Lucia's Compton requisitioned a meeting of Caricom heads of government, asking Trinidad and Tobago, the current chair, to hold it in Barbados. Instead, Trindad's Prime Minister Chambers, much to the irritation of Adams, called it for Port-of-Spain. The issue was where should the locus of regional decision-making on such a crucial matter rest. Chambers' decision reflected the developing tension between the broader Caricom— which, incidentally, has no formal mechanisms for conflict resolution— and the OECS, which had already informally moved toward a solution to the crisis, a solution that could be rationalized under the security mechanisms formalized within the OECS.

The OECS meeting was held in Barbados on October 21 (Friday) and the Caricom meeting in Trinidad the next day and into Sunday. The OECS Defense and Security Committee, of which Grenada was a member, met first and later transformed itself into a meeting of the general authority in order to ratify its decisions. At that time, Barbados was invited in and formal cooperation between Barbados and the OECS was decided. The next day, the prime minister of Jamaica joined the meeting.

The decisions publicly announced on that Friday night were the cutting off of further supplies of banknotes from the Eastern Caribbean Currency Authority and the suspension of all air and sea contacts between the OECS countries and Grenada.[16] The one not publicly announced was to support outside intervention in Grenada. The prime ministers had discussed various options, but according to one (private) source, minds were already made up as to the need for physical intervention. O'Shaughnessy notes that Lester Bird of Antigua and Barbuda raised objections to the invasion,[17] but no one else objected to the idea per se. The alternative of negotiation was also discussed, but half-heartedly at best, with some participants needing some persuasion to discuss it. In particular, the OAS was ruled out as peacekeeper because neither Barbados nor the OECS countries were members of the Rio Treaty. According to participants, there was a realization of the dangers of inviting in a superpower, and some leaders expressed a preference for intervention by a power other than the United States. Compton himself, the initiator of the idea (according to Adams), felt strongly that the United States should leave Grenada immediately after the intervention. Compton is also said to have favored intervention by France because of its reputation in conducting quick surgical strikes elsewhere and, of course, its legitimacy as a power with a direct political stake in the Caribbean, given its presence in nearby Martinique and Guadeloupe. On the other hand, Adams, who was invited to join the meeting of the governing council, preferred a British surgical strike, given the region's close ties with the head of the Commonwealth and the former colonial power.

Another area of debate was the validity or legality of the action. The need to legitimize the intervention was clear: Most of the prime ministers were lawyers, albeit not international lawyers, and they understood the importance of getting the consent of someone in authority inside Grenada— in this case, the Governor-General Sir Paul Scoon. (Although the Dominican prime minister indicated at the U.N. that Scoon had requested help on October 21, before the OECS meeting, Scoon's own statement that he issued a call for assistance two days later is more plausible. Scoon appears to have responded to OECS/United States initiatives rather than initiated his call for help himself.) The prime ministers also felt that Article 8 of the charter, which gives the Defense and Security Committee responsibility for coordinating efforts for "collective defence and the preservation of peace and security against external aggression,"[18] could be stretched to justify the intervention. As it turned out, they underestimated world opinion and were truly surprised at the negative international response their action received.

An important point must be made concerning the conduct of these meetings, and that is the fact that the discussions took place in a very calm atmosphere. The traditional "rational" model of decision-making, which sees decisions as the best alternatives rationally chosen, presupposes that decisions be made with a clear head.[19] Of course, few decisions are in reality made that way, and it would be too much to suggest that OECS decisions conformed to this "best alternative" ideal model. In fact, we noted that minds were already made up by the time the OECS meeting was held. However, the calmness of the atmosphere is significant in highlighting the fact that the prime ministers did not rush heedlessly into their decision and were not particularly pressured into making a particular decision. On the other hand, one participant pointed out that once the decision was taken, there was limited time to do the preparatory work needed, including justifying the decision to the missions abroad. There was no time to inform friendly countries, and relations with many of these suffered as a result.[20]

The OECS meeting over, the prime ministers, except for Adams, went on to Trinidad. Adams was presumably piqued at the decision to call the meeting for Trinidad. In any event, according to him, he met with Trinidad and Tobago's High Commissioner and told him that he "could not come to Trinidad because a military intervention in Grenada was being contemplated by the OECS, Barbados and others, in which the participation of all Caricom countries would be invited. He said he needed to stay in Barbados to negotiate with countries taking part and to take decisions on the military details."[21] The Trinidadian prime minister later indicated that he had never received any invitation to participate, and indeed neither the Eastern Caribbean participants nor Jamaica's prime minister seems to have made the OECS decision clear to Caricom participants.

The Caricom meeting can be quite easily recreated from the information available in primary and secondary sources. From the outset, certain countries had eliminated the option of the use of force, Trinidad and Tobago among them. At the Caricom meeting, according to chairman Chambers, there seemed at first to be general agreement on the non-involvement of any external element in the resolution of the Grenada situation and consensus on the need for a wholly regional (Caricom) solution pursued in conformity with international law and the U.N. Charter. The participants decided to seek the restoration of normalcy in Grenada by contact with the governor-general aimed at establishing a broad-based civilian government that would hold elections shortly; the acceptance of a fact-finding mission comprising eminent nationals of Caricom states; the putting into place of arrangements to ensure the safety of nationals of other countries in Grenada and/or their evacuation where desired; and the acceptance of the deployment in Grenada of a peacekeeping force comprising contingents contributed by Caricom countries.[22] Chambers indicated afterward that the only significant disagreement among the participants was over what to do if Grenada's military council rejected these proposals. Some members wanted to use force, others—Trinidad included—did not.[23]

Payne et al. quote inside sources as noting that Jamaica's Prime Minister Seaga and the OECS leaders were particularly quiet at the meeting—not surprising, given the fact that the debate was essentially marginal to their concerns. They also point out that the next morning's meeting convened an hour late because the OECS and Jamaican leaders and the Barbadian foreign minister were meeting with the U.S. ambassador, "presumably to be told that the Reagan administration had decided to respond positively to their 'invitation.'"[24] In any event, at Sunday's meeting, the consensus supposedly achieved at the last meeting broke down and two other proposals were tabled: one by Eugenia Charles calling for approval of the OECS sanctions, and the second, a not very germane proposal by Seaga calling for the restructuring of Caricom to assure ideological homogeneity. The participants finally agreed on suspension of Grenada from Caricom and adoption of the sanctions on Grenada proposed by the OECS. These decisions were reached over Guyana's objections. Guyana's Prime Minister Burnham argued that since Grenada, a member of Caricom, was not invited to the meeting, no binding decisions could be taken. Also, since Guyana disagreed and the Caricom treaty calls for unanimity on important issues, a majority decision was worthless.[25] The OECS leaders then went on to Barbados, having decided to pursue their plans on the basis of their own close institutional and other relationships with Grenada.

The four countries that opposed the invasion were Trinidad, Guyana, Belize, and the Bahamas. It is doubtful whether the proponents of intervention were much concerned with the position of Guyana, which was to be expected, or the Bahamas or Belize, which were viewed as too remote from the issue, but they were disappointed with the position of Trinidad. The OECS and Barbadian leaders were motivated both by concern for the besieged Grenadian people, who were closely linked to their own people by sociocultural ties, and by fear that the new regime in Grenada would be worse than the last (that is, more hard-line Communist). The Grenadian threat, for which they invoked Article 8 of the OECS charter, was not one of imminent aggression or even of contagion but a threat to the Caribbean way of life, to Caribbean ideals and morality. Eastern Caribbean leaders felt they had a moral right and duty to intervene, both to save the Grenadians in the immediate sense and to save them from foreign (Soviet) domination. In this they found common cause with Jamaica and the United States. Although concerned for Grenadians, Jamaica was less motivated by cultural closeness than by ideology. The United States was clearly ideologically motivated, glad to seize the opportunity to get rid of an unfriendly pro-Soviet regime.

OECS leaders assumed that the leadership of Trinidad and Tobago, sharing the same closeness to Grenada and similar anti-Communist sentiments, would support the decision to intervene. Instead, Trinidad did not. Prime Minister Chambers cited as justification the fact that Trinidad and Tobago's foreign policy is based on "non-interference in the internal affairs of other States and the avoidance of the use of force in conduct of international relations and in the settlement of disputes."[26] As we have seen in earlier chapters, Trinidad has been quite principled in its international political positions, as reflected in U.N. voting patterns. Its stance on Grenada conformed to the position of most of the international community and benefited Trinidad as a result. (Trinidad's success in being elected to a seat on the U.N. Security Council in 1985, and Barbados' failure to do so in 1984, as well as its failure in the same year to get its candidate Valerie McComie elevated from deputy secretary-general of the OAS to secretary-general, can all be attributed to the "fallout" from the Grenada events.) Yet the principled arguments do not suffice to explain the attitude of a country so close to Grenada geographically and socially. In fact, Grenada had even once sought unitary statehood with Trinidad.

Other factors may also have motivated Trinidad's decision-makers in opting for non-intervention. One was probably the style of George Chambers who was widely viewed as a weak prime minister, in comparison with his formidable predecessor Eric Williams. Chambers was not fully supported by his party, was less knowledgeable on foreign affairs, and was presiding over a declining oil-based economy. He was clearly in a less dominant position than his Caribbean counterparts and therefore was more likely to seek a "safe" way out. Second, though pro-U.S., Trinidad and Tobago has historically kept some distance from the United States. That fact, coupled with Trinidad's relative economic independence in the late 1970s and early 1980s, made its decision-makers less likely to choose to ally themselves with the United States in a military adventure into another country. Third, Chambers and his advisers lacked political astuteness in underestimating the sentiments of the Trinidadian people on non-involvement. Chambers was aware that Trinidadians would be averse to committing troops on any large scale— hence his correct assertion that he would have to consult parliament before sending troops to "war" in Grenada.[27] But he and his advisers were unaware of the extent of popular support for an action such as that taken by the OECS in which Caribbean troops were not in the front line. The OECS action was supported primarily because it was decisive; the proposals for diplomatic measures seemed to the public not to address the immediate problem.

In contrast to the Trinidadian decision, the motivations of the decision-makers of Guyana and Belize were fairly clear-cut. Leaders of both countries knew that standing firm on non-intervention was the only way to protect their own territorial integrity, given their border disputes with Venezuela and Guatemala. In addition, Belize has historically been sufficiently remote from the Caribbean core that its decision-makers could view the situation more objectively. Moreover, because Belize is dependent for its security on the U.K. forces stationed there, Belize was unlikely to take a stance that differed from Britain, which opposed the intervention; in any event, Belize could not commit forces into any other country without the concurrence of the U.K.[28] Guyana's Forbes Burnham was the most vociferous critic of the use of force and, in fact, of any sanctions against Grenada: Grenada was a socialist ally, and a hard-line government was preferable to a non-socialist one. Moreover, non-intervention was an important principle to Burnham, who had often felt himself besieged both by anti-Communist forces and by opponents of his authoritarian style.

Bahamian motivations in opposing the intervention pose an interesting case. The official Bahamian position was, like that of the other opponents, legalist—that is, that the Bahamas opposed any act of foreign intervention designed to affect the sovereignty of any state. But non-intervention may have taken on special significance for the Bahamas just then: As we saw in Chapter 5, the government was embroiled in a drug scandal initiated by a U.S. television report that high government officials, including the prime minister, were involved in drug trafficking. The prime minister and other government officials responded by invoking the sovereignty issue. Pindling may have used the Grenada issue to reinforce his message to the United States.[29] Geography was also a factor: Like Belize, the Bahamas was sufficiently remote to allow its policymakers to make legal, objective decisions. Nevertheless, the coauthors of one paper on the subject point out that Pindling was confused as to how to react. In an interview with them, Pindling stated:

> We're twelve hundred miles away. That was another difficulty we had with the Grenada situation, because we tried to point out to them that it's unfair for you to ask me to make a decision [about what to do with the Marxist government there] because I don't know, I don't feel what you feel. I'm a little way away from this ball game.[30]

The authors infer from the prime minister's confusion and the fact that he has never made a public statement opposing the invasion that it is possible that the then foreign minister, an outspoken person who had

had public differences with the U.S. diplomatic staff in the Bahamas in the past, may have played a major role in crafting the anti-invasion policy.[31] However, it is probably safer to assume that the foreign minister simply "took the ball and carried it" in his own fashion.

From the above description of the decision-making environment, what can we say about the process? First, the definition of the situation: Both the OECS and Caricom meetings took place amid an atmosphere of regional tension and crisis. Both were emergency meetings so there was a sense of urgency to the decision-making process. Yet, in terms of the effects of the crisis atmosphere on the process, the decisions taken at these meetings appear to have been reached in a relatively rational manner. Second, a large part of this rationalism was attributable to the fact that the stances were already fixed by the time the formal meetings were held. The OECS countries, Barbados, and Jamaica had already decided on military action through informal communication, and as one participant noted, some participants had to be persuaded to at least go through the formality of discussing other alternatives. Before the Caricom meeting, some countries had also already decided to oppose the use of force. Although the pro-invasion forces apparently were thrown off track during the first day of the Caricom meeting, they reinforced their decision when they held their own informal meetings that night. The result was that neither the OECS nor the Caricom meeting was really a decision-making forum in terms of the decision to invade. The OECS meeting was a decision-*formalizing* forum, and the Caricom meeting was irrelevant to the final decision, since open discussion of the invasion option was precluded from the start.

Third, Paige's hypothesis that the greater the crisis, the greater the harmony among decision-makers is true for the OECS, if not for the larger grouping. In fact, the harmony of the OECS states can better be defined in terms of the phenomenon of "groupthink."[32] There was no major opposition to the decision to use force (except from Lester Bird, who was brought into line by his father), and one bureaucrat aptly described his government's decision-making in the issue as "follow fashion" (imitative) decision-making. The great harmony within the OECS group was not only attributable to the crisis atmosphere but to the characteristics of the grouping: The OECS is a relatively cohesive group of small, closely linked islands. Most of the leaders have held their positions for a long time (or else, like Compton, their fortunes have revived), have long known one another, and share a strong conservative orientation. On the other hand, the Caricom decision unit was looser, comprising states of different political orientations and, as we have seen, different perceptions of their roles in the crisis. We can therefore say that the greater the crisis *and* the more cohesive the decision-making unit, the greater the harmony among the decision-makers.

Paige also assumes that the greater the crisis, the greater the search for information and the more the solicitation of subordinate advice and interdepartmental collaboration. By the very fact that the crisis was regional, calling for decision-making in regional forums, it was clear that the prime ministers would be the dominant decision-makers in the Grenada crisis. But it is difficult to ascertain how much information and advice they sought from others. The early stages of decision-making involved the various cabinets and, in some cases, the foreign policy committees. Thus, if Saint Lucia is used as an example of Eastern Caribbean decision-making, on the day after Bishop was executed, the prime minister called a meeting of the ad hoc Foreign Affairs Committee, composed of the permanent secretary in External Affairs, the attorney general, the commissioner of police, and the deputy prime minister. After discussing the options, this group decided to support the convening of the OECS meeting. The decision was then reinforced in cabinet. Our analysis supports the contention that more advice was sought by the prime ministers (at this stage) than would normally have been the case. The roles of the foreign ministers and the attorneys general seem to have been particularly important. As previously noted, in the Bahamas case, the foreign minister appeared to be more certain of the correctness of the Bahamian position than the prime minister himself. Advice was also sought from the permanent secretaries through the Foreign Affairs Committee (as in Saint Lucia) or, as in St. Vincent, through the foreign minister's request for suggestions.

For those who favored the military intervention, the search for information and advice seems to have diminished once informal consultations were begun. In part, this would have been attributable to the felt need for secrecy. But this was also due to the fact that the decision to use force originated in the personal preferences of the prime ministers rather than in rational ends-means considerations. Thus the prime ministers screened out negative considerations brought up by those Caricom heads who did not favor invasion, seeing such arguments—we can speculate—as self-serving (in the Guyana case), weak (Trinidad), or lacking in understanding (Belize, Bahamas). Since most of them were lawyers, they felt no need to seek international legal advice on the ramifications of the intervention. They did not seek expert national or international advice or "feel out" international opinion through their ambassadors. At this stage, cabinets and foreign ministers played mainly supportive roles, again except for Lester Bird.

One technician who was an active participant in the process was the director-general of the OECS. However, in his role as international civil servant, the director was not a decision-maker but rather a facilitator and coordinator. As head of the secretariat, he had to assist in the implementation of the OECS decision.

In the information aspect of the decision-making process, the flow and pattern of communication are also legitimate areas of analysis. Paige suggests that the greater the crisis, the greater the felt need for face-to-face proximity among decision-makers. In the Grenada conflict, the decision-makers were separated by oceans. The need for proximity thus was translated into frequent telephone communications during the early stages of the crisis and later a pattern of informal meetings by the OECS states, Barbados, and (even later) Jamaica, to complement the formal meetings of the OECS and Caricom. Although communications among the "in" group were adequate, there were several failures with respect to those outside the intimate circle. For one, the British High Commissioner in Barbados was supposedly told of the impending invasion and his government was invited to participate, but the official OECS request, delayed by a faulty telex machine, was not sent to the British government until the afternoon before the invasion. (Payne et al. posit that the British government probably knew of the requests but did not take them seriously and then assumed that the Caricom decision had overriden the OECS view.)[33] The problem, in terms of our decision-making analysis, is not so much that these procedural failures occurred, as the fact that in not having talked seriously with the British well beforehand, the OECS members may have closed off certain options before they needed to.

Again, the Barbados prime minister insisted that the High Commissioner for Trinidad and Tobago had also been told of the contemplated OECS action. No doubt the High Commissioner assumed that the proposed action was by no means assured and was superseded by the decisons taken at the Caricom meeting. Interestingly, according to one OECS bureaucrat, OECS officials made every attempt to contact Trinidad on the eve of the invasion, but all telexes were jammed and all the telephones were busy. The lines apparently miraculously cleared after Chambers addressed parliament on October 26, an address in which he emphasized the fact that he had not been informed of the invasion.[34] The half-serious implication here is that Trinidad may have deliberately avoided being forced into a difficult situation, but it is difficult to see what Trinidad would have gained by this. In any event, the inability to reach Trinidad stemmed from the last-minute nature of the attempt to communicate. OECS leaders could have informed Trinidad and others anytime after the ending of the Caricom meeting on Sunday, October 23, especially as the legitimizing call from Governor-General Scoon to the United States for assistance was supposedly made that night. These communications failures were therefore not unavoidable; they contributed to diplomatic tensions that might have been minimized, albeit not eliminated, had they not occurred.

Despite the secrecy of the meetings held during the crisis, the public was not completely absent from the decision-making process. While decision-makers tended to ignore public opinion against intervention, they were not immune to public pressure. One analyst noted that "as the events in Grenada unfolded, churches, radio stations, and ordinary citizens in the rest of the Caribbean—all pleaded with their governments to do something to help."[35] A bureaucrat interviewed credited opposition calls for action for the policies his government implemented, and indeed governments seemed anxious to appear active. In the circumstances, decision-makers probably concluded—correctly as it turned out—that the public would approve a decisive action such as the one contemplated. Note that although opposition pressure may have hastened the governments' urge to act, opposition *perspectives*, particularly left-wing perspectives, were not a significant influence on decision-making, given the parliamentary dominance of most ruling groups. Opposition views were more important in cases (Belize, Bahamas) where opposition sentiment coincided with popular opinion. Thus Caribbean decision-makers were acting under a certain amount of popular pressure, and this may have helped propel them toward a decisive solution. Those governments that misjudged popular reaction lost political ground as a result.

In sum, the decision-making process in this extraordinary crisis was in many ways no different from decision-making at normal times: Prime ministers were dominant, opposition influence was weak, bureaucrats were only minimally involved, and decision-makers were calm and rational. Nevertheless, there were some differences: More input was sought from others, particularly foreign ministers and attorneys general, in the early stages, and popular pressure may have been more important than at other times. In addition, the special situation of crisis and urgency led to some misjudgments and communications failures. Finally, major decisions were actually taken outside of the institutionalized channels, and decisions taken within Caricom channels fell within the lowest common denominator (sanctions) rather than representing full assessments of costs and benefits, as might be expected in decision-making on less divisive issues.

The final level of foreign policy making is the implementation of policy. In Chapter 8, we therefore turn to some of the bureaucratic problems Caribbean states have encountered in their attempt to maintain a reasonable international presence and to convert decisions into policy.

Notes

1. See R. C. Snyder, H. W. Bruck and Burton Sapin, eds., *Foreign Policy Decision-Making: An Approach to the Study of International Politics* (New York: Free Press, 1962); James Robinson and Richard Snyder, "Decision Making in International Politics," in Herbert Kelman, ed., *International Behavior* (New York: Holt, Rinehart and Winston, 1965): 433–463; M. Brecher, B. Steinberg, and J. Stein, "A Framework for Research on Foreign Policy Behavior," *Journal of Conflict Resolution* 13 (1), March 1969: 75–101; M. Brecher, *The Foreign Policy System of Israel* (London: Oxford University Press, 1972); Brecher, *Decisions in Israel's Foreign Policy* (London: Oxford University Press, 1974); Brecher, *Crisis Decision-Making: Israel 1967 and 1973* (Berkeley, Calif.: University of California Press, 1980).

2. Brecher, *Decisions in Israel's Foreign Policy*, 6–7.

3. Bahgat Korany, with contributors, *How Foreign Policy Decisions Are Made in the Third World* (Boulder, Colo.: Westview Press, 1986). See 39–60 for the entire critique.

4. See Graham Allison, *Essence of Decision* (Boston: Little, Brown, 1971).

5. Glenn Paige, *The Korean Decision* (New York: Free Press, 1968): 273–309 passim.

6. For detailed descriptions of the events in Grenada see, among others, Hugh O'Shaugnessy, *Grenada: An Eyewitness Account of the U.S. Invasion and the Caribbean History That Provoked It* (New York: Dodd, Mead, 1984); and Anthony Payne, Paul Sutton, and Tony Thorndike, *Grenada: Revolution and Invasion* (New York: St. Martin's Press, 1984).

7. For text of "The Grenada Declaration" of November 1971, see Guyana Ministry of External Affairs, *Dialogue of Unity: A Search for West Indian Identity*, Address of Attorney General and Minister of State for External Affairs, S. S. Ramphal, to Caribbean Ecumenical Consultation for Development, Trinidad, November 16, 1971.

8. Harry Partap, "Caricom Marriage on the Rocks, Says Kamal," *Trinidad Express*, February 26, 1984, pp. 19, 55.

9. Interview with Vaughan Lewis, Director-General of the OECS, January 22, 1986.

10. *Trinidad Guardian*, October 29, 1983, p. 5.

11. Ibid.; and O'Shaugnessy, *Eyewitness Account*, 171.

12. Payne et al., *Revolution*, 148.

13. *Newsday* (New York), March 24, 1985, p. 3.

14. *Trinidad Guardian*, October 29, 1983, p. 5.

15. Trinidad and Tobago Ministry of Information, *Info*, September/October 1983, p. 8.

16. O'Shaughnessy, *Eyewitness Account*, 158–159.

17. Ibid., p. 159.

18. For text of OECS treaty, see Jack Hopkins, ed., *Latin America and Caribbean Contemporary Record*, vol. 1, 1981–1982 (New York: Holmes and Meier, 1983): 686–697.

19. For a brief critique of the model, see Sidney Verba, "Assumptions of Rationality and Non-Rationality in Models of the International System," in James N. Rosenau, ed., *International Politics and Foreign Policy* (New York: Free Press, 1969): 217–231, especially 227. For an elaboration of the rational model and comparison with other models, see Allison, *Essence of Decision.*

20. Interview with Vaughan Lewis, January 22, 1986.

21. *Trinidad Guardian*, October 29, 1983, p. 5.

22. *Info*, September/October 1983, p. 8.

23. Statement of Prime Minister Chambers to Parliament, October 26, 1983.

24. See Payne et al., *Revolution*, 151.

25. Quoted in O'Shaughnessy, *Eyewitness Account*, 168.

26. *Info*, September/October 1983, p. 8.

27. Cited in O'Shaughnessy, *Eyewitness Account*, 165.

28. Opinion given by Assad Shoman, former Belize Minister of Health, Housing, and Cooperatives at Caribbean Studies Association Annual Meeting, Puerto Rico, May 29–June 1, 1985.

29. Steve Dodge and Dean Collinwood, "Foreign Policy Making in the Bahamas: A Case Study of Nassau's Anti-U.S. Reaction to the Invasion of Grenada," paper presented at the Caribbean Studies Association Annual Meeting, Puerto Rico, May 29–June 1, 1985.

30. Cited ibid., p. 33.

31. Ibid.

32. On the phenomenon of "groupthink," see Irving Janis' classic work, *Victims of Groupthink* (Boston: Houghton Mifflin, 1972). He asserts that in times of crisis, there is strong group cohesiveness and participants tend to submerge any doubts they may have about their decisions. Members who do not are subjected to strong expressions of disapproval and may even be excluded from future discussions. According to Patrick Morgan (*Theories and Approaches to International Politics* [Palo Alto, Calif.: Page-Ficklin, 1975: 81], "a false unanimity emerges, based on the feeling that the group is undoubtedly correct, is inherently moral in its decisions, is clearly better informed than outsiders, has all the relevant information, and has picked the best possible course of action."

33. Payne et al., *Revolutions*, 153.

34. Interview with Earl Huntley, Permanent Secretary in the Ministry of External Affairs, Saint Lucia, January 21, 1986.

35. Robert A. Pastor, "The Impact of Grenada on the Caribbean: Ripples from a Revolution," in *Latin America and Caribbean Contemporary Record*, vol. 3, 1983–1984: 16.

8. The Caribbean Diplomatic Machinery

Caribbean foreign policy has traditionally carried a strong executive stamp. However, the need for skilled foreign policy bureaucrats and for an efficiently managed diplomatic machinery has grown as Caribbean countries have become more embroiled in an increasingly complex international environment.

Small size has traditionally carried with it financial and human limitations that have prevented states from participating actively in the international system. But today small states are expected to be able to carry out their basic international responsibilities. Moreover, in order to achieve even their most basic goal of development, they have found that they need to maintain a global, not just regional, presence. Financial limitations mean that this presence will be small, but it need not be unimpressive. Small states can compensate for other limitations by developing their human resources. Singapore, for example, has acquired much international respect through the ability and dynamism of its diplomats. Hand in hand with skill is the need, recognized by countries such as Singapore, to ensure job satisfaction and provide adequate incentives for good people to join the diplomatic service or accept diplomatic appointments.

Diplomatic Infrastructure

Although the complexity of the diplomatic infrastructure clearly depends on the size and financial resources of the state, a more important factor in the Caribbean is the perception of government leaders as to the role of the foreign affairs bureaucracy. In all the Caribbean countries, foreign affairs units were initially established—either before independence, as was the case with Trinidad and Tobago, or immediately after, as was the case in most other countries—as units within the prime minister's office. As indicated in Chapter 6, prime ministers bore the major responsibility for foreign affairs. Later, independent foreign ministries were developed but as we will see their growth has been stymied in many cases by lack of official interest, not in foreign affairs per se but in expanding the role of the foreign ministry.

Though each is slightly differently organized, the foreign ministries of the larger Caribbean countries all contain sections that deal with political and economic matters, protocol and consular matters, administrative issues, and information. The political section is usually further subdivided by geographic sectors and also deals with relations with international organizations. The economic division handles relations with the international financial institutions and organizations such as Caricom and the ACP-EEC arrangement. Only Trinidad and Tobago has a separate Caricom division. The protocol and consular sectors deal with diplomatic conferences and visits, passports, visas and other matters affecting nationals abroad, and residence and citizenship requirements. The administrative unit deals with accounts, personnel, promotions and transfers, and matters relating to the rules and regulations of the service. And finally, the information division is charged with publicity and communications and usually includes a cultural section and library services.

Beyond the basics, the additional units vary by country and provide an insight into the priorities of each country. In Jamaica, there are foreign trade and legal sections, including a law of the sea sector; Trinidad and Tobago has legal, marine affairs, science and technology, and international trade divisions; Guyana has a legal sector and a frontiers division; and Barbados has a policy planning sector and until 1986 had an international trade division. Legal and marine affairs gained in significance as a result of the law of the sea negotiations of the 1970s. Trinidad's technology sector is a response to the relatively recent rise of issues of great Third World interest, such as technology transfer and research and development matters, being discussed in U.N. forums. Although Trinidad's is the only ministry with a separate division for this, it should be noted that Guyana's foreign ministry works in close cooperation with the government's Institute of Applied Science and Technology. But by far the most popular addition has been international trade divisions, to correspond to the relatively new economic thrust of Caribbean countries toward export promotion.

Traditionally, matters of international economics have been dealt with by technicians within other relevant ministries, a fact that, as we will see, has caused some difficulties for foreign ministries. But now there is a general recognition that in matters of trade, even more than in the more traditional financial area, foreign ministries can be valuable in serving "as a link between local Ministries, Agencies and private firms and the international intergovernmental organisations [GATT, UNIDO, UNCTAD, ITC and regionally, the CBI] geared to disseminate information and provide technical assistance and advisory services in export promotion and development."[1] Still, the continuing uncertainty as to whether External Affairs should be entrusted with such an important technical area is reflected in the decision of the Barbados government to remove the international trade portfolio from the ministry in 1987.

Overall, the range of issues dealt with by the ministries of the larger countries is impressive and shows a good response to the increasing complexity of the international environment. However, the proliferation of divisions often stretches the capacity of staffs, both in terms of quantity and quality—the latter because staffs are not necessarily adequately trained for dealing with some of the newer issues. In addition, adequate information is not always available: In many cases, financial or staff constraints mean that libraries are not properly stocked. Moreover, they tend to be underused, especially by the older staff members. Also foreign policy staffs tend to be more occupied with administrative work than with research activities. At least at the formal level, Barbados probably is the most progressive bureaucracy in this regard; its appropriately named "Policy Planning, Research and Information" division includes specific activities relating to the preparation of reviews and reports on foreign affairs. As long as the foreign service bureaucracy remains more occupied with implementation and coordination, its input into the formulation of foreign policy will remain reduced.

The rationality of the organization of the ministries must be considered an important factor in their efficiency. In these larger foreign ministries, there are several levels of management: At the top is the permanent secretary, next are the heads of the various divisions, and the general staff is at the third level. This seems to work quite well from a managerial perspective, except for a few problems. One is that the political division has traditionally been larger than others, creating some organizational imbalance. Ministries seem to be dealing with this by subdividing the division into sections with separate directorships. More problematic has been the overburdening of the permanent secretary, who traditionally has been responsible for both administration—including control over appointments (except ambassadors), promotions, and transfers—and policy. In part this is being dealt with by the appointment of highly experienced senior officers as deputy permanent secretaries, with these deputies often heading the main political divisions. But Guyana has gone further in revising its organization so that there are two permanent secretaries: one is in charge of administration, which includes protocol, information and legal sections, and the other in charge of policy matters dealt with under the political, economic, and international organization sections (see Figure 8.1).

A less easily addressed problem is the organizational uncertainty caused by changes in the political system. Many Caribbean states have not had to deal with this problem until recently because past regimes have been long-lived. Now that political change is occurring, it tends to be matched by administrative changes as new governments reorganize and experiment to suit their perceived priorities. Foreign ministries are especially vulnerable because new foreign policy strategies or new twists

198

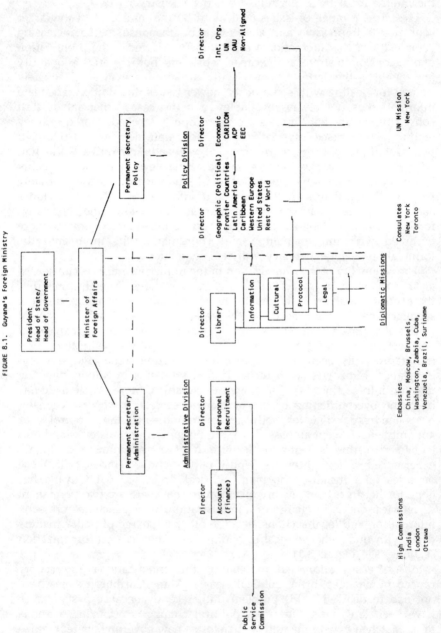

FIGURE 8.1. Guyana's Foreign Ministry

Compiler: Cecilia Rose, City University of New York

on old strategies are adopted by each administration. An example of the organizational confusion that may result is the case of Trinidad and Tobago after a new government came to power in 1986. The ministry was reorganized to incorporate tourism and international marketing, but about six months later, tourism was dropped so that energies could be concentrated on international trade. As noted, in Barbados the international trade portfolio was dropped in mid-1986. Accompanying these organizational changes are inevitable ministerial or sub-ministerial changes and changes in the individual responsibilities of bureaucrats. As in all countries, there is a bureaucratic core in the larger Caribbean states that is relatively immune to change. However, patronage governs certain major personnel appointments. The state of flux in which some foreign ministries are caught contributes to a lowering of morale and reduces organizational efficiency.

A final problem for the foreign ministries of all Caribbean countries, both large and small, lies in the area of coordination. In the smaller countries, as we will see, the problems are unique, grounded in competitiveness among ministries, but in the larger countries, the coordination problem has less to do with competitiveness and more to do with organizational deficiencies. We noted in Chapter 6 that the growing technicality of foreign policy has meant that many ministries other than external or foreign affairs now participate in international affairs. Among these are agriculture, commerce, health, and energy ministries as well as the office of the prime minister, which either consults with other ministries or exercises its inherent authority, depending on the demands of the situation. More than a decade ago, Basil Ince pointed out that in Trinidad and Tobago, "some ministries view the Ministry of External Affairs as a post office to which information should be sent after all action has already been taken." He blamed this on personnel jealousy, on the belief that the foreign ministry does not have the expertise to be part of other ministries' decision, and on the general lack of interministerial coordination mechanisms.[2] The situation has not changed substantially in the 1980s (although the jealousy factor may have abated) and can in fact be generalized to the rest of the Caribbean. In most instances, ministries take their foreign policy initiatives without special consultation or coordination with the foreign ministry. Reports may be passed along to be filed, but in these cases, the foreign ministry does not even act as a clearinghouse. While it is unrealistic (and not even desirable given staffing concerns) to expect that all external initiatives of all ministries should be conducted through the foreign ministry, certainly greater efforts at coordination of major initiatives would result in greater efficiency in the conduct of foreign policy.

The bureaucracies of the smaller Caribbean territories have somewhat different characteristics from those of the larger countries and are therefore considered separately here. Most claim to be functionally specific, usually divided along the same basic lines as the larger bureaucracies. (The

Bahamian organization differs from others in including a "legal and security" division and in being much better staffed.) But the range of matters handled is considerably smaller than in the larger bureaucracies, and for many states the divisions exist only in theory because inadequate staffing precludes specialization. Thus in Grenada in 1986 only two persons were assigned to the political and economic section, two to the protocol and consular section, and three to administration and general services. Of these personnel, at least two were junior clerical officers. One of the two persons—the senior officer—assigned to protocol was temporarily on leave. At the same time, in Saint Lucia the two officers for political and economic affairs were on assignments abroad, and the one person assigned to protocol was studying abroad. As is the case in most of these countries, the administrative division was the strongest and best trained. The extreme in 1986 was represented by St. Vincent, where there were no functional divisions and, in fact, only one bureaucrat directly dealing with foreign affairs.

The problem in these small states is not just a question of inadequate staff but, as one bureaucrat noted in an internal memo, a "lack of clarity" as to the role of foreign ministries.[3] Foreign ministries are clearinghouses rather than agencies performing crucial coordinating and advisory roles. Eastern Caribbean governments, in particular, tend to believe that because the most crucial area of foreign policy is the economic area, and these issues are handled by the technical ministries, the foreign ministry is somewhat irrelevant. For example, the prime ministers of Saint Lucia and St. Vincent have openly espoused this view, reducing the staff and status of their external affairs ministries in favor of the finance sectors. Moreover, we noted in Chapter 6 that the importance of economics and finance is reflected in the fact that most prime ministers in the Eastern Caribbean also hold finance portfolios, and many hold the external affairs portfolio as well. This situation has tended to engender competitiveness between the foreign ministries and the ministries of finance in that there are no provisions for coordination of policy between the two areas. Foreign affairs personnel complain that the finance and other ministries take initiatives without consultation with them and merely use them whenever convenient. Although the complaints about coordination are not very different from those heard in the larger countries, the difference in the smaller states is that there appears to be a zero-sum situation between the relevant ministries, with the one being upgraded at the expense of the other. In such circumstances, rationalization of the structure of the foreign ministries is unlikely to occur without fundamental changes in governments' perceptions of the importance of the ministry.

One somewhat positive aspect of the situation in the smaller territories is that permanent secretaries appear to have more independence in administrative and minor policy matters than do their counterparts in the larger countries. Ironically, this is especially the case where the prime minister is in charge of the foreign ministry and other portfolios, simply because the prime minister is so often overburdened with portfolios and absorbed in pressing political affairs that little time is left for day-to-day foreign policy. But the independence of the permanent secretaries in these countries has to be balanced against the fact that they are often bypassed in policymaking and are frequently the last to know about their prime ministers' foreign policy initiatives.

The diplomatic infrastructure also includes the missions of Caribbean states abroad. In Chapter 5, we saw that Caribbean countries maintain few missions, the number ranging from 13 for Guyana, Trinidad and Tobago, and Jamaica to 3 for the smallest countries. This, of course, in itself limits the international effectiveness of these countries, but it can be countered by adequate representation in multilateral forums and by personnel quality, as discussed in the next section. The small size of the missions also precludes organizational complexity. The staff of the larger missions of the larger countries usually comprises the ambassador, a minister, one or two counselors, a first secretary, one or two second secretaries and/or a third secretary, and a few attachés. The missions of developed countries are similarly structured in terms of hierarchy, but there is usually more specialization of the staff in different technical areas. Understandably, financial limitations prohibit this for most Caribbean states. Moreover, given their small size, Caribbean missions are quite loosely organized, which in some cases gives the impression of a lack of coordination and efficiency. Most missions do maintain a certain organizational hierarchy necessary for effective decision-making, but the atmosphere is usually very informal.

The main structural difference between the larger and smaller states in overseas operations has been the inability of the smaller states to provide individually all the facilities needed for effective representation. Eastern Caribbean countries have tried to overcome this problem by establishing joint missions in London and Ottawa. In the beginning, this meant both shared facilities and joint (really, collective) representation—that is, the sharing of one ambassador. However, a regional ambassador is almost inevitably bound to displease one or more constituents, and this, coupled with the pull of nationalism, has led to individual representation with shared facilities in London, although the regional arrangement in Ottawa remains. In view of financial and staffing difficulties that led to the closing of the Dominica mission to the U.N. in 1986, Belize and the Eastern Caribbean states, excluding Antigua, St. Kitts, and St. Vincent, agreed in 1987–1988 to a Commonwealth proposal that offered funding, on a five-year trial basis, of certain shared facilities (for example, a common reception area and library) and basic staff at the United Nations. It is worth noting, however, that the arrangement does not relieve these countries of the bulk of the financial burden of maintaining a mission in New York. On the whole, collective arrangements make a great deal of sense and are beneficial in helping to counteract some of the structural limitations of small states. Unfortunately, they do not appeal to the more nationalistic states. They are also limited to the few geographic areas that participants can agree on as being crucial targets of their foreign policy.

Finally, in all countries, the efficiency of the foreign service depends on the clarity and ease of communications among the various units involved. Caribbean heads of missions generally communicate with headquarters on a weekly basis, more if the occasion warrants. Ambassadors vary in the degree to which they perceive themselves to be (or actually are) constrained in making independent decisions. The more seasoned and self-assured the diplomat, the more the person is likely to use initiative. However, before making major decisions or giving major speeches, all ambassadors clear their positions with the ministry at home. The correct line of communication is between ambassador and permanent secretaries, and on the whole this seems to be followed. However, especially in some smaller islands, political appointees may bypass the permanent secretary and go directly to the minister or prime minister. Within the missions—to generalize across the twelve states of our study—ambassadors tend not to schedule regular meetings with staff but instead to schedule them as the occasion demands. Thus for example, at the U.N. missions, more meetings are naturally held during the convening of the General Assembly than at other times. Ambassadors seem to meet frequently with individual staff members; so, given the small size of the missions, efficiency depends rather heavily on interpersonal factors.

At the headquarters end, permanent secretaries should meet regularly with the foreign minister as well as with their staffs. In some of the smaller countries, permanent secretaries are more likely to initate contacts with the foreign minister than vice versa, and there are cases in which the foreign minister bypasses the permanent secretary and deals instead with other senior officers. Permanent secretaries themselves seem to prefer one-to-one contacts with staff rather than formal meetings. As for meetings between the minister and the general home staff, only a few ministers have made regular provision for this, and there is evidence that this does not provide the minister with the feedback expected. On the whole, the senior foreign policy staff members in the smaller countries are more likely to approach the ministers directly with an initiative than are their counterparts in the larger countries.

Finally, effective communication and coordination should be global in scope—that is, among ambassadors and between them and the minister and senior home staff. Regular meetings of all these individuals can provide opportunities for the constant reassessment of foreign policy goals and strategies. The larger countries attempt to do this by scheduling review meetings between all ambassadors and the minister and the home staff, especially the permanent secretary. However, except for Guyana, these meetings have not been held on a regular basis, and often the attendance is only partial. In Guyana, heads of missions conferences are held annually, but there is evidence that they do not produce meaningful results. Unless the discussions and reports presented at these conferences lead to changes or improvements in policy, the meetings will simply be viewed by participants as paid vacations home rather than as crucial to policymaking.

Bureaucratic Limitations on Effective Policymaking: An Example[4]

In order to clarify the actual impact on decision-making of the problems described in the previous section, we have chosen to focus briefly on some of the bureaucratic difficulties encountered in one of the small states, Saint Lucia. Saint Lucia is a pivotal state among the Eastern Caribbean islands. It is exhibiting a strong interest in foreign policy, judging from the fact that it has hosted several important conferences, including the Organization of American States General Assembly of 1981 and the Caricom summit of 1987, and is the headquarters of the Organization of Eastern Caribbean States. Yet, as we will see, foreign affairs has limited bureaucratic priority in Saint Lucia.

Scholars have noted that because foreign relations was the last realm of competence that colonial powers handed over to newly independent nations, there is a lack of machinery and skills for foreign affairs in the period immediately following independence.[5] The Caribbean states were no exception to this situation, but the transition was less abrupt than for many other emerging nations. In most cases, departments of external affairs were established under the prime minister's office just before or after independence. Moreover, for the Eastern Caribbean countries, a limited external competence had existed under the Associated Statehood agreement. Associated States were given authority to apply for membership in international organizations of which the U.K. was a member; to negotiate trade agreements and send and receive visits for commercial purposes; to negotiate aid agreements with the United States and members of the Commonwealth; to sign agreements relating to emigration; and to negotiate agreements of local concern. Specific competence was granted for the negotiation of the Caricom agreement. Although none of this could be equated with the grant of true international responsibility, at least the seeds were planted for the growth of the organizational and policy structure.

As was the case in almost all the Caribbean countries, Saint Lucia's limited international relations were handled before and just after independence by the prime minister's office. In fact, after independence in February 1979, Prime Minister John Compton assumed the portfolio of minister of external affairs. In July 1979, a new government came to power, headed by Allan Louisy of the Saint Lucia Labor Party. Deputy Prime Minister George Odlum then became minister of external affairs, as well as of trade, industry and tourism. At that time, a separate ministry of external affairs was created, headed by an assistant secretary, pending appointment of a permanent secretary.

The first problem for the ministry, in terms of its influence on the decision-making process, was its physical location next to the prime minister's office and across town from the foreign minister's office located in the ministry of trade. The significance of this was that the channels of communication remained between the prime minister and foreign affairs staff rather than between the foreign minister and his staff. Between 1979 and 1981, Saint Lucia underwent a high level of elite instability. An agreement between Louisy and Odlum that the former would step down as prime minister after six months was refuted by Louisy. According to analysts, Louisy had the support of the party executive but his cabinet was divided.[6] In the ensuing battle for power, Louisy abolished the post of deputy prime minister and redistributed Odlum's ministries, other than the external affairs portfolio. However, continuing friction and social unrest eventually led to Louisy's resignation, while Odlum left to form his own party. The interim government of Winston Cenac was dissolved in January 1982, and an interim coalition government was formed. This government was voted out of power and John Compton returned as prime minister and foreign minister in May 1982.

These governmental changes were reflected in changes in the foreign policy bureaucracy's organizational structure. Under the Cenac government, Odlum's foreign affairs portfolio was assumed by a former agriculture minister, Peter Josie, who also became minister of trade. The foreign ministry was moved to the trade building just before Saint Lucia hosted a major OAS meeting in 1981. A permanent secretary was finally appointed, and communication between the foreign minister and his staff improved. Interestingly, it was an external event, the OAS assembly, that served as a catalyst for the rationalization of the organization of the ministry. Considerations of image led to greater interest in the fate of the foreign ministry.

The governmental unrest of 1979 to 1982 did not affect the day-to-day operation of Saint Lucia's foreign policy because the technocrats remained in place both at home and abroad. In fact, the political problems placed the technocrats at the center of decision-making. Thus, for example, at the United Nations, Saint Lucia had a better record of voting attendance in 1981 than in 1982–1984. (It was absent 116 times in 1979, 34 times in 1980, 22 times in 1981, 76 in 1982, 27 in 1983, and 54 times in 1984.)

The return of John Compton, who had served as prime minister for fifteen years until 1980, represented a return to the dominance of the prime minister in foreign policy decision-making. Indicative of this was his assumption of the important portfolios of finance, foreign affairs, home affairs, and planning. The foreign ministry remained located in the trade building, whereas the prime minister operated out of government headquarters. The lines of communication were reorganized, working again to distance the foreign minister from his staff. In the absence of close communications—by 1986 the prime minister had reportedly visited the foreign ministry only twice—the permanent secretary was forced to use his initiative in making day-to-day decisions. But major decisions remained the prerogative of the prime minister.

Given the dominance of Compton, it is not surprising that the foreign ministry has often been bypassed in decision-making. For example, when the prime minister was planning to visit West Germany and France in 1985, the foreign ministry learned about it through a political officer of the U.S. embassy to the Eastern Caribbean and through the West German ambassador's inquiries as to the nature of the visit. In another example, the prime minister took the decision to invite the pope to Saint Lucia in 1986 in consultation with the local church but without informing the ministry. The prime minister also approved the appointment of a lobbyist in Washington without any input from the ministry.

The failure to tap ministerial expertise leads not only to embarrassment (which is not fatal) but to uncoordinated policy. Thus, for example, the prime minister opposed the foreign ministry's stance against U.S. sanctions on Nicaragua. While the prime minister has been concerned about relations with the United States, the foreign ministry's concern was— at least partly—that sanctions against Nicaragua could lead to its flooding the market with bananas, Saint Lucia's chief export. On such an issue, greater discussion between the foreign ministry and the prime minister's office is called for, even if the prime minister's view remains dominant.

Like many other small states, Saint Lucia's ambassadors are political appointees, and given the prime minister's personalized style of governing, the advice of these appointees has often superseded the advice given by the foreign service bureaucrats. For example, the ambassador to London's opinion was important in the decision not to establish diplomatic relations with the U.S.S.R. The advice of the ambassadors to the U.K., the United States, and Canada also appears to be taken very seriously and to supersede any contrary advice given by the ministry. Again, the coalescing of the prime minister and foreign minister portfolios has meant that potential foreign affairs personnel have been absorbed into the prime minister's office, not the foreign office. It is important that the prime minister is also in charge of finance and planning, the department that handles all aid projects and has become the focus of attention. In such an atmosphere, the foreign ministry is reduced to protocol functions.

Saint Lucia's prime minister has reportedly said that he opposes "posturing" on the international stage, and during his 1982 election campaign, he talked about closing the U.N. mission. He has resisted the demands from the ministry for more staff and has instead instituted cutbacks. These are not irrational actions: Given Saint Lucia's relative poverty, it must operate with a certain austerity. In addition, since Prime Minister Compton sees his country as vigorously pro-West, it is logical to focus on a few Western missions rather than seek diversification. Moreover, because Saint Lucia needs to emphasize economic development, it makes sense to focus on aid and trade and to employ the technicians in the finance and trade ministries to the greatest advantage. The point, then, is not so much whether the policy makes sense but whether the decision-making process is effective. The downplaying of the foreign ministry means that the main channel of external information and coordination is lost. The permanent secretary does not play the necessary screening role, and important feedback information is absent. Since the bureaucratic role in foreign affairs is downplayed, foreign operations become dependent on the vagaries of politics. Clearly, very small states need to have foreign policy structures that are proportional to their size. But perhaps more so than in larger countries, small states need to work toward rationalizing their foreign policy bureaucracies in order to promote maximum efficiency under conditions of resource and personnel scarcity.

Personnel

The Caribbean is fortunate in having a great base of human potential. Literacy levels are high, and primary, secondary, and higher education are relatively accessible compared to other developing countries. When Britain pulled out of these states, it left them with little or no experience in the handling of external relations and with few personnel trained in international relations. As Dominica's Eugenia Charles stated in a private interview, Britain should have been responsible enough to train adequate personnel at least two years prior to independence.[7] None of the countries lacked pools of potential diplomats, either experienced civil servants or young persons with higher-education degrees, but the smaller the island, the smaller the pool, so that the catch-as-catch-can early years after independence have been more difficult for the smaller islands than for the larger states. Nevertheless, the Caribbean was fairly fortunate in being able to draw from their pools a small number of individuals who had previously worked with the West Indies Federation, the Eastern Caribbean Commission, and the West Indies Associated States (WISA) secretariat. These persons have either substituted experience for formal training or else have benefited from additional specific diplomatic training. Typical of the first type was the permanent secretary of one smaller state who had no direct training in diplomacy but whose federal experience led to jobs as personal assistant to the governor, then assistant to the High Commissioner to Caricom, and finally to permanent secretary in the ministry of external affairs. Of the second type, Basil Ince writes that

> Trinidad and Tobago benefitted from the demise of the Federation since the short-lived Federal Government had begun to train candidates for its

prospective diplomatic service. Those Trinidad and Tobago candidates who had benefitted from diplomatic training became the nucleus of the career diplomats in the Ministry of External Affairs. Their training, which included stints at universities in North America and Europe, was supported by attachments in British Embassies and Consulates, in such diverse locations as Italy, Brazil, England, Spain and Australia. Since the training of individuals slated for employment in the External Affairs offices is an expensive proposition, many candidates received their training with the financial support of interested non-governmental organizations in North America. Thus the new Ministry's composition included senior civil servants, the nucleus from the Federal days and lower-level recruits, some of whom came from other civil service departments.[8]

Gerald Samuel makes similar observations about Barbados, where the process of establishing a ministry was somewhat more hurried than in Trinidad. (In Trinidad, an external affairs division was established in the prime minister's office a full year before independence.) In the four months between independence and the establishment of the ministry of external affairs, Barbados cast around for suitable diplomatic personnel:

Barbados possessed a relatively large number of university graduates in its well-developed government service. Several public servants who worked in senior posts in Ministries existing much longer than the Ministry of External Affairs were transferred to help form the nucleus of the new foreign ministry. These local civil servants and personnel from the West Indies Federation and the Eastern Caribbean Commission coupled with politicians recruited from among the senior ranks of the ruling Democratic Labour Party membership comprised the core staff of the Barbados Ministry of External Affairs.[9]

In the larger countries, the foreign service was created as a parallel unit of the civil service, but in the smaller countries, foreign service personnel have usually maintained civil service ranks. In all cases, after the initial recruitment of seasoned bureaucrats, recruitment has been limited to persons with university degrees, usually in languages, economics, international relations, political science, or other relevant fields. Still, the recruitment process has remained far from professionalized: Given the small size of these countries and the prevalence of patronage politics, ascriptive criteria ("who you know") have been determining factors in job hiring in general, and the foreign service is no exception. Social status and correct political links have in the past been particularly important. In the smaller countries, the application of ascriptive norms has not necessarily worked toward the exclusion of qualified people, given the small pool of qualified applicants to begin with. However, in larger countries, the problem has been more serious. Fortunately, as the services become more professionalized, this is slowly changing.

So far, Trinidad and Tobago is the only country that has introduced an objective foreign service exam, and this only recently in the early

1980s. In all countries, prospective candidates are interviewed, but this does not preclude partiality. While the size of the interviewing panel varies with the size of the country, it usually comprises senior foreign service and/or civil service officials, including the permanent secretary in the ministry of external affairs. In some cases, the minister of external affairs himself participates. Interestingly, in Trinidad and Tobago, a psychiatrist has been included in the panel, ostensibly to weed out persons with undesirable personality traits. This may be worthwhile for persons entering positions that will involve them in high-level decision-making, but as we have seen, foreign policy personnel are implementers of decisions more than initiators. In such circumstances, the inclusion of a psychiatrist is irrelevant, especially since the normal hiring process may involve some examination of an applicant's psychiatric record. In any event, the interview may be only a formality in some cases, and in all cases there is no screening of interviewers themselves to ensure impartiality.

Perhaps because of ascriptive hiring patterns and also because in the initial stages foreign service personnel were poorly trained, the Caribbean foreign service has been heavily dependent on in-service training. Often persons already trained in diplomacy are bypassed in favor of those with barely adequate qualifications who can be trained while in service. This ensures that they are molded to suit the prevailing norms of conservatism (commitment to the status quo) and conformism that characterize the foreign service both in the Caribbean and elsewhere.[10] Caribbean foreign service personnel thus for the most part lack the initiative and innovativeness needed to cope with the many international challenges that Third World nations face.

Ince also pointed out in the early 1970s that in terms of rewards, it was better to do graduate work while in service than before. Speaking of Trinidad, he noted:

> The way in which the promotion system currently works discourages individuals doing post-graduate work since such work will be rewarded with one of two increments in the lowest salary scale. The individual who joins with an undergraduate degree and spends the time to gain a post-graduate degree in the Ministry received nearly the same salary as the post-graduate appointee and in addition is blessed with seniority.[11]

Our own research suggests that the situation still pertains, not only in Trinidad but throughout the Caribbean. Still, it should be added that graduate work is generally viewed highly and encouraged. Many Caribbean countries appoint Ph.Ds to their most visible positions, including ambassadorships, without regard to experience. Since many of the Ph.Ds (or professional degrees) are not in international relations, the tendency to appoint such persons—not only career officers but even political appointees—to high positions must be attributed to the general esteem for education that pervades the Caribbean.

Caribbean governments have placed a relatively strong emphasis on the training of their career diplomats. A major training center has been the Institute of International Relations of the University of the West Indies (Trinidad), established in 1966, which offers year-long courses in international relations. Foreign service officers have also been regular participants in short courses in diplomacy offered by the United Nations Institute for Training and Research. Other training opportunities have been offered by Britain and the Commonwealth, Canada, the EEC., private U.S. foundations such as the Carnegie Endowment for International Peace, and, for the Eastern Caribbean islands, by Barbados. It is interesting to note that the smaller islands, in gaining independence later, could draw on the experience and advice of those in the larger countries. Barbados has been especially helpful to the Eastern Caribbean states both formally and informally through regular contacts between permanent secretaries and other personnel. In other instances, Eastern Caribbean personnel working for foreign services in the larger countries returned home at independence to offer their skills to the new governments.

Despite these training opportunities, Caribbean foreign policy personnel suffer from a number of limitations that prevent them from dealing effectively with some of the complexities of international affairs. In the first place, the dearth of specialists, pointed out by Ince over a decade ago,[12] continues, even though the exigencies of external relations in developing countries demand the hiring of more specialists, especially in international economics and finance and international law. The continuation of this preference for generalists was attributed by one diplomat to bureaucratic inertia, the unwillingness of bureaucracies and bureaucrats to change. Despite the trend noted earlier for foreign ministries to become more involved in matters of international trade and finance, the ministries have coped by encouraging their current personnel to gain some knowledge in these areas (along with the general knowledge they have gained in other areas of international affairs) rather than by hiring personnel trained in these fields. The result is that technocrats from central banks and ministries of finance continue to deal more or less independently with crucial international economic matters, and the attorney general's office deals with matters of international law in which it is not really qualified. It can be noted, however, that since the protracted law of the sea negotiations of the 1970s, there has been a greater awareness of the need to hire specialists in international law. As a result, the larger countries have recruited personnel in this field. However, the smaller countries continue to rely on the domestic law specialists in the attorney general's or prime minister's office. In a few cases, experts have been hired from the outside.

In addition to specialization in certain fields, language training should be a logical focus, given the heterogeneity of the Caribbean area itself. Knowledge of Spanish is particularly important because, as we have seen, so much of Caribbean policy is oriented toward Latin America.

But here again, Caribbean foreign services are lacking. Even though quite a few foreign service officers have undergraduate degrees in languages and others have received some in-service training, language fluency is rare on the part of Caribbean diplomats. It is not that language training is not encouraged: some services such as Guyana's pay for officers to take language courses, and all encourage the practice. Rather the problem is that language training is not emphasized, although Barbados may be an exception in this regard. Also, bureaucratic inefficiencies in some countries lead to anomalies in placements—French-speaking persons, for example, are as likely to be assigned to a Spanish-speaking country as to a more suitable location. Meanwhile, there is strong evidence that language training pays off in terms of diplomatic benefits: Among the diplomats surveyed for this study, those who spoke Spanish well were more likely to get along well with their Latin American colleagues. In particular, Guyana's permanent representative to the U.N., Noel Sinclair (now in charge of policy matters at headquarters in Guyana), was widely respected within the U.N.'s Latin American group not only because of his long tenure but because of his fluency in Spanish. Barbados' Valerie McComie, deputy secretary-general of the OAS, also cited his language fluency as a major factor in his acceptance by the Latin Americans. At the time this research was done, Barbados also was reaping the advantages of having a Spanish-speaking ambassador to the United States and OAS.

Ambassadorial skills deserve special mention because it is ambassadors who, in representing their country abroad, are most important in projecting the Caribbean image to others. The tension between career diplomats and political appointees is a well-known problem in all foreign services. The career diplomat brings experience and skills to an ambassadorial position, but the political appointee often has access to the highest levels of the decision-making structure and knows how to work with sensitivity to the particular political climate. For the smaller states of the Eastern Caribbean and Belize, the lack of experienced career diplomats has meant that all ambassadors are political appointees. Most of these ambassadors are well educated; some have graduate or professional degrees, a few in a field related to international relations. But being political appointees, they lack diplomatic training and experience. This would in no way be a fatal flaw if they could draw on experienced staff for help. However, given the training problems previously elaborated and the staffing problems described in the next section, this is unfortunately usually not the case.

For the larger countries, the debate between political and career appointees becomes relevant. The ratio of career to non-career ambassadors varies, of course, according to the level of personalization of the political leadership and the extent of its use of patronage. Barbados, Jamaica, and Guyana have made special efforts to promote career diplomats so that the ratio of these to non-career ambassadors was either about even or leaning toward more career appointees in the mid-1980s. Taking into account that political appointees may be very skilled and politically astute, it is not wise to eliminate their appointment altogether. Nevertheless, the country's diplomacy is likely to be more effective if career diplomats outnumber political appointees.

The practice of political appointments also raises another personnel problem that can adversely affect the morale of the officers, and here the situation is particularly applicable to Trinidad and Tobago. The high level of political appointments in Trinidad has led to frustration among senior foreign service officers who have reached the top with nowhere to go. The result is job dissatisfaction and a lowering of productivity as officers while away the time until retirement. Trinidad and Tobago also appears to have the only foreign service in which there are serious bottlenecks in the promotion process. Because of the stagnation of the older officers, promotions of younger officers are slowed so that it currently takes seven or eight years to move from the second rank of the foreign service into the third, and more to move into the fourth and fifth. (Promotion from the first rank to the second is relatively swift.) To a large extent, this is reflective of a general problem in Trinidad's padded civil service bureaucracy, but the bottleneck problem is also compounded by the closure of Trinidad and Tobago's diplomatic service—that is, because the service is autonomous, there is little or no horizontal movement to other sectors of the civil service. In most other Caribbean countries, the foreign service is an integral part of the civil service, and promotions can therefore take place "out" as well as "in."

Morale, and thus performance, is also affected by other considerations, including the availability of opportunities for demonstrating initiative and assuming responsibility; proper work distribution so that overloading does not take place; financial compensation; availability of opportunities for appointment to prized posts abroad; and perception of the country's effectiveness in foreign policy. Each of these will be discussed in turn.

We have already noted that foreign service officers are called upon to implement policy. Yet job satisfaction is dependent on the extent to which foreign officers are consulted by their ministers, ambassadors, and permanent secretaries and the extent to which their opinions, once given, are taken into account. This issue has already been discussed in Chapter 6 on influences on decision-making. Generalizing across the twelve countries, we can say that permanent secretaries and their deputies are least likely to be dissatisfied, given the fact that they exercise administrative control and policy oversight. But their level of satisfaction depends on the extent to which they are bypassed in important matters— as we saw, ministers sometimes communicate directly with other ministries, and prime ministers often make external affairs decisions without consulting the foreign ministry—and the access they have to the foreign minister (permanent secretaries often have to take the initiative to meet with the minister rather than vice versa). At the next level, because one-to-one contacts seem to be preferred by permanent secretaries as well as by ambassadors, the job satisfaction of their staffs will depend on their responsibilities and on the personal relationship with the superior. Our research indicates that foreign officers abroad generally have more room for growth and use more initiative than those at headquarters.

A major problem for Caribbean foreign service bureaucracies is staffing. Even in Trinidad and Tobago, where there are bottlenecks in promotion, there is a need (or at least, the appearance of a need) for more staff at the lower levels. The situation is most acute for the smaller territories. In Saint Lucia, in early 1986, for example, the headquarters staff—which was supposed to comprise three foreign service officers in each of three divisions—was apparently reduced to six, all but two of whom were either on loan abroad or on study leave. (However, there were eight or nine support staff.) Moreover, the prime minister reportedly had indicated that he wanted to cut the staff to four people "on the telephone." At the same time, in neighboring St. Vincent and the Grenadines, the foreign ministry staff—which up to July 1984 consisted of a permanent secretary, three assistant secretaries, and an administrative cadet and junior staff—had been returned to the Prime Minister's Office and had been slashed to only one officer and support staff. The permanent secretary for foreign affairs was actually permanent secretary to the prime minister and also cabinet secretary. In Grenada, even with the attention being given to external affairs by the post-PRG government, there was only a permanent secretary, a senior assistant secretary, two assistant secretaries, and four officers, with a fifth officer on study leave. Of these persons, only two had undergraduate degrees and one had diplomatic training without having a first degree. Clearly, it is difficult to conduct international relations with any degree of effectiveness in the absence of staff, especially *trained* staff. To be fair, small states, concerned above all with achieving economic goals, can conduct international economic and functional relations through personnel in other ministries. But foreign policy bureaucracies provide competence and knowledge about specific aspects of the international environment, and they coordinate and facilitate linkages of all kinds between domestic agencies and individuals and the rest of the world. In an age of technology, it is generally assumed that technicians are needed to help conduct international relations, but no one has proposed eliminating diplomats themselves.

Of the larger Caribbean countries, Guyana has the most staffing problems because its weak economy has led to a shortage of both skilled and unskilled staff. In addition, all the Caribbean states, but the smaller ones in particular, maintain very small missions abroad. Trinidad's embassy in Nigeria, for example, has only two officers and some support staff, who do consular as well as diplomatic work. Economic problems reduced Guyana's U.N. staff from eleven in 1980–1981 to five in 1986–1987. St. Vincent has only two representatives, other than the ambassador, at the United Nations to service the seven basic committees of the General Assembly. If, as some international relations specialists maintain, size of missions reflects influence, then the Caribbean states are far from influential. This understaffing and overloading not only minimizes diplomatic effectiveness but also reduces the morale of diplomatic personnel. Table 8.1 gives the size of the missions of the Caribbean states at the two postings generally considered most important to these states—Washington and the United Nations, New York.

Jamaica has the largest mission at the U.N., trailed by Trinidad and Tobago, which, incidentally, at the time of writing had received a boost by the addition of two more officers after its election to the Security Council in 1985. Noteworthy is the fact that Grenada has a larger mission at the U.N. than Guyana or Barbados. St. Kitts also has a mission that appears proportionally well staffed considering that the island is the smallest of the independent Caribbean states, but this is deceiving in that the mission services Washington and the OAS as well. On the other hand, Grenada's mission in Washington is surprisingly small, a lingering effect of the poor relations with the United States prior to 1983. Saint Lucia is also proportionally understaffed in both New York and Washington. Finally, the four more developed countries are relatively well staffed in Washington.

Some peculiarities in the distribution of personnel must be noted. St. Kitts does not actually have three officers in Washington and four at the U.N. because the same staff, except for one, is shared by the two missions. This means that St. Kitts has only one additional person servicing Washington. Similarly, although ambassadors are listed in both missions for St. Kitts, Saint Lucia, and Dominica, the same person serves as ambassador to both the U.N. and Washington. In addition, the ambassadors of St. Kitts and Dominica are listed as resident in the islands, an odd arrangement that in actuality means that they are rarely present at the missions. Also, the U.N. list was compiled before Dominica closed its U.N. operations for lack of staff and money. In 1987, one officer was continuing to run operations informally, but officially there was no mission. At the time of writing, Dominica was planning to reopen the mission under a Commonwealth arrangement previously described, but its problem appears to be not only a financial one but also a staffing issue.

None of the Caribbean missions can be considered well staffed in terms of the capacity to service a wide variety of areas. This can easily be seen by comparing the size of the Caribbean missions with those of other countries considered influential internationally (Table 8.1). It must also be remembered that many Caribbean embassies are also burdened with consular work. Shortage of staff has even led the smaller countries to recruit nationals who are residents abroad for service on a contract basis. Still, work overload is normal. Thus, at the U.N., doubling up on committee work is common, even for Jamaica. The smaller states

TABLE 8.1. Size of Caribbean Missions to U.N. and Washington[a]

	U.N. Mission	Washington Mission
Antigua/Barbuda	4	2
Bahamas	3	2
Barbados	5	7
Belize	3	2
Dominica	2[b]	2
Grenada	6	9
Guyana	5	8
Jamaica	13	3
St. Kitts/Nevis[c]	4	3
Saint Lucia[d]	2	--
St. Vincent/Grenadines	3[e]	
Trinidad and Tobago	7	9
United States	72	--
United Kingdom	26	83
India	21	45
Nigeria	17	31
Venezuela	25	24

[a] Numbers refer to professional staff, including ambassadors and attaches. U.N. figures are as of October, 1986 and U.S. figures as of May, 1986.

[b] Dominica closed its U.N. operations in 1986. The permanent representative to the U.N. was also ambassador to the U.S. but was resident in Dominica.

[c] Permanent representative to the U.N. is also ambassador to the U.S. and is resident in St. Kitts.

[d] Permanent representative to the U.N. is also ambassador to the U.S.

[e] At the time of writing, one of these officers had been temporarily assigned elsewhere; St. Vincent's U.N. staff also services Washington.

Sources: United Nations, Permanent Missions to the United Nations, No. 259, October 1986; United States Department of State, Diplomatic List, May 1986.

have coped by targeting the areas of most interest to them and confining their activities to these. At the U.N., they usually try to service the two political committees, the second (economic) committee, and the fifth (administrative and budgetary) committee. When handled in this manner, the smallness of a nation and its staff does not preclude it from pursuing an effective foreign policy. It only prevents it from having a highly visible international presence.

Some of the effects of small size can be countered by skilled diplomacy. The Caribbean has indeed produced its share of internationally visible diplomats, including Valerie McComie of the OAS; Alister McIntyre, former deputy secretary-general of the United Nations Conference on Trade and Development; S.S. Ramphal, secretary-general of the Commonwealth; and Edwin Carrington, deputy secretary-general of the ACP-EEC group. But by and large, few Caribbean ambassadors have the capacity for diplomatic maneuvering attributed, for example, to Singapore's diplomats, and most ambassadors are not highly experienced. Skill is also not the strong point of most lower-level personnel, who tend to go to meetings unprepared and not to participate actively. In part, this must be blamed on the attempt by governments to save money by sending representatives who are already on the spot to important international meetings. Money is indeed saved but at the price of international invisibility.

The morale of the foreign service officers also depends on monetary rewards, prestigious postings, and the perception of their countries' effectiveness. While most diplomats at home find their financial situation quite adequate, many diplomats abroad express dissatisfaction when questioned about these matters. Because of unfavorable foreign exchange rates, salaries are considered inadequate, and poor economic conditions at home have in many instances precluded salary increases for diplomats. However, salaries are supplemented by quite generous perquisites, including (usually) a 90 percent housing allowance and an entertainment allowance of a few hundred dollars. Complaints about "perks" tend to center on the fact that small entertainment allowances do not allow diplomats to engage in much of the self- (and country) promotion that brings international visibility.

Despite complaints, financial considerations do not appear to be a major negative factor in Caribbean diplomacy. According to one Jamaican diplomat, monetary reward is not highly important in the determination of job satisfaction, and the Jamaican service has no lack of candidates seeking admission. This downplaying of the monetary factor can be generalized across the Caribbean; as with other foreign services around the world, the attraction of the service is in its presumed glamor and prestige. Interviews with diplomats affirm that, although they are naturally more realistic than the general public about their jobs, they do perceive their profession as giving them a measure of prestige.

On the issue of prestige, the availability of desirable postings is a major factor in morale. Some diplomats refuse to rank posts, but others openly admit that the U.N. and Washington are the most desirable posts, followed by London (where, for some, the work is more varied), Ottawa, Brussels, and Caracas. The few African posts were not rated highly, although diplomats who had done a tour of duty there usually seemed quite satisfied. The U.N. was considered most desirable not only because of the attractiveness of New York but also because the U.N.'s activities are perceived as being very important to small states, enabling them to have some impact on the international environment. Washington tended to be selected by those who felt that bilateral relations were more important than multilateral diplomacy.

Given the attractiveness of most of the overseas locations, Caribbean diplomats do not have to worry about "hardship" postings the way diplomats from the United States or other large countries do. Also, the rotation system ensures that most officers get a chance of being posted to desirable locations. In fact, the complaints encountered in this area are the reverse of what might be expected: Officers may tire of the frequent moves, and there are also complaints about the selectivity of the system. The rotation system does not function in the smaller countries where organizational procedures have not yet evolved. But in the larger countries, there are unwritten rules governing postings. Newly recruited officers are expected to first spend two or three years at home rotating within the various sections of the headquarters—another concession to the generalist preference. Then they may be posted abroad for one or two tours of duty of about three years each before returning to head-quarters. This circular rotation pattern is the norm in most foreign ministries of the world, allowing officers to familiarize themselves with a variety of overseas duties without losing touch with the "home base." However, in the Caribbean, the rules have generally been applied with great flexibility, because of the realities of staff shortages. There is nothing intrinsically problematic about this, but abuses have occurred. Thus some persons have been favored with longer rotations abroad—for example, one diplomat was serving a fifth term abroad at the time of writing—whereas others, particularly female officers with families, have been favored with longer stints at home. When this happens, the unfavored have suffered by being blocked from desirable postings, and bottlenecks have occurred at the home office. Although most foreign offices have been working to correct the problem, they are today confronted with a modern version—namely, the difficulty of complying with the rules while reconciling the needs of two-career families. Many of the dissatisfied today are foreign service wives and husbands reluctant to leave their jobs to go abroad. It should be mentioned that the rules governing rotation *within* the various bureaucratic divisions have also been very flexibly applied and sometimes bypassed altogether.

On the final issue of officers' perceptions of their country's effectiveness, it is logical to assume that positive feedback—that is, recognition from other countries, and concrete results—enhance diplomats' perceptions of themselves as doing a good job. The conclusions reached here are based solely on interviews with diplomats at the United Nations. Diplomats from Trinidad and Tobago, Jamaica, and Guyana are generally very positive about their countries' effectiveness. In the past, Trinidad's diplomacy was viewed as being too low-profile to be effective, but diplomats' self-esteem was considerably enhanced by Trinidad's membership on the Security Council in the 1985 and 1986 sessions. Jamaican and Guyanese diplomats display more self-assurance than the Trinidadians: Jamaica is the best known of the Caribbean countries and it has projected itself successfully in many international arenas in the 1970s and 1980s. Jamaican diplomats feel that their country has been very successful in its initiatives mainly because of the dynamism of individual diplomats and the high level of involvement of Jamaican representatives. They point with pride to the fact that Jamaica chairs the U.N. Development Program's Governing Council, has been regularly elected to the Economic and Social Council, and has been active on the International Law Commission since the mid-1970s. Guyana too appears to have projected itself internationally through able representation; at the time of writing, it was a member of ECOSOC, and was serving on the UNDP and UNICEF (Children's Fund) executive boards. Guyana had the distinction of being the only Commonwealth Caribbean country to serve two terms on the Security Council, and its permanent representative was the senior Latin American and Caribbean ambassador in 1986. Guyana has also gained recognition because of its commitment to the Non-Aligned Group and its involvement in committees dealing with such issues as Namibia and Palestine. All the Big Four countries have been active on apartheid issues at the U.N.

Barbadian diplomats vary in their perception of their country's effectiveness at the U.N. but the variation is attributable to the problems Barbados encountered in the wake of its stance on the Grenada issue. Having been unsuccessful in gaining a seat on the Security Council and in other initiatives mentioned in Chapter 7, Barbadians—at least until 1986 when the Barrow government returned to power—felt isolated at the U.N. In an interview, its ambassador to the U.N. downplayed the U.N. and emphasized the importance of bilateralism.[13] Perhaps not coincidentally, the Barbadian ambassador to Washington was positive about his country's effectiveness, reflected for example in its OAS initiatives, particularly on the admission of Belize and Guyana, and its able representation at the Washington-based multilateral organizations. (Barbadian effectiveness at the U.N. increased after 1986, largely because of able representation, but the country was unable to garner enough support to achieve a major goal—election to the presidency of the General Assembly in 1988.)

The smaller islands once again must be considered separately because their limited skills and resources have prevented them from projecting themselves on the international stage. Yet diplomats interviewed or

questioned were quite confident that they could and have gained recognition by concentrating on specific issues. One representative felt that
the Caribbean governments themselves were not sensitized enough to
the importance of the U.N. and the possibilities of gaining quid pro
quos on the international stage, and most realized that much remained
to be done, in particular in terms of getting their countries elected to
posts on major committees. St. Lucia's vice presidency of ECOSOC
(1983–1984) and St. Vincent's election to the vice presidency of the
General Assembly in 1987 and to the chairmanship of the Fourth
Committee in 1988 represented encouraging developments in this regard.
Overall, we can conclude that they appear relatively satisfied with their
countries' positions.

In sum, formulated foreign policies can only be effectively acted on
if the channels of implementation work efficiently. Caribbean foreign
policy planning is already constrained by small size and limited resources,
and goals and strategies must be formulated with these limitations in
mind. But smallness need not affect achievement, and one of the factors
that plays a role in counteracting the effects of size is human resources.
The Caribbean diplomatic service is in general understaffed, and there
are important gaps in training. However, despite some tensions stemming
from the politicization and personalization of the appointment process
and from economic constraints, the perception of the foreign service job
as prestigious, the opportunities for travel, and the conviction that their
countries, however small, are effective internationally, seem to compensate
for many of the structural problems diplomats encounter. How truly
effective Caribbean foreign policy is—as opposed to the perception of
effectiveness—is a question that will be discussed in Chapter 9.

Notes

1. Vernetta Calvin-Smith, "The Role of External Affairs in the National Export
Promotion Thrust of Trinidad and Tobago," in Anthony P. Gonzales, ed., *Trade
Diplomacy and Export Development in a Protectionist World: Challenges and Strategies
for Caribbean States* (Trinidad and Tobago: Institute of International Relations,
1985): 53.

2. Basil Ince, "The Administration of Foreign Affairs in a Very Small Developing
Country: The Case of Trinidad and Tobago," in Vaughan A. Lewis, ed., *Size,
Self-Determination and International Relations: The Caribbean* (Mona, Jamaica:
Institute of Social and Economic Research, 1976): 328–329..

3. Interoffice memo regarding St. Vincent and the Grenadines' five-year
development plan, authored by Cecil John, permanent secretary in the Ministry
of External Affairs, St. Vincent.

4. I am indebted to Earl Huntley, permanent secretary in the Ministry of
External Affairs, Saint Lucia, for information on the conduct of foreign affairs
in that country. Earl is, however, in no way responsible for my critique of the
way the government handles foreign affairs.

5. See Ince, "Administration," 310.

6. Gary Brana-Shute, "Saint Lucia," in Jack Hopkins, ed., *Latin America and Caribbean Contemporary Record*, vol. 1, 1981–1982 (New York: Holmes and Meier, 1983): 615.

7. Interview of Prime Minister Eugenia Charles with a group of students from The City College of New York, January 1986.

8. Ince, "Administration," 321.

9. Gerald Samuel, *Barbados Foreign Policy from 1966–1978*, unpublished Master's thesis, Institute of International Relations, St. Augustine, Trinidad, p. 216.

10. Charles Frankel depicts the State Department's resistance to new ideas in his remarkable work *High on Foggy Bottom* (New York: Harper and Row, 1968).

11. Ince, "Administration," 334.

12. Ibid., pp. 330–331.

13. Interview with Ambassador Harley Moseley, permanent representative of Barbados to the United Nations, August 22, 1986.

9. Caribbean Foreign Policy: An Evaluation

General Evaluation

As small as the twelve independent Caribbean states are, they are nevertheless expected to carry out, to the best of their ability, the basic international responsibilities of all sovereign states. Independent states are expected to establish diplomatic linkages, to interact politically and economically with other states, and to participate in planned international activities. Moreover, all states, no matter how small, try to use the international environment to their benefit. Caribbean states, like most states, direct their international activity toward the goals of achieving security, economic development, and visibility or prestige. For them, security includes territorial, ideological, economic, and social concerns. With a few exceptions, economic development implies growth along Western capitalist lines; and prestige means effective participation on the international stage.

From an evaluative perspective, the Caribbean's goals are realistic, that is, achievable: Caribbean governments have been mindful of their small size and have not been overambitious in their goal setting. Territorial security has not, for them, implied territorial ambition but rather defense and preservation of existing boundaries. Similarly, economic development goals have been defined in gradualist and survivalist terms—managing to survive and even to progress a little bit. And prestige for most countries has implied "participation" rather than international influence.

In evaluating Caribbean foreign policy, our chief focus has to be on whether the *strategies* these states have adopted are capable of achieving the stated or implied goals. In the security area, the strategies have ranged from defense agreements with and aid from larger countries, most recently the United States, to the search for allies abroad, in the interest of territorial protection (Guyana) or, in the case of the socialist governments, protection from "imperialism." In the economic area, the strategy has primarily been to search for financial assistance from the West and from international organizations, for investment from abroad, and for export markets, and also to participate in relevant international

220

economic organizations. Finally, for visibility, Caribbean states have primarily relied on diplomatic activity, especially membership and participation in international organizations.

An evaluation of these strategies must rest on a somewhat detailed examination of their value. Territorial security has been defined broadly to include defense against secessionist attempts, mercenary attacks, smuggling, narcotics trade, and illegal immigration as well as boundary controversies. In this arena, Caribbean states have entered into bilateral treaties with the United States (Jamaica), and bilateral guarantees with the U.K. (Belize); regional arrangements with and without the U.S. (OECS, Regional Security System); treaties with the Eastern bloc (Grenada); international organization security systems (U.N., Rio Treaty); bilateral aid agreements (Brazil, United States, U.K., Canada); and general diplomatic linkages that have possible security ramifications, such as linkages with the Commonwealth.

Grenada has been the only country to establish strong security links with the Eastern bloc, a strategy that proved to be counterproductive—it not only did not preserve Grenada's territorial integrity in the long run, but actually engendered conditions that encouraged the violation of its sovereignty. For the rest of the Eastern Caribbean, the social and environmental concerns that supposedly underlay the creation of the security systems have so far been obscured by ideological issues. In the circumstances, we can only say that the systems have the potential to be useful tools in ensuring security collaboration on a regional basis, but that the aims at present go beyond regional capabilities. In another area, bilateral and international organizational security pacts represent the traditional methods adopted by small states to secure their territorial integrity. Jamaica and Belize are the only states that entered into formal bilateral defense agreements after independence. However, the Eastern Caribbean states and Barbados have now become tied into an informal but close relationship with the United States. Bilateralism in security matters, as in economic relationships, is problematic because it engenders dependence and imposes certain constraints on foreign policy. For example, because of the U.K.'s security guarantees, Belize is not free to make decisions that might antagonize the U.K. Bilateralism is especially problematic when the links are with the United States, simply because of the ideological perspectives that are deeply linked to U.S. assistance. Given these concerns, small states are better off relying on international organizations for their security needs. This permits them not only to take advantage of a security umbrella without major commitment but also to be involved in regional and even global decision-making on security issues.

On the specific boundary issues, Guyana and Belize have adopted some similar and effective strategies, specifically searching for international support, especially in the Third World and the region, while continuing bilateral negotiations and attempting to improve functional linkages with Venezuela and Guatemala. But the strategies have also differed in emphases: Guyana has relied heavily on international visibility, accompanied by some bilateral aid from the U.K., Brazil, and some socialist countries; Belize depends on bilateral support from the U.K. and the United States, accompanied by some international activity such as membership in the Non-Aligned Movement. Guyana's consistent international stance on non-intervention, its use of the United Nations forum, and its high level of non-aligned activity have produced some direct benefits, given the fact that Venezuela has itself been seeking a position of leadership in the Third World. On the other hand, Guatemala is not particularly Third World–oriented so that although Belize can certainly benefit from greater international visibility, it cannot rely on that only for protection against the Guatemalan threat. At the same time, the British security guarantee is only temporary. In the circumstances, Belize's strategy of seeking closer collaboration with the United States is probably a necessary one. Closer links to other Central American countries are also necessary since these are the countries most capable of containing Guatemala's ambitions.

In the area of economic security, the Caribbean states have joined with other Third World nations in international forums in affirming the right of all states to choose whatever economic and social arrangements they consider to be appropriate. Yet most Caribbean governments have chosen "traditional" arrangements in this regard. The affirmation has had significance primarily for the left-leaning governments that have found themselves at odds with Western financial institutions and multinational corporations and the governments that back these agencies. For the other countries, economic security has really meant economic development.

Although a strong Third World orientation has gained the left-wing governments wide support for their economic and social policies, this support has not proved sufficient to minimize external pressures, simply because for small states economic security rests heavily on bilateral political relations. Those Caribbean states that have been subject to external pressures have generally had governments that failed to understand the importance of maintaining good bilateral relations, however superficial, with the United States.

As we can see, economic concerns have been intimately tied to ideological concerns. Left-wing governments have relied on a strong global presence, on diplomatic support from Eastern bloc countries, from the Third World, and from less rigidly ideological Western governments. However, as is the case with economic security, these strategies have failed to ensure them ideological security—that is, the right to adopt socialistic changes without pressure from outside. The primary reason for this failure has been the Caribbean socialists' neglect of geopolitical realities—these governments have gone too far beyond the implied limits of political acceptability. Moreover, their goals and strategies have outrun their capabilities.

As we noted earlier, geopolitical considerations go beyond concerns about the relationship with the United States, to include as well the political concerns of neighbors in the Caribbean and Latin America. The failures in the foreign policies of left-wing Caribbean states in this geopolitical realm have stemmed partly from naïveté and partly from a misreading of the hemispheric, regional, and international environments. In sum, in the formulation of goals and strategies, left-wing Caribbean governments have generally overestimated their ability to achieve their foreign policy goals without Western and/or U.S. support, have over-estimated the value of Third World and Eastern bloc support, and, specifically in the case of Grenada, have attempted to conduct a global and anti-U.S. policy without sufficient awareness of the limitations imposed by size and weak economies. Of the three socialist governments—Jamaica, Guyana, Grenada—the one that has survived has been able to do so because the radical nature of the opposition groups has ensured it Western support. Even so, it is important to note that the Guyana government has maintained a pragmatic (or opportunistic) foreign policy and has sought at most times to retain a link with the United States. Guyana has actively sought alternative linkages but there has been a recognition of the fact that these cannot completely supplant bilateral accommodation. On the other hand, Guyana's policy appears to have evolved ad hoc rather than being the result of long-range planning.

The other aspect of ideological security that we discussed in the book was the perception of the majority of Caribbean states or governments that the Caribbean should be free from "foreign" socialist influence. In response to the rise of socialistic states in the 1970s, the conservative governments allied with one another and with the United States. (Neither the OECS charter nor the Memorandum of Understanding is specific about ideological security, but these priorities are deduced from Caribbean concerns prior to 1983, and from the consolidation of the role of the RSS after the Grenada invasion.) Analysts can well wonder if these strategies are achieving the implied goals. First of all, the Caribbean experience already suggests that there is difficulty in defining the goal itself—that is, whether ideological security entails action against un-friendly governments in the core region or whether it is to be applied strictly against an external (Soviet or Cuban) threat. If the former, as the Grenada case showed, the strategy of military involvement is bound to generate regional discord at high cost, especially for the smaller countries that rely more heavily on regional economic and functional mechanisms. As we have seen, Caribbean states also suffered a loss of international prestige by acting against one of their own. If the latter, the Caribbean would be drawn into costly global conflict. In both cases, the Caribbean states, which themselves have almost no military capacity, have to ally with the United States, as they have indeed been doing. But entering into a dependent security relationship with the United States simply adds more limitations to a foreign policy already circum-scribed by size and geography. Arms transfers and other military linkages usually increase the leverage and influence of the donor, but small states like those in our study do not have the capacity for "reverse" leverage that a country such as Saudi Arabia has. (For example, the Saudis linked oil production to arms sales in the early 1980s.)[1] Finally and most crucially, the security threat, vague to begin with, does not exist in 1988, which makes the military investment costly in terms of the diversion of resources, the internal social ramifications, and the dependence on the United States, without sufficient return on the investment.

This is not to say that Caribbean states could not benefit from a strategy of military linkage with the United States. If the Caribbean were important enough strategically to the United States, Caribbean countries could request quid pro quos for their support. In fact, there is evidence that at least some countries are thinking along these lines. But the history of U.S. relations with the Caribbean and Latin America is one of neglect at non-crisis times. Caribbean governments that expected aid for military cooperation have been disapppointed so far. Yet American policy is to link economic cooperation with military cooperation, locking Caribbean countries into a catch-22 situation. Overall, then, these particular foreign policy strategies appear to be counterproductive.

In economic development, Caribbean strategies have focused on searching for external assistance and markets, primarily in the West. Given the weak state of most Caribbean economies, these strategies have not worked very well. The Caribbean experience can be generalized throughout the Third World: External assistance is insufficient to meet needs and a high level of borrowing simply aggravates the cycle of dependence; conditions within these countries are not attractive enough for investment, or if they are, investment does not generate the anticipated return to the country; aid is politically and economically tied; and developed-country markets are protectionist. The whole question of development carries with it philosophical and economic ramifications that cannot be discussed here,[2] but we can say that Caribbean economic foreign policy is flawed in underestimating Caribbean capabilities. Caribbean states tend to work within perceived historical and geographic constraints that are not necessarily applicable. Thus while there is recognition of the need for diversification, there has so far been little success in achieving it. A "natural" affinity with traditional partners and donors is perceived, whereas barriers are presumed to economic alliances with Latin America and Afro-Asia. In fact diversification needs to be pursued much more aggressively.

Caribbean states also generally recognize the need for international solutions to some of the Third World's economic problems and have joined with the Third World in supporting various measures sought within the context of the New International Economic Order. In this, the Caribbean is following a correct policy. Unfortunately, many states are doing so passively rather than actively. In part, this is because of the overestimation of the geopolitical factor: Those states that have defined economic development in terms of independence from the West have been put to the test by pressures from the United States and the Western-controlled international institutions. This fear, however, is based on the presumption that an independent policy must be an anti-West one, and this has not been proved. We should add that policies of extreme self-reliance, as reflected in the Guyana experience, have not achieved the goal of economic development any more than the more open model has. Caribbean countries therefore face the challenge of devising more appropriate strategies to achieve their economic goals. Finally, bilateralism is not precluded by diversification, but Caribbean states need to be more aggressive here as well. At least two Caribbean states, Saint Lucia and Bahamas, have appointed lobbyists in Washington, and this might be a pattern to be followed. In any event, the Caribbean needs to have more effective representation in important capitals and to collectively work toward exercising some leverage at the bilateral level.

Finally, in the prestige or visibility area, Caribbean states are limited by lack of resources. But although their diplomatic network is narrow, they can achieve visibility in international organizations and at international conferences. Guyana and Jamaica have been most effective in projecting themselves internationally. Despite its poor human rights record, Guyana has achieved international prestige by activity in the Non-Aligned Movement as well as at the U.N. Jamaica has at different times projected a Third World image *and* gained visibility by being "sponsored" by the United States. Of course, Jamaica began its independent career with the advantage of being the largest Caribbean country and the one most internationally known, so its success in achieving visibility is understandable. As for the other Caribbean countries, analysis indicates that they need to promote themselves more on the international stage through more active participation at high level in major conferences, and through better use of skilled personnel to counteract financial limitations.

Caribbean foreign policy has been largely targeted toward or interactive with the following countries: the United States, the United Kingdom and other EEC countries, and Canada, followed by Caricom countries. Our research shows that in the effort to diversify linkages, the most important region for the Caribbean has been Latin America. A few countries have deepened relations with Eastern bloc countries, but for most, relations with these countries are quite superficial. As for Afro-Asia, there have been a few economic linkages with Middle Eastern (West Asian) countries, the newly industrializing countries of Asia, and China and some diplomatic links with West Africa, Ethiopia, and the Organization of African Unity. Nevertheless, these links have only begun to scratch the surface. Although preferred targets vary by country, Caribbean strategies overall have been too influenced by a perception of the developed countries as being the most important targets. Caribbean policymakers need to rethink this orientation, especially in view of the clear economic imperative for diversification.

This book has also considered the influences and influencers of Caribbean foreign policy, the decision-making process, and the role of the bureaucracy which coordinates and implements policy. In evaluating the impact and effectiveness of these, we can make the following conclusions. The decision-making process in the Caribbean is still too personalized and politicized, primarily because the Westminster system allows a prime minister and his cabinet carte blanche in an environment in which oppositions have traditionally been weak. In particular, crisis decisions tend to be personal decisions with little attention paid to opposition sentiment and not enough alternative information and opinion solicited. Nevertheless, there is evidence that personalism has decreased in importance in the larger countries since the 1960s and early 1970s, especially as post-independence leaders are replaced by those with less stature and longevity. Foreign ministers, high-level bureaucrats, elites, and interest groups have increased their influence, and external influence is more forthright. Public opinion too is better informed, if not much more influential. The smaller countries have the longest way to go in opening up their decision-making processes and rationalizing their decision-making structures. Prime ministers in these states tend to make decisions on the basis of personal preferences and personal relationships with advisers and ambassadors, often bypassing fledging foreign policy bureaucracies.

In the larger countries, foreign policy bureaucracies have become more functionally complex to meet the increasing complexity of international relations. Functional complexity has not necessarily been accompanied by efficiency because the need for trained and specialized personnel has not been fully met. In the smaller countries, governments are still trying to address the issue of whether foreign policy bureaucracies are needed and if so, why. Moreover, there is an acute need in these countries for trained staff. For all countries, international effectiveness is limited by their inability to maintain more than a few relatively understaffed missions abroad.

Although some Caribbean diplomats have acquired international recognition, there is a need for more skilled personnel and a more visible diplomatic presence. The recruitment process is still haphazard in many states and personalized in others. While the service appears to attract many candidates eager to travel, it needs to be made more attractive for those with advanced skills and training.

A Theoretical Evaluation and Model

We began this book by taking note of the dearth of theoretical studies of the foreign policy of small states in general, and of the Caribbean in particular. We also noted that although it was not intended in this book to develop a "grand" theory of Caribbean foreign policy, it *was* intended that the analysis of Caribbean foreign policy undertaken here would be undertaken within the context of a critical evaluation—and modification if necessary—of the available theoretical literature in international relations.

Caribbean foreign policy cannot be understood from a unidimensional perspective. From the "mainstream" point of view, size and its related poverty and powerlessness might provide sufficient explanations of small-state foreign policy. But from the small-state point of view, size is relative and cannot explain variations in behavior among "small" states, and clearly not all small states are poor. There are also examples enough of states that have overcome the limitations of size in carrying out effective foreign policies. From the decision-making perspective, also considered "mainstream," psychological and perceptual factors are most important in explaining foreign policy in general and that of small or Third World states in particular. Yet these states take decisions within operational contexts that have their own objective dynamic.

From other less traditional perspectives, the behavior of the Caribbean states might be understood by considering the dynamics of their historical links to global capitalism and their consequent dependence on the industrialized countries. This approach would also consider policy to be the product of certain class divisions within Caribbean societies. Indeed, Caribbean capitalist links both explain and *are* a part of the foreign behavior of Caribbean states. It might even be said that the economic history of the Caribbean provides an overarching influence or determinant of Caribbean behavior, not only on the economic dimension but also in the security and diplomatic areas. Yet it is not enough to say this, because dependency or world-systems theories do not tell us about the dynamics of the decision-making process or anything about national responsibility in policy formulation or why some decision-makers perceive their countries' capabilities and choices differently from others. Finally, some analysts would explain Caribbean foreign policy primarily in terms of systemic influences, stressing changes in the East-West relationship and, especially, changes in the U.S. role of world policeman. Again, these are important factors that influence the content and direction of Caribbean foreign policy. But they are not sufficient in explaining that policy. Caribbean states are not simply puppets or pawns in the East-West game. As small as they are, they have a wide range of foreign policy actions and a similarly wide range of foreign policy influences.

An initial framework to guide the analysis given in the book was provided in Figure 1.1. At this point, we can elevate the framework to the status of a model by drawing on the results of our study. Figure 9.1 suggests that there are three important processes, general policy formulation (goal setting and adoption of appropriate strategies), the making of actual decisions, and the implementation of those decisions.

FIGURE 9.1. A Model of Caribbean Foreign Policy

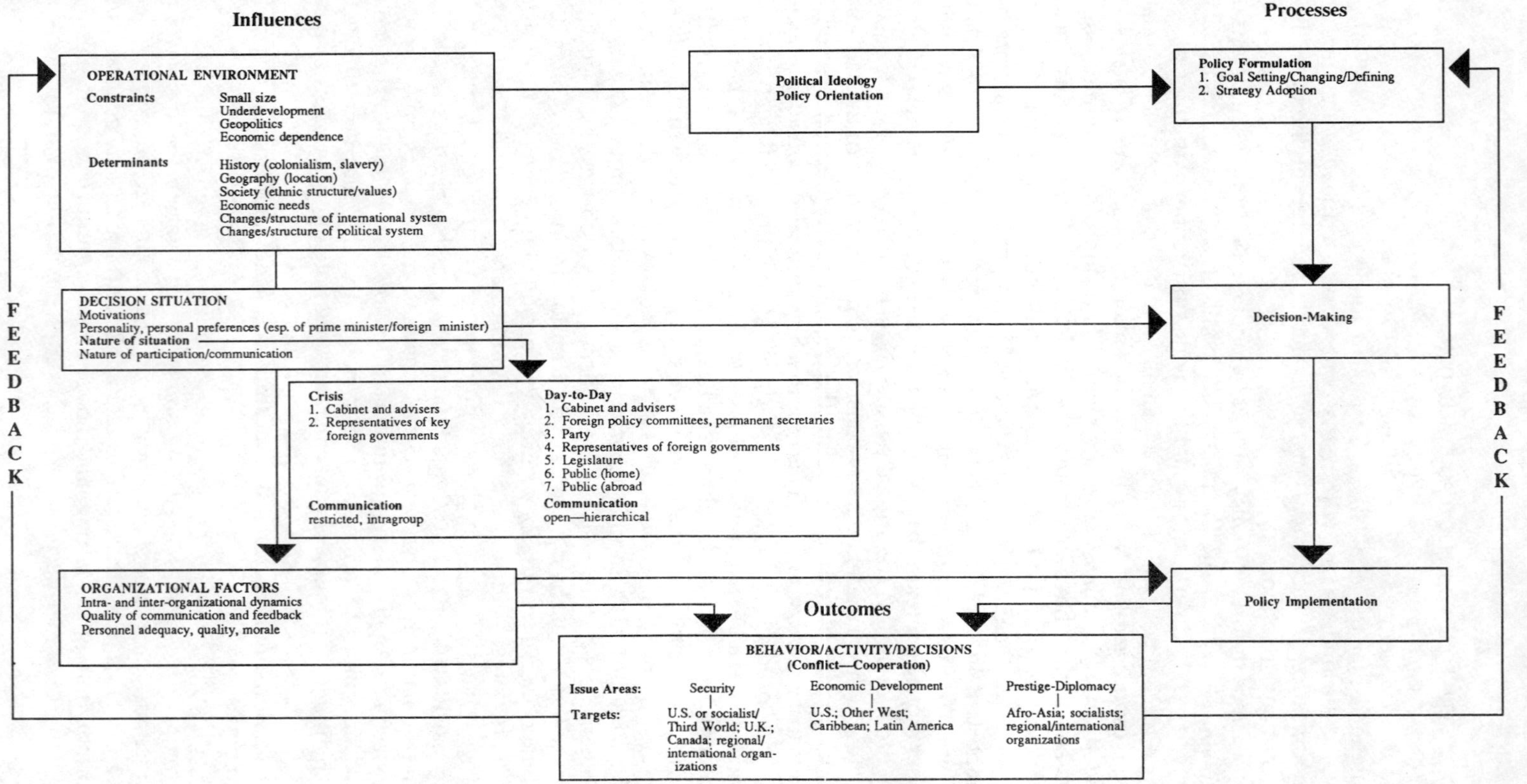

Influences

OPERATIONAL ENVIRONMENT

Constraints
- Small size
- Underdevelopment
- Geopolitics
- Economic dependence

Determinants
- History (colonialism, slavery)
- Geography (location)
- Society (ethnic structure/values)
- Economic needs
- Changes/structure of international system
- Changes/structure of political system

Political Ideology
Policy Orientation

DECISION SITUATION
Motivations
Personality, personal preferences (esp. of prime minister/foreign minister)
Nature of situation
Nature of participation/communication

Crisis
1. Cabinet and advisers
2. Representatives of key foreign governments

Communication
restricted, intragroup

Day-to-Day
1. Cabinet and advisers
2. Foreign policy committees, permanent secretaries
3. Party
4. Representatives of foreign governments
5. Legislature
6. Public (home)
7. Public (abroad)

Communication
open—hierarchical

ORGANIZATIONAL FACTORS
Intra- and inter-organizational dynamics
Quality of communication and feedback
Personnel adequacy, quality, morale

Processes

Policy Formulation
1. Goal Setting/Changing/Defining
2. Strategy Adoption

Decision-Making

Policy Implementation

Outcomes

BEHAVIOR/ACTIVITY/DECISIONS
(Conflict—Cooperation)

	Security	Economic Development	Prestige-Diplomacy
Issue Areas:			
Targets:	U.S. or socialist/ Third World; U.K.; Canada; regional/ international organizations	U.S.; Other West; Caribbean; Latin America	Afro-Asia; socialists; regional/international organizations

F E E D B A C K

In the Caribbean, goal setting, definition, and strategy adoption are or should be done within the context of the indicated operational constraints and influences on policy, screened through the policy orientation of various governments. These goals and strategies and the operational environment within which they have been adopted are taken into account by policymakers who are in turn influenced by the dynamics of the decision-making process—the perceptual, situational, and organizational characteristics of the decision-making unit. The implementation phase is itself influenced by organizational dynamics, communication, and personnel considerations. Finally, decisions taken can be analyzed in terms of the three issue-areas that correspond to the goals set, and the geographic targets of foreign policy activity.

The first use of this model is as an aid in understanding the dynamics of Caribbean foreign policy. The next step is to build on the model to generate theoretical propositions that might be tested not only in the Caribbean context but in the context of other small-sized states. Some testable propositions might be: that small states for which security is a major concern are likely to be more active than others in the international arena, especially in the diplomatic issue-area; that small socialist states will be more active diplomatically than non-socialist states; that the economic dependence of small states affects the nature of their diplomatic and security linkages as well; that smaller, poorer states are more likely to depend on bilateral and regional relationships than on global activity; that decision-making in small states is likely to be highly personalized and "closed" in terms of the input of the public and of bureaucrats; that the foreign affairs bureaucracy will receive low priority in small states relative to the economic and finance bureaucracy; that recruitment to the foreign service will be personalized and politicized in small states; and that wealth and diplomatic expertise will offset the limitations imposed by size.

There are many other propositions that can be generated by the results of our research on the specific Caribbean area. Theoretical breakthroughs will require the testing of their relevance to other small-state groupings, such as the Pacific islands. Meanwhile, Caribbean foreign policy researchers can also usefully utilize the model presented here to assess future changes in strategies, describe in more detail the relationships between influences and behavior, and add or rearrange the list of influences and the patterns and direction of relationships as changes occur across time.

Notes

1. For an enlightening analysis of the effects of arms sales, see Andrew J. Pierre, *The Global Politics of Arms Sales* (Princeton: Princeton University Press for the Council on Foreign Relations, 1982): 14–24 especially.

2. See J. Braveboy-Wagner, *Interpreting the Third World: Politics, Economics, and Social Issues* (New York: Praeger, 1986): 165–182.

Name Index

Subject Index